great court-martial cases

great court-martial cases

by joseph di mona

introduction by
senator birch bayh

GROSSET & DUNLAP
A NATIONAL GENERAL COMPANY
Publishers   *New York*

Contents

Introduction by the
Honorable Birch Bayh,
United States Senator from Indiana

An author who attempts to examine the American military court-martial through nearly 200 years of history has a large task before him. He obviously cannot deal with all of the literally millions of courts-martial that have taken place in our history. He must choose carefully to present a selection that has some significance for today's reader. He must be historically accurate, but he must go beyond mere "reporting" of the facts in order to place each case in its proper historical perspective. And he must deal with his subject not simply from a legal viewpoint, but from a human viewpoint as well: cases of law are notoriously dull unless handled with a deft touch.

Joseph DiMona has succeeded admirably in achieving these goals. In *Great Court-Martial Cases* he has produced an eminently readable book—one that should be read with interest and enjoyment not only by historians and lawyers, but by servicemen past and present. Indeed, I commend this work to all those concerned about the fairness and integrity of American justice, interested in the reform of an increasingly criticized military justice system three times the size of the federal criminal justice system.

As Mr. DiMona himself has concluded, that system does not—despite nearly 200 years of gradual reform—function in a uniformly equitable manner. Its flaws are many. It is in serious need of major reform. The very fact that well over half of the cases documented in this book (all of which were chosen for their legal and historical significance) raised questions of justice and fairness which to this day remain unsettled, should give us all cause for concern. How can we in good conscience draft and maintain a standing army, impose upon them rigid rules of military life, order them into combat—sometimes to pay the supreme sacrifice—and provide them anything less than a first-class system of justice?

As a United States Senator, lawyer, and former service-man, I share Mr. DiMona's concern about the quality of justice we are providing our military men and women. The question of its quality is perhaps more important today than ever before. The men and women now in uniform serve in an army which has changed substantially over the years. Most of them will not see combat. Many live off post and serve in a military capacity only during normal working hours. In many ways there is an increased similarity between military service and skilled civilian occupational pursuits, a fact reflected in the difficulty of moving toward an all-volunteer army. We cannot continue to subject these men and women to a second-rate system of military justice.

Moreover, there are now more than three million American citizens under arms. Most of these citizens are young and impressionable, and some will be confronted with American justice for the first time while serving in the Armed Forces. The 1969 Report of the Judge Advocate General of the U.S. Army noted that in the Army alone there were 76,320 courts-martial that year, 94 percent of which resulted in convictions. If we are to preserve the integrity of our civilian system of justice, we must see to it that these citizens return to civilian life with a view of criminal justice that recognizes the fundamental principles of fairness and human dignity. We must see to it that no person is convicted and confined, his life perhaps ruined, without having been accorded full procedural and substantive safeguards.

Our system of military justice has always been viewed as separate and distinct from our civilian legal system. It has its own substantive provisions, its own procedure and its own constitutional source. Its basic aim has always been the maintenance of discipline, and one of its dominant features has always been control by the commander. But such control carries with it the serious danger that the commander may use his influence improperly. The temptation is certainly great.

Just consider how overwhelming is the influence that commanders hold over courts-martial-procedures which may, after all, impose numerous penalties, including dishon-

orable discharge, lengthy imprisonment, or even death. In a
court-martial, the commander determines whether to prosecute, controls the court-martial procedure, and plays an
integral role in the appellate process. He authorizes searches and arrests, convenes the court-martial, and decides
whether the accused serviceman shall remain in pretrial
confinement. He chooses the prosecuting attorney and, in
some instances, the defense counsel. He chooses the men to
serve as members of a court, the military equivalent of
jurors, reviews the findings and sentence, and decides
whether a sentence to confinement shall be deferred pending appeal.

In addition to the threat presented by command influence, the military justice system denies a defendant other
rights fundamental to a free society. He may be denied
credit for time spent in confinement before trial. His military counsel may be precluded from seeking collateral
relief. He must apply to the prosecuting counsel, rather
than an independent military judge, for subpoenas.

These shortcomings must be remedied, and they must be
remedied quickly. We ask our young men by the millions to
give their time and their energies to strengthen our national
defense. And we have asked them by the tens of thousands
to give their lives on our behalf. We can delay no longer in
giving these citizens a first-class system of military justice.
What is urgently needed, it seems clear, is a comprehensive
revision of the Uniform Code, a reform which will make
military justice conform as nearly as possible to the civil
system we find in our state and federal courts.

Early in 1971, I introduced such a reform in the United
States Senate: The Military Justice Act of 1971. Although it
is not the ultimate answer—as Mr. DiMona points out, the
process of judicial reform will continue as long as this nation
has need for a system of military justice—I believe my
proposal would go a long way toward insuring every American serviceman and servicewoman the kind of speedy, fair,
and impartial judicial system to which they are entitled. My
bill would do so by eliminating completely all danger of
command influence over courts-martial—the possibility, or
even the appearance, that the commanding officer of an

accused man could affect the outcome of his court-martial. All parts of the Uniform Code of Military Justice dealing with courts-martial, from the moment of arrest to the final disposition of appeals and the completion of confinement, would be revised. Among other provisions, the bill would establish an independent courts-martial command, thereby greatly reducing the influence of commanding officers; extend to servicemen certain basic rights now accorded their civilian counterparts; establish a system of random selection for members of courts-martial, military jurors; abolish the requirement that two-thirds of the jurors be officers; and eliminate completely the much-criticized summary court-martial, under which one man acts as prosecutor, defense counsel and jury.

It is my judgement that the overwhelming majority of commanding officers in our military forces try their best to be fair. They try to see that those whom they command are treated justly, whether on the battlefield, in the barracks, or in the military court. But military laws need to be structured in such a way that those few commanding officers who might yield to the temptation are denied the opportunity to affect the case of even one of those who serve in their commands. And the system must be structured not only so that it *is* fair, but so that its fairness is *absolutely clear* to all Americans—in and out of the military.

Mr. DiMona, I believe, would agree with me that we owe it to the men and women of our armed forces, we owe it to the image of our nation as a land of "justice for all," to create a better system of military justice, a system which will not only bear scrutiny but which will invite admiration. As General Samuel T. Ansell, the then-acting Judge Advocate General of the Army, said over fifty years ago: "[The Army as] an institution has got to be based on justice, and it has got to do justice if it is going to survive, and if it is going to merit the confidence and approval of the American people." Mr. DiMona has written an excellent book which points to the need for a system "based on justice" and "doing justice." In so doing, he has done us all a great service.

Foreword

A book which covers the entire history of military justice in this country as seen through actual courtroom confrontations requires for its research a friend in court. Joseph E. Ross, the former head of Military Justice in the U.S. Navy, is the man chiefly responsible for aiding the author through the archives and into many byways in search of the trial transcripts, many of them never before unearthed. Although Mr. Ross is responsible for none of the opinions embodied in this book, it was he who helped stir my interest in the history of military justice.

This is a book about a system of justice which has been improved dramatically over the years, but still does not work. From Benedict Arnold to Mylai, spectacular trials have highlighted flaws and led to changes in this system, changes that are still being made. After three years of research it is the author's conclusion that, despite many critics, there *is* a need for military justice, but that very much still remains to be revised if a Uniform Code of Military Justice is to function in a uniformly fair manner.

There have been thousands of courts-martial in this nation's history; this book contains twelve selected for their legal significance and historical importance. Wars have resulted from the courts-martial in this book, traitors have been born, generals humbled, dissenters become martyrs, privates shot, and a Negro sailor kept alive against his wish. In effect, the emerging history of America and its changing social consciousness can be seen in the panorama of these trials through the unique viewpoint of military justice.

This book could not have been written without the encouragement of editor Lewis W. Gillenson, the perceptive research of my wife Barbara, and the untiring aid of editor Jonathan Bartlett who combines a sharp wit and a sharp pencil with a broad knowledge of all things American.

Joseph DiMona
New York City
September, 1971

1
Background to Treason

Prologue

In the mid-1700s, America was a cluster of colonies along the Atlantic coast, beset by Indians in the West, threatened by the French from the north, and protected by the mother country, England, far across the sea.

But differences were beginning to arise between the colonies and their protector. In King George's court, political advisers argued that "the plantations" were draining off too much English money, that they were not carrying their share of the financial burden. So began the imposition of taxes and with them portents of American rebellion fired by such men as Samuel Adams, Thomas Paine, and Patrick Henry—portents which were to become real in a volley of musket fire exploding into a crowd of Boston citizens.

A prosperous shipping merchant arriving in the West Indies heard about the "Boston Massacre" and quickly dispatched a furious letter: "I was very much shocked the other day on hearing the accounts of the most wanton, cruel, and inhuman murders committed in Boston by the soldiers. Good God, are the Americans all asleep, and tamely yielding up their liberties, or are they all turned philosophers that they do not take immediate vengeance on such miscreants?"

The author of this letter was soon to be known as one of America's foremost patriots. His name: Benedict Arnold.

The story of military justice in this country begins with the saga of this strange, brilliant officer. His was the first significant American court-martial. In those days the Army operated under a loose code of justice copied from the British. This code dated from 1689 when, with the acceptance by William and Mary of the Bill of Rights, Parliament had acquired the power to define the jurisdiction of courts-martial. At first, it had granted court-martial jurisdiction only over mutiny, sedition, and desertion. But gradually, British military commanders had expanded its scope to take in some civilian offenses committed by military men.

During the Revolution, the whim of the American commander was even more controlling as to the jurisdiction of military law. But considerable confusion clouded the question. What, for example, constituted a civilian and what a military offense? And indeed what was legal and what was not? Sea captains, for instance, were permitted to share in the prize money of any ship they captured, yet army generals were not expected to profit from their commands. Yet many high-ranking officers had been merchants and speculators, including Arnold himself. If a commander indulged in a private financial speculation, risking his own money, was he committing an offense? And if so, was it civil or military? Arnold's court-martial brought the problem into focus and, in effect, set a legal precedent that would last almost two hundred years.

But this was a court-martial of far more than legal significance. Arnold was a man with legitimate grievances against the civilians running the war. Almost from the first they had dogged him. Time and again, despite his brilliant battle record, he found himself placed under a talentless hack appointed for political reasons. He had been passed over for promotion while lesser men went up in rank. At

Saratoga he had been ordered out of action by the "political" General Horatio Gates, and the Americans only won the action when Arnold disobeyed his orders and rallied the troops. Gates, who was scheming to supplant Washington as Commander in Chief, took credit for the victory.

Time and again, as Arnold squabbled with the Continental Congress and various State councils, Washington had interceded for him. But Arnold had another failing that even Washington could do little about. Arnold simply did not keep adequate books. At that time a sum of money was advanced to a commander out of which he was to pay all salaries and all expenses of a specific campaign. An accounting was then to be made to the Continental Congress. Arnold's accounts were constantly questioned. Congressmen complained that in Arnold's hands money "disappeared." Arnold retorted that he could hardly keep accurate books while making a forced march through swampland to Quebec or while fighting in the wilderness around Lake Champlain.

As the War progressed, Congress constantly disputed Arnold's finances, tied up his accounts, and withheld his salary. By 1779, the proud general was an embittered man. The charges that the Pennsylvania State Council brought against him must have seemed the final insult to a man who had considered himself a patriot and who had proved his heroism time and again in battle. Within weeks of the filing of the charges Arnold entered into correspondence with the British.

But no definite arrangement was made. Arnold was apparently waiting for the outcome of the trial.

Benedict Arnold was born in Norwich, Connecticut, on January 14, 1741, and named for a great grandfather who had been a colonial governor of Rhode Island. As a young man Arnold showed drive and promise. He opened a small drugstore in New Haven and within a few years had built it into a commercial trading company of considerable size. Much of his trade was with the West Indies, and Arnold—the man of action—often sailed as captain of one of his own ships.

Then came first the "Boston Massacre," and then the Battle of Lexington, and Arnold abruptly abandoned commerce for the service of his country.

Few in this nation's history have been so impressive on the battlefield as Benedict Arnold. He joined with Ethan Allen in the victory at Fort Ticonderoga, then led a march through swampland and forest—one of the classic marches in military history—to Quebec in 1775. Wounded at the unsuccessful Battle of Quebec, he fell back with his ragged, starving band to Lake Champlain. There Arnold occupied his troops in cutting timber for rudimentary ships, barges, and rafts. With this makeshift fleet, he surprised an invading British force, causing so much damage that the British withdrew and returned to Canada, putting off the invasion until the following year. Had Arnold failed here, the British would have sailed down the Hudson, cut off New England from the rest of the Colonies, and quite possibly put an end to the Revolution.

The following year the British again struck south from Canada, following the chain of lakes that leads to the Hudson River. The British moved confidently. They had already taken New York and Philadelphia and only awaited the success of their northern campaign to fatally split the Americans.

But at Saratoga, Arnold, recovered from his wounds, once again played a decisive role. An American detachment was besieged by the British; Arnold raised the siege, taking a heavy toll of British officers and men. And on October 2, 1777, in the critical Battle of Saratoga the Americans were being relentlessly forced back by a British advance. Arnold led a spontaneous cavalry charge into the British lines that scattered the redcoats in confusion and turned the battle around. The British retired, were surrounded, and surrendered. France, taking note of this astonishing victory, decided to come to the aid of the Americans.

With the entry of the powerful French fleet into the war the

British could no longer roam the Atlantic coast unhindered. Fearful of a blockade across the Delaware, their first decision was to abandon Philadelphia and move their headquarters to New York.

The momentum of victory was now swinging to the side of the colonies. Arnold had been on the battlefield from the first. Now, still recovering from his wounds, a national hero, he was chosen by General Washington to take command of the Philadelphia area. For the rest of the war, it seemed certain, Arnold could rely on his hard-won combat laurels to obtain a series of such comfortable commands behind the lines. All should have been serene. The hero had received his just reward. But Arnold looked at it differently. His back pay was still in dispute and tied up in Congress and he desperately needed money.

The snow was gone from Valley Forge and a bleak spring brought promise of better weather as a man named Robert Shewell came into Arnold's temporary headquarters. At this time the British were still moving out of Philadelphia, and the Americans were waiting to take over. Shewell had a proposition in which Arnold was interested.

Shewell was a respected Philadelphia merchant, although suspected by some of Tory leanings. But then most Philadelphians of good family were suspected of the same attitude. And in this case, it seemed, Shewell wanted to help the Americans—by saving his ship's cargo. The ship was the *Charming Nancy*, currently loaded and tied up in Philadelphia. Shewell was worried, he said, that the British would confiscate his cargo and take it to New York.

Arnold could hardly have believed this story. It was well known that the British in their haste to move had little space aboard their ships for their own cargo, let alone the cargo of the *Charming Nancy*. In reality, all that Shewell had to do was wait a few weeks and the Americans would take over the port.

What was unspoken was that Shewell wanted to take the cargo to New York himself where it would claim a higher price from the British than the Americans would pay in Philadelphia. But he could not sail his ship through the American lines without a pass. All parties to the deal would later deny this motive. But the fact is that Arnold granted Shewell the pass, and, in return, eventually received a fifty-percent share in the proceeds of the cargo.

The *Nancy* set sail, the last British soldier embarked from Philadelphia, and Arnold assumed command. His first move brought irritation to the citizens of the city. He chose as his official residence the same mansion that the British General had just evacuated, and soon was living there in baronial splendor with a coach-and-four and liveried servants.

To make matters worse, there was widespread fear of looting in the lull between the exit of the British and the arrival of the Americans, and Arnold had been asked to close all shops and places of business. This brought added financial hardship to many Philadelphians, and they blamed it on the high-living American commander.

Nevertheless, Benedict Arnold, a short stocky man in uniform with a limp and an indefinable air of heroism, was soon a familiar sight at social gatherings in Philadelphia. And at one of these he met one of history's most intriguing women, azure-eyed, golden-haired Peggy Shippen, the eighteen-year-old daughter of one of Philadelphia's first families. And apparently, she couldn't keep her eyes off Arnold.

When the British had occupied Philadelphia the year before, Peggy hadn't been able to keep her eyes off another handsome officer, British Lieutenant John André. Years later one of her grandsons wrote, "Poor André was in love with her but she refused him for Arnold, keeping a lock of André's hair, which we still have."

Now André and his fellow British officers were gone, but the American hero Arnold seemed a worthy replacement, even at the age of forty-two. And her feelings for him were reciprocated. Soon Arnold was addressing decidedly non-military letters to the girl: "Suffer that heavenly bosom to expand with a sensation more soft, more tender than friendship." To her father, he was writing to ask Peggy's hand in marriage, claiming that his fortune was "sufficient."

But Arnold's fortune was in truth not only insufficient, it

was just about to take a turn for the worse. In the midst of his courtship, he received disturbing news about the *Charming Nancy*.

Of all people, Peggy Shippen's good friend John André had come sailing down the New Jersey coast with a British squadron, burning vessels along the shore. The *Nancy* had hastily put into Egg Harbor, and its captain feared that the ship was in danger of being burned. He wanted Arnold to send wagons to the *Nancy* immediately to unload her and save her cargo.

The trouble was that there were no private wagons to be had; all had been commandeered by the State of Pennsylvania. Arnold solved this dilemma by commandeering the wagons under a military order, then arranging to pay for them privately. However, when the wagonmaster, Jesse Jordan, returned to Philadelphia with the goods, he fell into a dispute with Arnold over the amount of his bill. He complained to the Adjutant General, and eventually those complaints reached the Pennsylvania State Council.

The complaints were eagerly heard by a Council that had had its troubles with the military commander. Arnold handled all their grievances with arrogance; in some cases he did not even bother to answer them. As a result, Joseph Reed, the President of the Council, had become Arnold's bitter enemy. He and others of the Council had often marveled at Arnold's luxurious style of living; now they were certain something illegal was going on.

The Council investigated the matter of the *Charming Nancy* including the commandeering of State wagons, the character of Arnold's associate, Robert Shewell, and the affair of the closing of the shops. The evidence they compiled was considered by them strong enough to take to Congress. Congress turned the problem over to General Washington, who decided that he must bring his favorite officer to trial by court-martial.

The battlefield hero who had helped Washington so many times in the past was bitter almost beyond words. For what he considered a private financial speculation he was being destroyed by the same civilian politicians who had consistently disrupted his military career. To Washington he wrote:

"Let me beg of you, sir, to consider that a set of artful, unprincipled men in office may misrepresent the most innocent actions. . . . Having made every sacrifice of fortune and blood, and become a cripple in the service of my country, I little expect to meet the ungrateful returns I have received from my countrymen."

Nevertheless the trial was scheduled for December, 1779. And a brooding, bitter Arnold began to think of treason.

December 23, 1779. Snow fell softly òn the village of Morristown, New Jersey, headquarters of the American Army in the east. Major General Robert Howe and other officers of the Council entered Norris' Tavern where the court-martial would be held. On hand were the two chief accusers of Arnold: General Joseph Reed, President of the Pennsylvania State Council, and Timothy Matlack, Secretary of the Council, plus other witnesses. Benedict Arnold chose to conduct his own defense.

General Howe was the president of the court-martial panel, chosen by Washington because Howe had had some financial problems himself, and might be more lenient with Arnold than any other officer. Three brigadier generals, eight colonels, and one lieutenant colonel made up the rest of the panel.

Arnold was brought up on four charges. They included giving permission for a vessel belonging to "persons of disaffected character" (i.e. Tories) to enter a port of the United States without the knowledge of the State of Pennsylvania or the Commander in Chief; with having shut the stores and shops of Philadelphia while privately making considerable purchases for his own benefit; with imposing menial offices upon the sons of freemen; and with using public wagons of the State for the transfer of private property.

The prosecution called Timothy Matlack to testify to the first charge. The confusion at the time concerning private speculations by military officers is such that Arnold was not even charged with profit sharing in the deal. The charge, instead, hinged on the accusation that Shewell was a Tory, and that, by implication, Arnold was aiding the enemy by granting him a pass.

Matlack testified that Shewell was not only generally regarded to be a Tory but had, himself, told Matlack of being ordered to leave George Washington's camp by the General "on pain of imprisonment."

On cross-examination by Arnold, Matlack admitted he did not know whether Arnold was aware of this fact when he gave the pass. And Arnold asked, "Have you understood that upon several alarms, Captain Shewell turned out with the militia and did duty with them?"

"I know nothing of the matter."

But Matlack did know other evidence of Shewell's alleged "disaffection." Property belonging to Shewell had been seized by American forces in Virginia because Shewell was deemed unfriendly to America. But again, cross-examination drew from him the admission that Arnold might have been unaware of this circumstance, as he was far from the scene at the time, with the Army in the north.

Arnold chose not to cross-examine Matlack further, and the Judge Advocate moved to the second charge, the closing of the shops while Arnold allegedly bought goods for his private benefit. The prosecutor produced a deposition of Colonel John Fitzgerald, a former aide of General Washington, dated May 7, 1779.

Fitzgerald's deposition read, in part:

"On the evening of the day on which British forces left Philadelphia, the deponent and Major David S. Franks, aide-de-camp to General Arnold, went to the house of Miss Brackenberry, and lodged there that night; that the next morning the deponent went into the front room of that house to view Colonel Jackson's regiment marching into the city, and saw lying in the window two open papers . . . the deponent was surprised to find one of them contained instructions to Major Franks to purchase European and East India goods in the city of Philadelphia to any amount, for the payment of which the writer would furnish Franks with the money, and the same paper contained also a strict charge to the said Franks not to make known to his most intimate acquaintances that the writer was concerned in the property purchase.

"These instructions were not signed, but appeared to the deponent to be in the handwriting of General Arnold.

"The other paper signed by General Arnold instructed Franks to buy some necessaries for the use of his table. The deponent compared the writing of the two papers and found them identical."

General Arnold's aide, Major David S. Franks, was placed on the stand to verify this astonishing story. He proved to be a reluctant witness.

"At or before General Arnold arrived in Philadelphia did you receive orders from General Arnold to purchase goods?"

"I did receive that paper which Colonel Fitzgerald had mentioned . . . several days before the enemy evacuated the city . . . . But upon our coming into town we had a variety of military business to do. I did not purchase any goods . . . . The paper was entirely neglected; neither did I think anything concerning it until I heard of Colonel Fitzgerald's deposition."

As far as the court was concerned, the key to this charge was clearly the timing of the note. If Arnold's order to purchase goods privately had been given to Franks *before* Arnold was appointed commander of the city—and therefore before he was ordered to close the shops—then the note was just an innocent instruction to buy.

"Are you certain that the order for purchasing the goods was given to you *several* days before you went to Philadelphia?"

"It might have been three, four, five, or twenty days."

"Did you understand from General Arnold that he was to have command of the city on evacuation?"

"I did, but it was a *short* time before."

"Were the orders to purchase goods given to you before the General mentioned the matter to you?"

"I believe they were."

On cross-examination Arnold was quick to exploit the

opening his aide had given him. He asked Franks if he did
not "suppose my showing you the instrument from General
Washington ordering me to take command a *countermanding*
of the previous order I had given you to purchase goods."

Franks merely said he had formed no supposition on the
subject, but Arnold had made his point. In fact, so far had he
succeeded that after court adjourned Timothy Matlack sat
down to write a lugubrious note to a friend in Philadelphia:

"Every day turns up something new relating to the course
of this Phenomenon; and I shall send you the further
proceedings in this case as soon as they are closed, as it is
probable they will produce important consequences one way
or another."

The next charge, on giving menial offices to freemen, was
disposed of rather briefly by the military court, all of whose
officers had had trouble enough with the independent men of
the militia. William Matlack, Timothy's nephew, took the
stand to tell his story. It seemed that General Arnold's aide,
the ubiquitous Franks, had asked him to search for his
barber and bring him back. Matlack was Franks' orderly, yet
he did not take kindly to this order. Indeed, after two
unsuccessful searches for the barber, he had complained to
Arnold about being assigned "menial" chores. But Arnold
apparently did not think the order was "menial." He asked
young Matlack:

"Was any *menial* office imposed upon you, or upon any
orderly sergeant, to your knowledge?"

"I conceived the office that was imposed on me as
menial."

The prosecutor had gained nothing on this charge and the
next day the Judge Advocate turned to the most damaging
accusation against Arnold: "Using public wagons of the State
for the transfer of private property."

Now the prosecution began to introduce evidence showing
that while no wagons were available for private transport,
General Arnold had used his high military office to comman-
deer no less than twelve wagons for a personal chore. First
came a deposition from the wagonmaster who had gone to
Egg Harbor to unload the goods, Jesse Jordan.

Jordan said that Deputy Quartermaster General John Mitchell had sent him to General Arnold where he received orders, signed by Arnold's aide, Major Franks, to proceed directly to Egg Harbor. The implication was that he was going on a military project. He said that he proceeded with twelve empty wagons to the forks of Egg Harbor and until they arrived within about twenty or twenty-five miles of the forks he was confident they were employed "in the public service of the continent," and expected they were to take in a loading of public stores. The first cause of his doubting was that they were denied provisions by the commissary of issues there, who said he was sure it was *private* property they were going for.

In Egg Harbor he had loaded sugar, tea, coffee, six swivel guns, nails, linens, chests, sailcloth, and other articles from the *Charming Nancy* and brought them to Philadelphia. Then he applied to Colonel Mitchell with his payroll and Colonel Mitchell said he would have nothing to do with it, that he must apply to General Arnold.

When he did apply to General Arnold, the General argued over the amount of the bill, saying that he thought he should pay only for the actual days of employment, not for Jordan's travel time from home to Philadelphia.

The Judge Advocate then stood up to say that his key witness on this charge, Deputy Quartermaster John Mitchell, had been delayed on his way to the trial, and he asked permission to place him on the stand later. Permission was granted, and Arnold began his defense.

Arnold's defense case was vigorous, brief, and to the point. In the middle of a war, in a time when travel was difficult and long and witnesses had a hard time getting to Morristown, he conducted his defense in many cases by calling the prosecution witnesses to the stand and challenging them with questions that left their own mark.

On the first charge, for example, which concerned his dealings with "a disaffected person," Arnold recalled Timothy Matlack for two pointed questions. He wanted to know if Matlack was aware that Captain Shewell had taken an oath of allegiance to the State of Pennsylvania and that he had produced a certificate of this oath to the President and Council of the State of Pennsylvania.

Matlack said he didn't know about that and Arnold excused him, aware that the questions would leave their own impression with the court. Besides, he had a surprise witness on this same charge who was on his way to the trial, and would be placed on the stand later.

In defense of the second charge, shutting up shops while purchasing privately for his own benefit, Arnold placed his aide, Franks, on the stand.

"What do you know about shutting up the shops and stores in Philadelphia?"

"The day after I came into town, General Joseph Reed, who is now President of the Pennsylvania Council, and myself met. He told me they were selling goods in town, and advised me to send a crier to prohibit the sale of goods .... When Arnold came to town, General Reed came to his quarters, and upon consulting with him, wrote his proclamation."

"Are you certain that *General Reed* drew up the proclamation?"

"I saw General Reed at the table drawing it up."

"Do you know of my having given any licenses to purchase goods, though applications were made by my intimate friends for them?"

"I know that many applications were refused, and I know of no license being granted . . . to purchase goods."

"Do you know of any articles being laid by for my own use?"

"No."

Now the court had a question for Franks.

"Do you know whether General Arnold purchased any part of the *Nancy* or her cargo?"

"I do not, but I have heard General Arnold say he did, and I have also heard Mr. Seagrove say he did."

"Was it previous or subsequent to General Arnold's granting of the pass."

"It was subsequent."

This was a windfall for Arnold. He had never denied the allegation that he had split the proceeds of the sale of the *Nancy's* cargo. But now his aide had managed to get in the record the inference that Arnold had granted the pass before any sort of deal was made. The implication was that the pass itself was granted in good faith, and the deal made only afterward as a private speculation.

While this impression was sinking in, Arnold created a great sensation in the court when he brought in one of the most prestigious officers in Washington's Army as a defense witness: Alexander Hamilton, aide to General Washington.

Hamilton, lounging elegantly in the witness chair and smiling from time to time, did not disappoint Arnold. He was here to testify about the character of one of Arnold's partners in the *Nancy* affair, Mr. Seagrove, another business associate accused of being "disaffected."

"Do you know Mr. Seagrove's general political character?"

"I have heard it frequently discussed, and very different opinions entertained of it. Many were of the opinion that he was warmly attached to the American cause, and others that he was not. . . . My own opinion of him was favorable from a general idea of his integrity, and from a particular circumstance which happened.

"As our troops were evacuating New York, I was among the last of our army that left the city; the enemy was then on our right flank, between us and the main body of our army. At about three miles from town, on our march out, Mr. Seagrove was at a house . . . in company with several ladies and gentlemen. He left them and came up to me with strong appearances of anxiety in his looks, informed me that the enemy had landed at Haarlam, and were pushing across the island, advised us to keep as much to the left as possible to avoid being intercepted.

"The favorable impressions I before had of Mr. Seagrove were confirmed by this incident, not so much from the nature of the transaction, as from an appearance of sincerity and concern strongly pictured in his countenance; which had the more weight as he remained in this city and might have run some risk for what he did."

"Has not the political conduct of Mr. Seagrove since confirmed the favorable impression you had before of him?"

"It has, as far as it has come to my knowledge."

Hamilton's testimony left the civilian accusers of Arnold discomfited. Timothy Matlack's allegations about the character of at least one of Arnold's partners had been directly refuted by an officer of known integrity.

Perhaps sensing the mood of the court in reference to the charge of "giving menial offices to freeman" Arnold did not even bother to refute the charge. He proceeded directly to the most troubling charge, using State wagons for private business.

Once again his aide, Franks, was on the stand. Franks said that he had gone to Colonel Mitchell, the Deputy Quartermaster General, to see whether he could spare some wagons to transport "some goods that were in danger of falling into enemy's hands at Egg Harbor." Mitchell had told him that at present he had no spare wagons but would let him know.

After some days had passed, Arnold sent Franks again to the Quartermaster, this time armed with an order that Franks had signed with his official title, directing that the wagonmaster pick up the goods.

"Did you not view the request made for the wagons of a private nature, and not official?"

"I understood you were to pay for the wagons for the transport of the goods, and that it was a matter of favor of Colonel Mitchell to let you have them."

"Then how did it happen that you signed the order to Jesse Jordan *officially?*"

"I had no particular directions from you so to do; from custom I always signed aide-de-camp at the end of my name."

In other words, if this testimony could be believed, the criminal charges against Arnold had come about solely by Franks' routinely signing "aide-de-camp" after his name.

As to the financial woes of Jesse Jordan, Franks testified that Arnold had left money with an aide "to discharge that account" but that Jordan had never returned to pick up his fee. A possible reason he had not returned would be revealed by Arnold in his summation.

Finally the key man in the wagon transaction arrived in court to be placed on the stand belatedly by the prosecution—Deputy Quartermaster John Mitchell who had assigned the wagons to Arnold. But to the dismay of the prosecution, Mitchell's testimony turned out to be favorable to Arnold. Apparently, there had been plenty of wagons to spare for private jobs at the time of Arnold's request.

Mitchell told the court: "As there were at the time a greater number of continental teams coming in than I expected, it enabled me to comply with General Arnold's request without any inconvenience to the service."

Arnold, on cross-examination, made sure the court understood the point: "When I applied for the wagons, did not you tell me that there were frequently public wagons lying idle in town, when provisions did not arrive to load as expected, in which case they could be spared, and it would be a *saving* to the public as they were obliged to pay for the hire of the wagons whether they were employed or not?"

"Those circumstances have happened."

Arnold's vigorous defense was over. Now he stood up in court and stared at the officers on the board as he launched his summation.

"When the present necessary war against Great Britain commenced I was in easy circumstances and enjoyed a fair prospect of improving them. I was happy in domestic connections . . . which claimed my care and attention. The liberties of my country were in danger. The voice of my country called upon all her faithful sons to join in her defense. With cheerfulness I obeyed the call. I sacrificed domestic ease and happiness to the service of my country, and in her service have I sacrificed a great part of a handsome fortune. I was one of the first that appeared in the field; and from that time to the present hour have not abandoned her service.

"When one is charged with practices which his soul abhors and which conscious innocence tells him he has never committed, an honest indignation will draw from him expressions in his own favor which on other occasions might be ascribed to an ostentatious turn of mind."

Arnold then put into the record two resolutions of Congress thanking him for his bravery, and rewarding him with a horse to replace the one that had been killed beneath him; and many different letters and awards from General Washington, in which he was called "active, judicious, and brave, and an officer in whom the militia will repose great confidence. . . . I am persuaded his presence and activity will animate the militia greatly, and spur them on to a becoming conduct."

"Is it possible," asked Arnold, "that having won such honors I could sink into a course of conduct equally unworthy of the patriot and soldier?"

Yet, here he was being harassed by the Pennsylvania Council. "Such a vile prostitution of power, and such instances of glaring tyranny and injustice, I believe are unprecedented in the annals of any free people."

His only reason for giving a pass to the owners of the *Charming Nancy*, he said, was to save the cargo for the citizens of the United States.

As for closing the shops, he had been merely obeying the orders of Congress. The proclamation had actually been written by Joseph Reed, who was now criticizing it in court. If this charge were true, said Arnold, "The blood I have spent in defense of my country will be insufficient to obliterate the stain . . . . Where is the evidence of this accusation? I call upon them to produce it; I call upon them to produce it, under the pain of being held forth to the world and to posterity . . . as public defamers and murderers of reputation."

To the charge of giving menial offices to freemen of the militia, Arnold stated that he had always respected the character and exertions of the militia. He pointed out that he had taken command of the Pennsylvania militia in June, 1777, against British General Howe. "How far the good countenance of the militia under my command operated in deterring General Howe from marching to the city of Philadelphia I will not pretend to say."

On the issue of the public wagons, Arnold said simply that the wagons were not needed by the State at the time; their own Quartermaster had testified to that. And he had contracted to pay privately for them.

But this was only another example of the civilian vendetta against him, Arnold said. It was the Pennsylvania Council which had told the wagonmaster not to call for his pay—but instead to raise his charges to double the amount, and then to bring him into court.

"There is now an action against me, pending in one of the courts of Pennsylvania, for upwards of 1100 pounds for the hire of those wagons. Is it not very extraordinary that I should be accused and tried before this honorable court for employing public wagons, and at the same time and by the same persons be prosecuted in a civil court of Pennsylvania for employing the same wagons as private property?"

Arnold ended his statement with a plea aimed directly at the distinguished court of officers, several of whom had fought alongside him:

"I have looked forward with pleasing anxiety to the present day when, by the judgment of my fellow soldiers, I shall (I doubt not) stand honorably acquitted of all the charges brought against me and again share with them the glories and danger of this just war."

The court heard the Judge Advocate's summation, then adjourned to the 26th. On that day Arnold was brought in and, standing stiffly in front of the panel, heard the verdict.

The officers were clearly of opinion he had no right to give the permit to the *Charming Nancy*, "circumstanced as he was." His closing of the shops was justified, and they found the charge of private purchases "entirely unsupported, and they do fully acquit General Arnold of it."

Without comment, they acquitted him on the charge of treating militia men as menials.

"Respecting the fourth charge, it appears to the court that General Arnold made application to the Deputy Quartermaster General to supply him with wagons to remove property then in imminent danger from the enemy ... and it also appears that General Arnold intended this application as a private request and that he had no design of employing the wagons otherwise than at his private expense, nor of defrauding the public . . . but considering the delicacy attending the high station in which the General acted, and that requests from him might operate as commands, they are of opinion the request was imprudent and improper and that, therefore, it ought not to have been made."

In consequence of its findings on the first and last charges, the court sentenced him to receive a reprimand from his Excellency, the Commander in Chief.

A light punishment, but to a man of Arnold's pride, a devastating one—particularly as he had expected complete vindication. And Washington's reprimand, when it came, showed that despite his fondness for the high-spirited officer, he was angry at his actions:

"The Commander in Chief would have been much happier in an occasion of bestowing commendations on an officer who has rendered such distinguished services to his country as Major General Benedict Arnold; but in the present case a sense of duty and a regard to candour oblige him to declare that he considered his conduct in the instance of the permit as peculiarly reprehensible, both in a civil and military view, and in the affair of the wagons as imprudent and improper."

Epilogue

Embittered by Washington's reprimand, Arnold finally made his treasonous deal with the British. He would betray an important post. West Point, which commanded the full sweep of the Hudson, was the prize ultimately agreed upon. In August, 1780, Arnold asked Washington for command of that post and received it. On September 21, 1780, at Stony Point, New York, he finally met in person his wife's good friend John André to arrange details of the betrayal.

André was captured on his way back to New York and six incriminating papers he was carrying were discovered. News of the capture came to Arnold while he was breakfasting with

Washington, who had chosen that tense moment for a surprise visit. Arnold excused himself and disappeared.

He successfully made his way to the British and eventually went to England where he was greeted with scorn and neglect. He died in London on June 14, 1801, shorn of honor and despised forever by the countrymen he had once served so well in the field of battle.

2
The Other Pueblo

Prologue

*"Neither nature nor art has partitioned the
sea into empires, kingdoms, republics, or
states. There are no dukedoms, earldoms,
baronies, or knight's fees, no freeholds,
pleasure grounds, ornamented or unornamented
farms, gardens, parks, groves or forests there,
appropriated to nations or individuals, as there
are upon land. Let Mahomet, or the Pope, or
Great Britain, say what they will, mankind
will act the part of slaves or cowards if
they suffer any nation to usurp dominion over
the ocean, or any portion of it."*

John Adams

No matter how eloquently John Adams expressed his
opinion, eloquence was all he had to back it up, for it was
exactly Great Britain's intention "to usurp dominion over the
ocean." To the British it was as simple as life or death.

21

At the turn of the nineteenth century Great Britain was
in the midst of a bitter war with Napoleon, and her fleet
was the only potent weapon she had. Napoleon might be
able to rampage over Europe, but unless he could overcome
the British Navy, he could never conquer the British Isles.
In 1805 he assembled thirty-one French and Spanish ships
under Admiral Pierre Villeneuve, but at the Battle of Tra-
falgar, Admiral Horatio Lord Nelson led his twenty-seven
major British ships against it. The French lost twenty vessels,
the British none. British mastery of the seas was secure.

Great Britain's victory was not complete, however. Napoleon then set out to subdue all Europe and ordered that *no*
European nation trade with Great Britain, a nation that—
then as now—lived by trade. He moved quickly to annex
Holland, drove to the Baltic, raced across western Germany.
British trade with the continent dropped precipitiously. The
goods that Europe had formerly acquired from Britain now
came from the fledgling United States across the ocean. American trade with Europe rose to $108,000,000.

The British took action. Parliament passed a measure
known as "The Orders in Council" which prohibited neutral
powers from dealing commercially with the European continent, the order to be enforced by the British Navy. American
trade with Europe dropped to $22,000,000.

The British blockade of Europe helped exacerbate relations
with the United States that had been far from cordial before.
The question hinged on the concepts of nationality and desertion. To staff her fleet Britain needed men. "Press gangs"
had long scoured the streets of British cities seeking candi-
dates, willing or otherwise, but not even the supply of "Liver-
pool Wharf Rats" was unlimited. To maintain her hold
on her reluctant manpower, Britain abided by the an-
cient rule of perpetual allegiance—once a citizen, always a citizen, no matter what. The United States, on the other hand,
had been founded on immigration and was anxious to establish the principle that once a citizen is naturalized, he owes
allegiance only to his new homeland.

These conflicting viewpoints had led to a clash as early

as 1789, when a British vessel had stopped the American warship *Baltimore* off Cuba and taken off fifty-five men as British deserters. By 1807, almost 2,000 American seamen had been taken by the British.

But by 1807, the situation had become far less tense. President Jefferson's diplomatic efforts to come to an agreement with the British seemed to be prevailing. There had been no impressment incidents for some time and the British warships along the American coast were scrupulous in observing only their blockade activities.

With this background, the United States frigate *Chesapeake*, one of only six major warships in the U.S. Navy, was being refitted in Washington Navy Yard in 1807, preparatory to taking up a new assignment. No one contemplated that her upcoming voyage would be anything but peaceful.

June 22, 1807. The *Chesapeake*, a handy, Norfolk-built thirty-six-gun frigate, raised sail and pointed her bowsprit toward the Atlantic. Coming out of Hampton Roads she was an impressive sight, white sails billowing from three masts, sailors and officers bustling about their duties.

Pacing her quarterdeck was one of the most controversial officers in the Navy, Commodore James Barron, on his way to take command of the U. S. Naval Forces in the Mediterranean. Tall and lanky, he gave the impression of a man born to command. And he was. His father had been commander in chief of the Virginia State Navy during the Revolution; his brother was the widely respected Commodore Samuel Barron.

But fellow officers had already branded him a coward. In action against the Barbary powers off the North African coast two years earlier he had angered captains John Rodgers and Stephen Decatur, Jr., who were eager to invade the city of Tripoli. Barron had persuaded his brother Samuel, in command, to hold off attack until peace negotiations could be undertaken. A treaty was signed—and it was an

ignominious one for the Americans, leaving in force the
financial tribute that America would have to pay to sail the
Mediterranean free from harassment by Barbary pirates.
Rodgers blamed the "shameful" treaty on James Barron,
and from his cabin on the *Constitution,* he had hurled the
taunt of "cowardice."

Barron sailed as fleet commander on the *Chesapeake,*
which had been designated to be his flagship in the Mediterranean. As the flagship officer, he was senior in command on the ship. The captain of the *Chesapeake* was Master-
Commandant Charles Gordon. The division of responsibility
between these two officers was to become a crucial issue.
(Normally, the captain is responsible for making his ship
ready for sea—and for combat.)

A few miles to port—or larboard as it then was called—a
British squadron lay at anchor, but these ships, although
they bristled with heavy guns, were of little concern. The
British were always there. At war with Napoleon, they
ceaselessly sailed the Atlantic coast in search of French
shipping.

As the *Chesapeake* got under way, H.M.S. *Leopard,* a
fifty-gun frigate, raised sail and detached itself from the
squadron. Sailing ahead of Barron, it preceded him to sea.
Barron watched it awhile, but the *Leopard* seemed to take no
notice of the American ship. And, finally, he went below.

The *Chesapeake* tacked to take advantage of the breeze;
far ahead *Leopard* echoed the move. *Chesapeake* tacked
again, and *Leopard* came about also, always keeping the
"weather gage," which men on sailing ships knew as the
"fighting position."

More than once that day Barron came on deck to view the
Leopard in the distance. Both ships were sailing into the
same wind; both would normally tack at the same time. What
Barron could not see was that the *Leopard* was clearing for
action, tricing up gunports, removing tompions from the
guns, making ammunition ready.

About three in the afternoon, the *Leopard* abruptly stopped its cat-and-mouse maneuvers, bore around sharply, took
up a position on the American ship's windward quarter, and

hailed the *Chesapeake.* "Request permission to send an officer aboard with dispatches."

Bobbing on the blue water, a small boat pulled toward the *Chesapeake,* with a British lieutenant in the stern. Minutes later, the officer, Lieutenant Meade, climbed from the gig to the frigate's spar deck and was escorted below to the Commodore's cabin. There, beneath the oaken beams, stood the tall Commodore. Lieutenant Meade saluted, and handed him a one-page dispatch.

Admiral George Cranfield Berkeley, commander in chief of the Royal Navy on the North American Station, had listed six ships from which British seamen had deserted to the *Chesapeake,* and instructed his captains to search the American warship. Captain Salisbury Pryce Humphreys of the *Leopard,* in a note that accompanied the dispatch, conveyed his hope that an agreement could be reached without interrupting "the harmony subsisting between the two countries."

Barron discussed his reply with a passenger and old friend, Doctor John Bullus. At the request of the State Department, Barron had investigated all of his crewmen before sailing. As far as he knew all were American citizens. Mystified, he drafted a reply: "I know of no such men as you describe. It is my disposition to preserve harmony, and I hope this answer to your dispatch will prove satisfactory."

What Barron did not know was that one sailor—John Wilson—was indeed a British deserter sailing under false papers. And the British knew he was there.

The Lieutenant took the reply, climbed down to his gig, and began the trip back to his ship. Coming out on deck into the sunshine, Barron saw the British ship not 300 yards away, as the gig pulled up by its side—and for the first time discovered that the *Leopard* was in full battle array. Heavy guns poked from the ports, marines and muskets peopled the decks, gunners stood at battle stations.

Barron turned to Captain Gordon and told him to get the men to quarters quietly—so as not to alarm the British in case they were bluffing. Boys rushed below to the magazine for powder horns; men started clearing the gun decks. But not in time.

Big guns exploded in a cloud of fire and smoke from the *Leopard*; broadsides smashed into the *Chesapeake*, splintering her hull and masts, while secondary batteries swept her deck with chain and canister. Blood drenched the men cringing behind silent guns, unable to return the fire. Only seven powder horns were filled, matches were not primed, and the loggerheads were cold.

On deck, Barron was already wounded. Repeatedly he ordered his guns to fire; none responded. In the smoke and wreckage of the gun deck, crewmen were unable to find the matches; they had been stored, but not in the magazine.

As the *Chesapeake's* guns remained mute and the enemy broadsides continued, Barron called to Marine Officer John Hall: "Go down to the gun deck and ask them for God's sake to fire one gun for the honor of the flag. I mean to strike." Young Lieutenant William Henry Allen, frantic with frustration, picked up a hot coal from the galley in his bare hand and fired a lone gun at the very moment when the Commodore struck his colors.

And the firing stopped. The battered, splintered *Chesapeake*, wounded and dying men all over her decks, hove to as a British boarding party arrived. Barron bitterly informed the British officers that he was surrendering his ship as their prize. The British coolly refused. They searched the ship, and took off "John Wilson" and three Americans whom they also claimed were deserters. Then they sailed away. The action was over, but the drama had hardly begun.

In itself, the court-martial of James Barron was dramatic. Rarely—if ever—in the history of court-martial law has a naval defendant faced a court so packed against him. The president of the court was his old enemy John Rodgers, the man who had called him a coward. His other enemy from the Barbary days, Stephen Decatur, Jr., was also on the panel. To Decatur's credit, he tried to resign from the court. "It is probable that I am prejudiced against Commodore Barron," he wrote Secretary of the Navy Robert Smith. "Even prior to the attack my opinion of him as a soldier was not favorable." The Secretary denied his request, for there were already too few senior officers available to serve.

But Barron's troubles were not all in the panel of officers who would judge him. From his own crew, several men stood ready to betray him. Master-Commandant Charles Gordon was one. Gordon was an elegant young man with a reputation for wit. The Commodore considered him frivolous and unwilling to attend properly to his duties. Another hostile officer was Lieutenant Allen, who had fired the lone gun. He was an intimate of John Rodgers and had come aboard the *Chesapeake,* already predisposed against his commander, Barron.

In all, six of his officers had united in asking, in an official letter to the Secretary of the Navy, for a court-martial of Barron. They would be on hand to testify against him.

Barron, Gordon, Marine Gunnery Officer Hall, and Gunner William Hook were all to be tried separately for various offenses. Gordon, particularly, received a certain amount of deference: the Judge Advocate General, Littleton Waller Tazewell, was a close friend of Gordon's uncle in Congress. And if Barron was acquitted the guilt for not having the ship ready must fall on Captain Gordon.

As Barron saw it, he had ordered the guns to fire. Because the guns were not ready they had not fired. Captain Gordon, in a letter to Barron before the ship sailed, had certified that the *Chesapeake* was completely ready for sea. In Barron's mind, this was the key: his officers had been derelict in their duty, from the Gunnery Officer to Captain Gordon.

But the Navy had a different view, expressed in the charges read to Commodore Barron as his court-martial convened on the deck of the *Chesapeake,* lying in Norfolk harbor, on January 4, 1808.

Charge 1st For negligently performing the duty assigned him.

Charge 2nd For neglecting on the probability of an engagement to clear his ship for action.

Charge 3rd Failing to encourage in his own person his inferior officers and men to fight courageously.

Charge 4th For not doing his utmost to take or destroy the Leopard, *which vessel it was his duty to encounter.*

As to the first charge, the prosecution first attempted to

establish that Commodore Barron had not visited the *Chesapeake* as often as he should have before she sailed, to see whether her guns were properly fitted and her ammunition correct. Various witnesses testified that he had made only two brief visits to the ship before sailing. And Captain Gordon added: "The magazine I know he did not see."

The second charge hinged on how soon Barron should have realized that the *Leopard* intended to attack. The *Chesapeake* had sailed at seven A.M. The *Leopard* had gotten under way almost immediately thereafter. If Barron could not have known until the last few seconds of *Leopard's* hostile intent, he would be clear of the charge. But the two ships had sailed together for eight hours before the firing started. Had there been no clues?

Various officers testified that the action of the *Leopard* in getting under way was suspicious enough. For one thing, there had been signals in the British squadron. For another, the *Leopard* had tacked so as to always have the weather gage on the *Chesapeake*.

At two P.M., while these maneuvers were taking place and well before the *Leopard* had stopped and hailed the *Chesapeake*, a dinner was served in the Commodore's cabin. It was to play a pivotal role in the trial. The guests were Captain Gordon, Doctor Bullus, and Captain Hall. (Doctor Bullus, a civilian, never appeared at the trial.) Captain Gordon, testifying for the prosecution, gave his version of what happened:

"While we sat at dinner in the cabin, the *Chesapeake* having been tacked about this time, the *Leopard* also changed her position. This enabled us to see her through the larboard forward port in the cabin. Commodore Barron then observed (addressing himself to no particular person at the table that I recollect, but generally to the company) *that her movements appeared suspicious.*"

This appeared to be devastating testimony. If Barron at two P.M. had thought the British ship's movements suspicious, he would have had more than an hour to clear his decks for action. Barron's attorney, Robert B. Taylor, wasted no time attacking that testimony in cross-examination.

"Am I to understand that this remark produced no observation from you or any other person?"

"I don't recollect any."

"Did you, or any other person at the table then, express any suspicions of the *Leopard's* intentions to Commodore Barron?"

"I don't recollect any."

"Did you communicate the suspicions you then had to any person previous to the attack?"

"I did not. I had no conversation with any person upon this subject."

"Did these suspicions induce you after dinner to order the gun deck to be cleared away?"

"They did not."

After more questions of this kind, and more negative answers, the counsel asked:

"And yet you have stated you had suspicions?"

"I had suspicions—such suspicions as these remarks would naturally excite in my mind; but I did not think that an action must inevitably occur, in consequence of having heard this remark."

Marine Captain John Hall told a different story.

"Did you hear Commodore Barron say anything about the *Leopard* at dinner?"

"I heard Commodore Barron speaking of the sailing of the *Leopard*, say he thought we beat her; this is all that I heard him say."

"Did you hear any other persons at table express suspicions of her movements?"

"None."

This time it was the Judge Advocate who came forward to cross-examine.

"Did you remain at table the whole time Captain Gordon did?"

"I remained at table the whole time of dinner until the cloth was removed. I then left the table, leaving Commodore Barron, Captain Gordon, and Doctor Bullus still there."

So Barron could have made his remark after Hall had left, leaving only Bullus able to refute Gordon's testimony. And Bullus was not available at the trial.

But before Hall was excused another note entered the questioning. The Judge Advocate asked what had prompted Barron's remark concerning the *Leopard*.

"The two ships were standing on the same tack and as we were at table we could see the *Leopard* through the starboard port."

"Are you positive that you saw the *Leopard* through the *starboard* port?"

"I am pretty certain of it. I remember looking over my shoulder as I sat at table to see her, and from my situation at table I must have seen her in that situation through the starboard port."

The prosecution then moved to establish Barron's negligence in what the Commodore himself termed "the second era" of the trip, the time between the *Leopard's* hailing of the *Chesapeake*, and its opening broadsides.

Surely, the prosecution contended, any reasonable man would have known when the British sent an officer to demand deserters that they intended to use force to take them off. From the first moment the officer came aboard, the Commodore should have ordered his crew to battle stations. But what had happened?

About fifteen minutes after the British officer came aboard, Gordon was called to the cabin:

"While I was in conversation with the British officer, Doctor Bullus and Commodore Barron appeared to be in close consultation repeatedly which left me alone, ignorant of what was going on. In about half an hour after the arrival of the British Lieutenant, one of our officers came down to the cabin, and informed me the *Leopard* had a signal flying. This the British officer said was a signal for his boat, and appeared anxious to be off. On his showing anxiety the Commodore himself entered into conversation with him, and I left them and went on deck. In eight or ten minutes the officer came up and I saw him over the side."

Forty minutes—time enough to get the guns ready—had been wasted. Now, too late, Barron apparently realized what was about to happen. As Gordon testified:

"He remarked, as their demand appeared of a serious nature, I had better get the gun deck clear. I immediately went on deck and ordered the first lieutenant to have the gun deck cleared, and shortly after sent down the second lieutenant to assist him. About this time, Commodore Barron came on deck himself and went to the gangway. He then called me, and asked if I observed that the tompions were out of the *Leopard's* guns, and her guns pointed on us. I observed it and he then directed me to order the men to quarters but not to make use of the drum, or to let a man be seen out of the ports, adding at the same time, that if we were seen going to quarters, they would charge us with making the first hostile show."

The order to send the men to quarters without the use of the drum—the normal manner of calling to quarters—was made much of by the court. Underlying the trial was the unspoken feeling that Barron had acted throughout in a manner unbecoming a naval officer—and here was yet another apparent example. To add to the confusion, the drums had already started beating and Gordon had to stop them, confusing everyone just as the first broadside hit. The feeling of the Navy about this was revealed in a question to Gordon:

"Do you think that under the circumstances you have stated, a commander could order his crew to quarters secretly, without acting unbecoming to the character of an American officer?"

"I think that under the circumstances first stated, that is, after the British officer first came aboard, a commander might properly have got his crew to quarters secretly. But afterwards, when he had left the ship as he did, and the *Leopard's* guns were pointed into us, this was a time which required great decision and determination, and to order the crew to quarters secretly was not evincing such a disposition, and therefore was improper."

The third charge against Barron, failing to encourage his men to fight courageously, also implied personal fear or cowardice. The picture of Barron during the crucial moments of battle, as described by witnesses, showed a man in a

chaotic situation, trying any measure he could think of. He
must have been astonished to find that none of his guns
would fire. They were all loaded in port before sailing, so,
even though cartridges, wads, and sponges were not
available for continuing fire, they should have been able to
unloose one broadside. But the confusion below deck, vividly
testified to by witnesses, was a scene of men trying to find
powder horns and matches to fire the guns—and failing.

So there he was on the quarterdeck, with broadsides
smashing his ship apart. He tried hailing the British ship. He
attempted to lower a boat with an officer to go over to the
Leopard. The British ship didn't answer his hail, and the boat
got jammed while lowering. And still the broadsides poured
in, men writhed and fell, and no guns answered from his own
ship.

Perhaps the best description of Barron during these
moments was given by Marine Captain Hall:

"When I first came on the upper deck, I observed
Commodore Barron standing in the gangway, hailing the
Leopard. This was after the *Leopard* had fired one gun
athwart our forefoot but before her first broadside. Almost
immediately, after this, the *Leopard* fired a broadside into
us. By this broadside Commodore Barron was wounded . . . I
then went aft where my marines were, and asked the
sergeant if the marines were all ready, and their guns loaded.
He told me they were.

"I . . . saw Commodore Barron standing on the aftermost
gun, I believe, hailing the *Leopard,* saying he would send a
boat on board, just about which time a second broadside was
fired from her. Commodore Barron immediately turned
round, and said, as well as I recollect, 'have a boat lowered
down.' He then got down from where he was standing, and
observing some of the rigging cut away, he asked for God's
sake gentlemen, will nobody do their duty? Commodore
Barron then went forward and meeting Captain Gordon asked
if the gun deck was yet ready. Captain Gordon replied that it
was not. He then ordered Captain Gordon below to get the
gun deck ready, and told him to stay forward until it was
ready. Commodore Barron then continued going forward . . .

and when he returned aft, he called to me and said "Captain Hall will you go down to the gun deck, and ask them for God's sake to fire one gun for the honor of the flag. I mean to strike."

Another vivid picture was given by Sailing Master Samuel B. Brooke:

"When I came on deck, Commodore Barron was in the gangway with a trumpet in his hand, hailing the *Leopard*. He remained there during the height of the fire. Towards the latter part of it he came aft, and observed to me, 'Mr. Brooke, is it possible we can't get any guns to fire?' I replied I knew nothing about the guns, I had nothing to do with them. I then discovered that Commodore Barron was wounded in the leg. It was bleeding, and I asked him if I should tie it up. He said it was of no consequence. Commodore Barron then got on the signal locker, and I took my handkerchief and tied up his leg."

"Did Commodore Barron fail to encourage in his own person his officers and men to fight courageously?"

"I don't know what Commodore Barron may have said. He was in the gangway in the height of the fire, which is called the slaughterhouse. I thought he behaved very well there."

And Hall, in answer to the same question, said "Everything which he did, I thought, was calculated to encourage them—I never saw a man manifest more courage, so far as I could judge."

But the prosecution offered a different impression with the testimony of young Fitzhenry Babbitt, a midshipman.

"Did you hear Captain Barron use any language during this attack calculated to dispirit his crew?"

"I heard him say to the men who were standing on the weather guns while the *Leopard* was firing upon us, to keep down, we should all be cut to pieces."

Cross-examination brought out that the men were needlessly exposing themselves by standing on the guns to see the action—and that the remark might have been "*you* might all be cut to pieces."

The fourth charge, not doing his utmost to take or destroy the *Leopard*, was most eloquently pressed by Captain Gordon in his closing remarks, which wound up the case for the prosecution. He wished, he said, to amplify some of his testimony:

"In giving my reasons for saying the colors were prematurely struck, I observed it was because we were in readiness to return their fire . . . . I should have also stated other reasons which contribute to produce that opinion; had the Commodore determined to continue the action when he gave me orders to go down and get the guns to work myself, as I was gone but a few minutes, I think he should have waited my report of the gun deck, but I had scarcely time to go below and return, when the colors were hauled down. I wish also to say to the court that at that time I did not believe he had any knowledge of the state of the ship below to influence him in his conduct.

"To the best of my knowledge no deaths had been reported; no damage had been reported; no dismounting of guns from their being badly fitted to their carriages; no cartridges, wads, or sponges could have been found too large, because the charges in the guns had not been fired off, consequently no deficiencies could have come to his knowledge to have influenced his decision."

Gordon then brought out another point.

"In the course of my evidence, I stated that there was not much prospect of success at that time. I meant to convey by that answer, that there was not much prospect of succeeding in taking the *Leopard*—but not to convey an idea that as a national ship there was nothing for us to do but strike. In such a situation, I conceive that although we may be a little inferior, it is expected a commodore will exert himself to do his enemy all the injury in his power, and notwithstanding we could not expect to succeed in taking the *Leopard*, we had it in our power to retaliate, by injuring her very materially, and very probably killing as many of her men."

Following this, the record reads "All the evidence . . . being now concluded, the president informed Commodore James Barron that if he was prepared, the court would now hear any defense he might choose to make."

Barron's main witness was himself. Standing up to face a

court packed with his enemies, his eyes flashing angrily, his voice tinged with contempt and scorn for Gordon, he was an impressive figure. A man who had been caught in an impossible situation, who had acted for humane reasons— and not by the naval code—he looked into the eyes of Decatur, the "Hero of Tripoli," while he drove home one point, then challenged the huge and hulking Captain Rodgers, who scowled like a Naval Buddha, barely able to hide his own contempt.

And in a masterful, logical defense, he brought into play two superb weapons: his thoroughgoing knowledge of the Navy, and an eloquence born of outrage.

"Mr. President and Gentlemen of the Court—

"After serving in the navy of the United States for ten years, it is now my fortune to be brought before you on charges implicating my honor, and my life . . . . Conscious of my own innocence . . . I enter on my defense with the proud and confident anticipation of rescuing my reputation from unmerited reproach. In this defence you shall find no unmanly attempt to interest your feelings or your generosity. It shall be such a one as an officer may make without reproach and officers receive without a blush. It shall be directed wholly to your judgment and your reason.

"The first charge against me is for negligently performing the duty assigned me . . . . The charge presupposes . . . that it was my duty often to visit the ship; personally to superintend her equipments, and examine into her condition, while she remained in Hampton Roads.

"In examining the principle of this charge I will show that the duties which it presupposes to have attached to me were not in my province, but peculiarly and exclusively devolved on another officer . . . . My defence is that in the relative situations of Captain Gordon and me . . . the duties . . . exclusively pertained to *him* as captain and commander, and not to me.

"It was *his* duty to 'repair on board,' on *him* was the obligation of 'stationing and mustering the crew' . . . so as to have her 'constantly prepared for immediate action.'

"If these duties really appertained to me, I alone am

responsible for the injury sustained from their nonper-
formance. Yet by a strange perversion either of judgment or
feeling, the omission is in *general* terms imputed to me as an
offense, while all the details of omission are *specific* subjects of accusation against Captain Gordon in his approach-
ing trial.

"I proceed to the 2nd charge, For neglecting on the
probability of an engagement to clear the ship for action. . . .
The question presented to you by this charge is not whether
these circumstances appear *now* to you to have prognosti-
cated the subsequent attack; but whether they ought *then* to
have convinced me. On this subject, *you* have the benefit of
history; I could only speculate. That which is now fact to you,
was only inference to me. You judge from experience, I
reasoned only from probability.

". . . The first occurrences, in the order of time . . . are the
communications by signal from one of the British squadron;
the telegraphic communication between that ship and another; and the *Leopard's* getting under way.

". . . Those signals are as incomprehensible without a
book of explanation as were the hieroglyphics of Colonel Burr
without the aid of General Wilkinson's key . . . . But it seems
that, as the *Leopard* got under way, I ought to have inferred
. . . 'the probability of an engagement.' Why so? If I had been
permitted to conjecture the meaning of a signal, I should
certainly have inferred that the signal was designed not for
the *Leopard* . . . but for the *Melampus*, which remained at
anchor. For the *Leopard* is not represented to have made an
answering signal . . . while the *Melampus did* answer the
signal.

"But the *Leopard*, it seems, got under way, when no other
vessel but the *Chesapeake* was in sight, carried but little sail
. . . and the charge supposes that I should have inferred the
probability of an engagement from these appearances. To
this charge it would be a sufficient reply to say, in the
language of a poet—

'Trifles, light as air, are, to the jealous,
Confirmations strong as holy writ.'

". . . With respect to the evolutions of the two ships, the tacking, wearing, etc., I really know not how to answer them, because I cannot perceive their force and application.

". . . The change of the *Leopard*'s course was produced by the same circumstances which caused the *Chesapeake* to brace sharp, to wit: the change of the wind . . . . Surely it cannot be expected that such a movement in a ship, known to belong to a nation at amity with us . . . ought to have excited . . . suspicion.

". . . Against such a suspicion of any attack were opposed the recollection of numerous cases in which seamen had been demanded of our ships, and refused, without hostility; a temper in the British councils then more favorable to the United States than at any former period; the recent arrangement by a treaty of the difficulties between the United States and Great Britain; and, above all, the daring extravagance of the act itself. As well might I have anticipated an attack in Hampton Roads.

"I cannot but deem my situation peculiarly unfortunate when it is imputed to me as a crime, that from these trivial occurrences I did not infer the probability of an outrage which the whole American nation has pronounced unprecedented in audacity; and which Great Britain herself, has since disavowed.

"One circumstance I ought not to pass unnoticed. Captain Gordon has stated that at table I expressed my suspicions of the *Leopard*—I most solemnly affirm that I made no such communication. . . . Doctor Bullus and Captain Hall were at table; neither of these heard it. . . . That Captain Hall did not hear it is proved by his own oath.

"Another thing is remarkable. The witnesses who have stated that they discovered the indication of unfriendly intentions in the *Leopard* are the persons who originally preferred the accusation against me; and who have given a written pledge to the world to establish their charges . . . . Though I believe them honorable and just, I know them to be men; they are not exempt from the infirmities of our nature; it is not in human virtue to be indifferent to . . . a prosecution for which . . . they are pledged to the world.

"To the rising, not the setting sun, are offered homage and adoration . . . . I am stripped of all power—my accusers are continued in command over these witnesses. It may be said, however, that Captain Gordon is not among the number of my pledged accusers—most true, a stronger motive operates on him. The web of his destiny is interwoven with mine. My condemnation is the pledge of his acquittal . . . . To my enquiries, he replies that he is under prosecution; and is not bound to furnish evidence which may operate against himself . . . . His sensitivity is indeed so very delicate (not to say morbid) that he refuses to give information beneficial to me even on points in no degree connected with the charges against him. He has even refused to acknowledge a letter, since proved to be in his own handwriting—so keen is the perception of his own danger, from my acquittal. Surely, sirs, I have a right to expect that with these evidences of Captain Gordon's mind towards me, your justice will supply those restrictions to his statements which his own lips refuse to furnish.

"There is always, sirs, a surer test of the influence of motives upon men at a past time; than their present declarations—I mean their conduct.

". . . Can it be imagined that Captain Gordon, if his expectation of attack was really so strong as he now supposes it to have been, would have gone to sea expecting an engagement without having, even once, had his men trained to the exercise of the guns; and without any enquiries as to the state of the magazine?

"The last offence with which I am charged is for not doing my utmost to take or destroy the *Leopard*, which it was my duty to encounter.

"If you are to judge whether the surrender was necessary from the state of the ship, at that moment, no man can condemn me. Whatever differences exist in the statements of witnesses on other points, they all concur in declaring that at that moment they were not only unable to *continue*, but even to *commence* a fire. At that instant there were neither matches, heated loggerheads, powder horns, cartridges, or wads in any of the divisions.

"At that time, too, the hull and spars of the ship had
suffered materially; twenty of the crew had been killed or
wounded. . . .

"In judging of the necessity of the surrender you must
ascertain the relative situations of the two ships, at the
moment it was adopted. If our situation was such as to
furnish no hope of success or escape; if it precluded the
expectation of even annoying my antagonist; if it presented
no prospect but the wanton and certain destruction of the
crew . . . there is not on earth one man of sound judgment
and correct heart who will not declare that the surrender was
proper.

"I address myself not to that man who, speculating in
safety . . . spurns the dictates of reason and virtue; wickedly
sports with the lives of his fellow beings, and in the
arrogance of imaginary heroism proclaims that, in every
case, surrender is dishonor. I speak to him of true spirit and
pure intelligence who discriminates between the idle . . .
suggestions of false pride and the manly conclusions of
genuine honor.

". . . I have, sirs, but a few words more to add, my destiny
is in your hands—my life, my honor, the sole patrimony
which ten years of service enables me to bestow on my posterity, hang on your decision. I wait that decision with the
solicitude which those great considerations ought to inspire."

The record reads: "The court then adjourned till tomorrow
morning 10 o'clock, then to meet at the house of Mrs. Street,
in the borough of Norfolk."

The wind blew cold across Chesapeake Bay, causing ships
to rock at anchor. Men pulled up their coat collars and
plodded along their way to Mrs. Street's house, a capacious
red brick mansion big enough to hold the press. Everyone in
Norfolk seemed to be there; they watched in awe as high
officers in full uniform, and correspondents from as far north
as Boston and as far west as Pittsburgh, clambered off
horse-drawn carriages, and made their way through the
throngs.

Florid, pink-jowled, fussy of his appearance, Judge Advocate General Tazewell did not present a pretty picture that day. He was a man committed to Captain Gordon. (Years later, Marine Officer Hall told Barron that prosecutor Tazewell had actually *written* both Gordon's defense and his own in the trials yet to come.) Now he read off the charges and specifications against Barron and heard the court respond.

To the first charge the court voted negative. The second charge, neglecting to clear his ship for action, had six separate specifications and the court took up each one separately. To the first four, the vote was also negative. The fifth specification read:

"In that the said James Barron did receive from the commanding officer of the *Leopard* a communication clearly intimating that if certain men were not delivered up to him he should proceed to use force, and still, the said James Barron neglected to clear his ship for action."

The court voted affirmative.

The sixth specification read:

"In that the said James Barron did verily believe from the communication he received from the . . . *Leopard* that the said ship would fire upon the . . . *Chesapeake* . . . and still the said James Barron neglected to clear his ship for action."

Again the court voted affirmative.

This raised an interesting legal question. By voting "yes" on two out of six specifications, would the court rule that the entire charge was affirmative, thereby convicting the Commodore? Before considering the question, the court took up the two remaining charges. Both were turned down. There must have been great tension in the old house of Mrs. Street. The record, however, merely reads:

"The Judge Advocate, by the direction of the court, then read again the second of the said charges, and the several specifications annexed to same.

"The same being heard and duly considered, the Judge Advocate propounded the following question: Is the prisoner guilty or not guilty under this second charge preferred a-gainst him . . . and it was decided that he is guilty."

Monday was as cold as Saturday. A threat of snow stirred

the city. Inside the Street house, fires crackled in old fireplaces, and one reporter, caught in the crush, saw his coat start to go up in flames. A bitter naval officer, proud descendant of proud naval forebears, looked stonily above the heads of his enemies as he heard himself suspended for a term of five years from the Navy.

Epilogue

Commodore James Barron's court-martial reverberates through history. The firing by the British on an American ship was a major incident in the series of events that so angered President Jefferson that he slapped an embargo on British goods, closed American ports to foreign shipping, and tried to put the country on a course of total isolation. His actions led directly to the War of 1812.

And Barron himself was still to be heard from. His resentment at his court-martial was lifelong—and not without reason. In subsequent trials, Captain Gordon, whose ship was admittedly unready for battle, confessed his guilt and was given a "private reprimand," and the court even apologized for that. Barron, banned from command, brooded. In 1820 his resentment had reached such a pitch that he challenged his old enemy, Stephen Decatur, Jr., to a duel at Bladensburg, Maryland. Decatur accepted and was killed.

As to military justice, the trial was a landmark. It prompted a Naval Regulation prescribing exactly the responsibility of a commanding officer under such a situation: "The Commanding Officer shall not permit his command to be searched by any person representing a foreign state." This philosophy of the sanctity of the ship would be dramatically expressed five years later in the War of 1812 from the deck of the same *Chesapeake*. Mortally wounded, Captain James Lawrence ordered his men: "Don't give up the ship."

This regulation—and this spirit—dominated the Navy for 150 years, until a converted cargo ship lumbered along the coast of Korea and an American commander, Captain Lloyd

Bucher, faced the same agonizing decision: Do you surrender your ship or do you wait—unable to fight back—like a sitting duck until ship and crew are destroyed?

Bucher, like Barron, chose surrender. But the mood of the American public had changed and the Navy apparently knew it. Bucher was treated gently by a Court of Inquiry. He was not court-martialed. And the public at large, far from calling for vengeance, approved wholeheartedly.

3

They Hanged Philip Spencer

Prologue

"No commander shall inflict any punishment beyond twelve lashes . . . with a cat-o-nine tails. If the fault is to deserve a greater punishment he is to apply to the Commander-in-Chief of the Navy in order to the trying of him by court-martial, and in the meantime he may put him under confinement."
Art. 4
Navy Regulations c. 1840

In 1842 with the nation at peace, the Navy adopted a method of training future officers on the job, on actual cruises. The brig *Somers* was designated the first of such training ships and in October of 1842 set sail under the command of Captain Alexander Slidell Mackenzie.

Captain Mackenzie remains an elusive figure. A man of

letters (he was the author of several books, including a biography of his kinsman Oliver Hazard Perry) , described by his friends as "modest and unassuming," he was also apparently a martinet aboard ship. His unruly crew grated on his nerves, and no one more than Midshipman Philip Spencer, the son of the Secretary of War. Spencer, the Captain thought, was devious, dishonest, corrupt, always trying to undermine the authority of the Captain and his officers.

In describing Spencer's faults in a letter to the Secretary of the Navy, Mackenzie shows himself to be lacking in a sense of humor, a sense of proportion, perhaps even plain common sense, when he reports. Spencer's attempts to "seduce and corrupt" the crew "by availing himself for their amusement of an anomalous faculty which he possessed of throwing his jaw out of joint and by some strange mode of bringing the bones into contact to produce musical sounds, strange, mysterious, but as has been represented to me not unpleasant, and to play with perfect accuracy and elegance of execution a variety of airs."

It was an era when crews were large and the number of officers small, when the Captain was completely in charge once the ship had left port. It was an era when discipline was enforced by the cat-o-nine-tails, and according to the log of the *Somers*, the cat was used with great liberality by Captain Mackenzie. It was also an era when mutinies were a real and dangerous threat. And when the whisper of mutiny reached the captain of the *Somers*, he was prepared to take action.

On December 14, 1842, the tiny U.S. Navy brig *Somers*, under the command of Captain Alexander Slidell Mackenzie, made her way into the port of New York. A few days later, a New York citizen, Philip Hone, wrote the following entry in his diary:

"On our return today we found the city excited by the development of a dreadful story . . . . The . . . "Somers" . . . arrived in this port on Wednesday night from a cruise on the African coast . . . . During the whole of Thursday there was a

strange mystery about this vessel. She lay in the bay;
nobody, not even the near relations of the Officers, was
permitted to visit her . . . . The cause of all this is now
explained. A dreadful mutiny had been formed when the brig
left the coast of Africa . . . . Of this conspiracy, Philip Spencer,
a young man of eighteen years of age, son of the Hon. John
C. Spencer, Secretary of War, was the ringleader.

"The plan was to murder the Captain and Lieutenant,
convert the brig into a pirate, and come to the American
coast for the purpose of intercepting and robbing the packets
. . . . Two-thirds of the crew were engaged in the plot, but
Captain Mackenzie appears to have acted with the utmost
decision and bravery."

The tone of this diary was also echoed in the newspapers:
The New York *Express*, December 17, 1842.

". . . The story we learn is that young Spencer offered his
paper or roll of the conspirators to the master-at-arms to
sign, who signed it, to quiet their suspicions, then immediately revealed the facts to the Commander. The moment the
conspirators found they were discovered, they met in a body,
and went to the Commander demanding possession of the
ship, and young Spencer presented a pistol to his heart . . . .
The officers, after something of a struggle . . . overpowered
the conspirators, and regaining complete possession of the
ship, instantly caused the ringleaders to be tried by
court-martial, and young Spencer, within ten minutes of the
finding of the Court, was hung at the yardarm, along with
two of his men . . . ."

The New York *Herald*, December 18, 1842.

"These desperadoes might have eluded detection and
pursuit for years. . . we can hardly find language to express
our admiration of the conduct of Commander Mackenzie.
The public voice has already pronounced a verdict of
unqualified and unanimous approbation."

By the next day, the newspapers had come into possession
of some quite different information:

The New York *Herald*, December 19, 1842.

". . . There was no overt act . . . the plot was merely *in
embryo* . . . . In such circumstances a great difference of

opinion exists as to the necessity and legality of Mackenzie's conduct. . . . It also appears that there was no court-martial. . . . The officers would seem to have acted under a panic. . . ."

In Washington, the "official organ" of the Administration was the *Madisonian*. On Wednesday, December 21, a communication signed "S" was printed. Everyone soon knew that "S" was Secretary of War John C. Spencer, the father of Philip.

"The only account we have given by Spencer himself, is that *it was all a joke*. If it shall appear to have been the mere romance of a heedless boy . . . and if the execution of him and two seamen (against one of whom at least, there is not yet a particle of evidence) should prove to have been the result of unmanly fear, or of a despotic temper, and wholly unnecessary at the time to repress or prevent a mutiny—if all this can appear, it cannot be doubted that the laws will be vindicated. The laws of Congress prescribing the navy regulations forbid the taking of human life, even by the sentence of a court-martial . . . without the sanction of the President of the United States, of the commander of the fleet or squadron. This is believed to be the first instance in our history in which the law has been violated—the first in which prisoners—not of the enemy, but of our own citizens—have been put to death in cold blood."

What had happened on the *Somers?* Three men were dead. Had they been hanged without trial? And if so, why? A Court of Inquiry was called on December 28 to find out. The country was in an uproar, split up the middle in its opinion about the case. Prominent authors, including Richard Henry Dana and James Fenimore Cooper, argued in print; Dana defended the Captain, Cooper condemned him.

Secretary Spencer applied pressure for a civil trial in which Captain Mackenzie would be tried for first-degree murder. And Mackenzie, while the Court of Inquiry was deliberating, shot off a letter to the Secretary of the Navy pleading for a quick court-martial to forestall such action.

Sir:

I shall, if not tried by a court-martial, be liable as I am informed, after any lapse of time . . . to be arraigned for murder or manslaughter in the civil courts. Should there be any interval between the close of the Court of Enquiry and my appearing before a court-martial I shall, as I am also informed, be liable during that interval to similar arraignment.

Under these circumstances, I . . . request that the court . . . may be ordered to assemble before the dissolution of the Court of Enquiry, in order that there may be no such interval.

Mackenzie got his wish. Even before the Court of Inquiry published its findings a court-martial was ordered, to begin in Brooklyn on January 28, 1843. (The Court of Inquiry, as it turned out, completely cleared Mackenzie, a decision that normally would not have resulted in a court-martial.) Mackenzie was charged with murder, two counts of oppression, illegal punishment, and conduct unbecoming a naval officer. He denied all except the fact of the execution, stating:

"I admit that Acting Midshipman Philip Spencer, Boatswain's Mate Samuel Cromwell, and Seaman Elisha Small, were put to death by my order, but, as under the existing circumstances this act was demanded by duty and justified by necessity, I plead not guilty to all the charges."

James W. Wales, a purser's steward, was the first key defense witness. His testimony evoked a dark night in the South Atlantic. Wales had been taking his ease by the forward bitts watching the ocean break against the bow. There was no sound except muttered sailor-talk along the decks, the creaking of masts, and the whisper of ocean water. Then:

"Mr. Spencer came forward, and, after some few remarks relative to the weather, requested me to get on top of the booms, telling me at the same time that he had something very important to communicate to me. I accordingly got on top of the booms with him and he commenced the conversation by asking me was I afraid of death—and did I fear a dead man and dare I kill a person. I was very much surprised at these remarks and looked up to see if he was in earnest; I found that he was very serious and very much in earnest in what he said. I replied that I was not particularly anxious to die quite yet, that I had no cause to fear a dead person and that did a man sufficiently abuse or insult me, I thought I could muster sufficient courage to kill him if necessary. Mr. Spencer replied, 'I don't doubt your courage at all; I know it. But,' said he, 'can you keep a secret and will you keep one? If so,' he added, 'take the oath.' He then dictated an oath, of which I cannot recollect the whole; but the purport of it was that I should never make known to any person the conversation which was about to take place between us. I took the oath as directed by Mr. Spencer. He then went on to state that he was leagued with about twenty of the brig's company, to take her, murder all her officers, and commence pirating. The plan and stations of the men, he said, he had all arranged in secret writing, done up in his neck handkerchief. He requested me to feel of his neck handkerchief. I did so and there was a rumpling which showed that there was paper in the back part of it. He went on to state to me the plan he should pursue. The affray would commence some night when he had the midwatch. Some of his men would get into a fight on the forecastle. He (Spencer) was to bring them up to the mast and call Mr. Rogers, the officer of the deck, to pretend to settle the difficulty. A soon as Mr. Rogers had got to the gangway they were immediately to seize and throw him overboard. They would then have the vessel in their own possession. The keys of the arm-chest, he said, he could lay his hands on at any moment. The arm-chest was to be opened and the arms distributed to his men. He was then to station his men at the hatches to prevent anyone from coming up on deck, and he should proceed to the cabin and murder the Commander with the least noise possible. He should then proceed with some of his men to the wardroom, and then murder the wardroom and steerage officers.

"This accomplished, he said he should go on deck, have the two after guns slewed around so as to command, from a raking position, the deck. He would then cause all the crew to be called on deck, and select a number from them such as would suit his purposes; the remainder he should cause to be thrown overboard. This done, he should commence clearing the deck, beginning by throwing overboard the launch and all the spare spars and rigging of the vessel, as they only tended to lumber up the deck; that should they stand in need of any spare spars or rigging, they could take them from vessels that they would capture.

"This done, the brig was to proceed to Cape San Antonio, or to the Isle of Pines; and there take on board one who was familiar with their intended business, and who was ready and willing to join them. The name of this person was not mentioned. This done, they were to commence cruising for prizes; that whenever they took a vessel, after taking from her that which would be of use to them, they were to murder all on board and scuttle the vessel, so as to leave no traces of her. Should there be any females on board of the vessels they would take, they would have them removed to the brig for the use of the officers and men—using them as long as they saw fit, and then making way with them.

"Spencer then called up Elisha Small, seaman on board. He came and stood by the railing, but did not get up on the booms. (This was before I made any reply to what he said—because I could not reply.) He commenced talking to him in Spanish, but I could not tell what they were talking about, as I did not understand the language. Small looked surprised, however, at what he told him. I saw Small's face very plainly. Spencer then remarked to Small, in English, 'O, you need not be under any apprehension of fear on his (witness's) account, as I have sounded him pretty well and find he is one of us.' Small seemed pleased, and remarked that he was very glad to hear it.

"I took the first opportunity that I could to make the matter known to Commander Mackenzie."

Wales' conversation with Spencer took place on Friday night, November 25th, with the ship midway between the

Canary Islands and the West Indies. Hundreds of miles from land, with no radio communication to shore or to other ships, a real mutiny was indeed possible. But was this a real mutiny? The Judge Advocate asked on cross-examination:

"Did you tell Spencer he was taking a large job on hand with twenty men?"

"I did not."

The *Somers* crew consisted of 120 men, including twelve officers and midshipmen. Twenty associates in such a crew seemed unimpressive to the Judge Advocate.

"When Mr. Spencer told you he intended to make a scuffle some night . . . did you tell him it would be likely to rouse the men and prevent him from going on with his plan . . . considering he had but twenty associates in a crew of one hundred men?"

The defense counsel objected that the question was really an "argument." The Judge Advocate replied that he "was of opinion that the question was entirely legal, he having no right to assume the truthfulness of the witness." He wished to find out if the conversation would show whether the organization was complete, and if the mutiny, if existing at all, was to take place after further accomplices might be acquired. The witness, the Judge Advocate pointed out, had sworn that the mutiny was to break out before the arrival at Saint Thomas, and, he argued, "it is highly important to ascertain whether the mutiny was immature or not."

The Judge Advocate was overruled, but his statement touched on one of the major issues of the *Somers* case: the question of time. Saint Thomas was nine days to westward, time enough for a "mature" mutiny to erupt. But each day carried the ship closer to port and lessened Spencer's time to recruit, organize, and carry out such an elaborate plan. Guert Gansevoort, First Lieutenant on the *Somers*, took the stand to tell what happened the next morning, Saturday, November 26th.

"He (the Purser) asked me if I was aware that a plot existed on board to take the vessel out of the hands of her officers and murder them all? I told him that I was not aware of anything of the kind. He then gave to me the information that Mr. Wales had given him . . . . I was anxious to make it known to the Commander, and did not stay to hear all he had to say. I immediately entered the cabin and mentioned the circumstances. He received it with great coolness—said that the vessel was in good discipline, and expressed his doubts as to the truth of the report. I asked him if I should see Mr. Wales myself and get the information from him. He said no—he did not wish me to do so, or to say anything about it. He assigned no reason at this time for this, but ordered me to keep a strict lookout upon Mr. Spencer and the crew generally, which I did. About dinner time I missed Mr. Spencer from the deck. This was about two o'clock. I discovered that he was in the foretop, and immediately went up to see what he was about. He was sitting on the lee side of the top, with his chin resting on his breast—apparently in deep thought. He did not observe me till I had got into the top and was standing erect. He raised his head, and as soon as he discovered me got up and evinced some confusion. He asked me some questions about rigging, and about the foremast head, which I answered in my usual manner . . . I came on deck and left him in the top. I should think it was about an hour after that I discovered Green in the top with him. He appeared to be engaged in pricking India ink in Spencer's arm. The crew were employed in slinging clean hammocks. I was engaged in mustering the men for the purpose of having hammocks stowed. When I got abreast of the Jacob's ladder on the starboard side forward, I observed Mr. Spencer sitting on the ladder. I turned my eye towards him and immediately caught his eye, which he kept staring upon me for more than a minute, with the most infernal expression I have ever seen upon a human face. It satisfied me at once of the man's guilt. As soon as the hammocks were stowed, I reported the circumstances to the Commander, and told him that I thought something should be done, in order to secure him. He replied that we would keep a sharp lookout—that he did not wish to do anything hastily; and that by evening quarters he would decide what it was best to do. I think it was just before the drum beat to quarters, that he asked me what I would do if I were in his situation as Commander of the vessel. I told him that I would bring that young man aft (alluding to Mr. Spencer) and iron him and keep him on the quarterdeck. He told me that that was the course which he intended to pursue, and that he was very glad to find that I agreed with him."

Commander Mackenzie, thirty-nine years old, was by no means a typical naval officer. His talents ran to the literary; he was the author of several books of travel and biography. Appropriately, for one of such background, his testimony was given in a long narrative deposition. For his own reasons, Mackenzie took advantage of his legal right to refuse to take the stand in his own defense.

This is how he described the arrest, and the dramatic events which followed:

"At evening quarters I ordered all the officers to lay aft on the quarterdeck. I approached Mr. Spencer and said to him, 'I learn, Mr. Spencer, that you aspire to the command of the *Somers?*' With a deferential, but unmoved and gently smiling expression, he replied, 'Oh, no, sir.' 'Did you not tell Mr. Wales, sir, that you had a project to kill the commander, the officers, and a considerable portion of the crew, of this vessel, and convert her into a pirate?' 'I may have told him so, sir, but it was in joke.' 'You admit then that you told him so?' 'Yes, sir, but in joke.' 'This, sir, is joking on a forbidden subject—this joke may cost you your life. Be pleased to remove your neck handkerchief.' It was removed and opened, but nothing was found in it. I asked him what he had done with the papers containing an account of his project which he had told Mr. Wales was in the back of his neck hand-kerchief. 'It is a paper containing my day's work, and I have destroyed it.' 'It is a singular place to keep day's work in.' 'It is a convenient one,' he replied, with an air of def-erence and blandness. I said to him, 'You must have been aware that you could only have compassed your designs by passing over my dead body, and after that, the bodies of all the officers; you had given yourself, sir, a great deal to do; it will be necessary for me to confine you, sir.' I turned to Lieut.

Gansevoort and said, 'Arrest Mr. Spencer, and put him in double irons.' Mr. Gansevoort stepped forward and took his sword. He was ordered to sit down on the stern-post, double ironed, and, as an additional security, handcuffed. I directed Lieut. Gansevoort to watch over his security, to order him to be put to instant death, if he was detected speaking to, or holding intelligence in any way with any of the crew. That night the officers of the watch were armed with cutlasses and pistols, and the round of both decks made frequently, to see that the crew were in their hammocks, and that there were no suspicious collections of individuals about the decks. On searching the locker of Mr. Spencer, a small razor-case was found, which he had recently drawn with a razor in it from the purser. (Inside), the case was found to contain a small paper rolled in another; on the inner one were strange characters, which proved to be Greek, with which Mr. Spencer was familiar. It fortunately happened that there was another midshipman on board the *Somers*, who knew Greek. The Greek characters converted by Midship'n H. Rogers into our own, exhibited well-known names among the crew. The certain, the doubtful, those who were to be kept whether they would or not, arranged in separate rows; those who were to do the work of murder in the various departments, to take the wheel, to open the arm-chest."

Boatswain's Mate Cromwell had been a close friend of Spencer's, and Seaman Small was implicated by Wales' report. The Captain related how he had kept an anxious eye on both of them.

"The following day being Sunday, the crew were inspected at quarters at ten o'clock. I took my station abaft, with the intention of particularly observing Cromwell and Small. The third or master's division, to which they both belonged, always mustered at morning quarters upon the afterpart of the quarterdeck. The persons of both were faultlessly clean; they were determined that their appearance in this respect should provoke no reproof. Cromwell stood up to his full stature, his muscles braced, his battle-axe grasped resolutely, his cheek pale, but his eye fixed, as if indifferently, at the other side. He had a determined and dangerous air. Small made a very different figure. His appearance was ghastly, he shifted his weight from side to side, and his battle-axe passed from one hand to the other; his eye wandered irresolutely, but never toward mine. I attributed his conduct to fear.

"I had always been very particular to have no strain on the light braces leading forward, as the tendency of such a strain was to carry away the light yards and masts. While Ward M. Gagely, one of the best and most skillful of our apprentices, was yet on the main-royal-yard, a sudden jerk of the weather-main-royal-brace, given by Small and another whose name I have not discovered, carried the top-gallant-mast away in the sheare-hole, sending forward the royal-mast. I did not dream at the time that the carrying away of this mast was the work of treachery; but I knew it was an occasion of this sort, the loss of a boy overboard, or an accident to a spar, creating confusion, which was likely to be taken advantage of by the conspirators, were they still bent on the prosecution of their enterprise. To my astonishment, all those who were most conspicuously named in the programme of Mr. Spencer, no matter in what part of the vessel they might be stationed, mustered at the main-top-mast-head. Whether animated by some new-born zeal in the service of their country, or collected there for the purpose of conspiring, it was not easy to decide; the coincidence confirmed the existence of a dangerous conspiracy. The eye of Mr. Spencer travelled perpetually to the mast-head, and cast thither many of those strange and stealthy glances which I had heretofore noticed. By this time it was dark, and quarters had been unavoidably dispensed with; still I thought, under the circumstances, that it was scarcely safe to leave Cromwell at large during the night: the night was the season of danger. After consulting Lieutenant Gansevoort, I determined to arrest Cromwell; I met him at the foot of the Jacob's-ladder surrounded by the officers; on questioning him as to a secret conversation he had held the night before with Mr. Spencer, he denied its being he: he said 'It was not me, sir, it was Small.' Cromwell was the tallest man on board, and Small the shortest. Cromwell was immediately ironed;

and Small then pointed out by an associate to increased
suspicion, was also sent for, interrogated, and ironed. Increased vigilance was now enjoined upon all the officers;
henceforward, all were perpetually armed; either myself or
the first lieutenant was always on deck, and generally both of
us were."

The *Somers* was a training ship for midshipmen and
apprentices. Mackenzie did not spare the whip on these
apprentices, most of them boys of fourteen and fifteen. The
next day, Monday, November 28, he punished two of them
for breaches of discipline and took the opportunity to tell the
crew of Spencer's "plot."

"The effect of this upon the crew was various: it filled
many with horror at the idea of what they had escaped from:
it inspired others with terror at dangers awaiting them from
their connexion with the conspiracy. I now considered the
crew tranquillized and the vessel safe. Having noticed Mr.
Spencer's attempt to hold intelligence with the crew, I
directed that all the prisoners should be turned with their
faces aft. I also directed that no tobacco should be furnished
them after the supply they had on their persons when
confined should be exhausted. . . . The day after Mr.
Spencer's tobacco was stopped, his spirits gave way entirely.
He remained the whole day with his face buried in the grego,
and when it was for a moment raised, it was bathed in tears
. . . . But the whole crew was far from being tranquillized: the
most seriously implicated began once more to collect in
knots: during the night, seditious words were heard through
the vessel, and an insolent and menacing air assumed by
many . . . . Mr. Wales detected Charles A. Wilson attempting
to draw out a handspike from under the launch, with an
evident purpose of felling him, and when Wales cocked his
pistol and approached, he could only offer some lame excuse
for his presence there. I felt more anxious than I had yet
done, and remained continually on deck. At twelve o'clock,
when the watch was called and mustered, M'Kinley, Green,
and others seriously implicated, missed their muster. That
they should have been asleep at all that night, was not likely:
that they should have missed their muster on that particular

occasion, having never done so before, otherwise than intentionally, was impossible. Those who missed their muster had all some lame excuse: there was probably an agreement to meet around the officer of the deck, and commit some act of violence . . . . At four o'clock, others of the implicated also missed their muster. I could not contemplate this growth of disaffection without serious uneasiness. Where was this thing to end? Each new arrest of prisoners seemed to bring a fresh set of conspirators forward, to occupy the first place. With fine weather and bright nights, there was already a disposition to make an attack and rescue the prisoners. When bad weather should call off the attention of the officers—when the well-disposed portion of the crew should be occupied in shortening sail, and utter darkness should withdraw everything from view, how great the probability of a rescue. If the most deeply implicated were ironed, would all the dangerous be in custody? What sympathy might not be excited by the suffering of the prisoners? These grave considerations, the deep sense I had of the solemn obligation I was under to protect and defend the vessel which had been intrusted to me, and the lives of the officers and crew . . . all impressed upon me the absolute necessity of adopting immediately some further measures for the security of the vessel . . . . Under these circumstances, I addressed the following letter to all the officers on board.

U.S. BRIG SOMERS,
Nov. 30, 1842.

GENTLEMEN: The time has arrived when I am desirous of availing myself of your council in the responsible position in which, as commander of this vessel, I find myself placed. You are aware of the circumstances which have resulted in the confinement of Midshipman Philip Spencer, Boatswain's Mate Samuel Cromwell, and Seaman E. Small, as prisoners, and I purposely abstain from entering into any details of them, necessarily ignorant of the exact extent of disaffection among a crew which has so long and so systematically and assiduously been tampered with by *an officer.* Knowing that suspicions of the gravest nature attach to persons still at large, and whom the difficulty of taking care of the prisoners we already have, makes me more reluctant than I should otherwise be to apprehend, I have determined to address myself to you, and to ask your united council as to the best course to be now pursued, and I call upon you to take into deliberate and dispassionate consideration the present condition of the vessel, and the contingencies of every nature that the future may embrace, throughout the remainder of our cruise, and enlighten me with your opinion as to the best course to be pursued.

I am, very respectfully, gentlemen, your most obedient,

> Alex Slidell Mackenzie
> Commander.

The next morning, the officers handed this letter to the captain:

> U.S. Brig Somers
> Dec. 1, 1842

Sir: In answer to your letter of yesterday, requesting our counsel as to the best course to be pursued with the prisoners . . . we would state, that the evidence which has come to our knowledge is of such a nature as, after as dispassionate and deliberate a consideration of the case as the exigencies of the time would admit we have come to a cool, decided, and unanimous opinion, that they have been guilty of a full and determined intention to commit a mutiny on board of this vessel of a most atrocious nature; and that the revelation of circumstances having made it necessary to confine others with them, the uncertainty as to what extent they are leagued with others still at large, the impossibility of guarding against the contingencies which "a day or an hour may bring forth," we are convinced that it would be impossible to carry them to the United States, and that the safety of the public property, the lives of ourselves, and of those committed to our charge, require that (giving them sufficient time to prepare) they should be put to death, in a manner best calcu-

lated as an example to make a beneficial impression
upon the disaffected. This opinion we give, bearing in
mind our duty to our God, our country, and to the
service.

We are, sir, very respectfully, your obedient servants,

> Guert Gansevoort, Lieutenant,
> R. W. Leecock, Pas'd Ass. Surg'n,
> H. M. Heiskill, Purser,
> M. C. Perry, Act'g Master,
> Henry Rogers, Midshipman,
> Egbert Thompson, Midshipman,
> Chas. W. Hays, Midshipman.

"I at once concurred in the justice of this opinion, and in
the necessity of carrying its recommendation into immediate
effect . . . . The three chief conspirators alone were capable
of navigating and sailing her. By their removal, the motive to
a rescue, capture, and carrying out of the original design of
piracy, was at once taken away . . . . In the necessities of my
position I found my law, and in them also I must trust to find
my justification.

"I gave order to make immediate preparations for hanging
the three principal criminals at the main-yard-arms; all hands
were now called to witness punishment . . . . The officers
were stationed about the decks according to the watch-bill I
had made out the night before, and the petty officers were
similarly distributed, with orders to cut down whoever should
let go the whip with even one hand, or fail to haul on it when
ordered. The ensign and pendent being bent on and ready for
hoisting, I now put on my full uniform and proceeded to
execute the most painful duty that has ever devolved on an
American commander—that of announcing to the criminals
their fate. I informed Mr. Spencer that when he had been
about to take my life . . . without cause of offence to him . . .
it had been his intentions to remove me suddenly from the
world in the darkness of night, in my sleep, without a
moment to utter one murmur of affection to my wife and
children, one prayer for their welfare. His life was now

forfeited to his country, and the necessities of the case, growing out of his corruption of the crew, compelled me to take it . . . . If there yet remained to him one feeling true to nature, it should be gratified. If he had any word to send to his parents, it should be recorded and faithfully delivered. . . .

"This intimation overcame him entirely. He sank, with tears, upon his knees and said he was not fit to die. I repeated to him his own catechism, and begged him at least to let the officer set, to the men he had corrupted and seduced, the example of dying with decorum.

"This immediately restored him to entire self-possession; and, while he was engaged in prayer, I went and made in succession the same communication to Cromwell, and Small. Cromwell fell upon his knees completely unmanned, protested his innocence, and invoked the name of his wife. Mr. Spencer said to me, 'As these are the last words I have to say, I trust they will be believed, Cromwell is innocent.' The evidence had been conclusive, yet I was staggered. I sent for Lieutenant Gansevoort and consulted him; he said there was not a shadow of doubt. I told him to consult the petty officers. He was condemned by acclamation by the petty officers. He was the one of whom they had real apprehensions; the accomplice at first, and afterward the urger-on of Mr. Spencer, who had trained him to the act by which he intended to benefit.

"I returned to Mr. Spencer; I explained to him how Cromwell had made use of him; I told him that remarks had been made about the two not very flattering to him, and which he might not care to hear, which showed the relative share ascribed to each of them in the contemplated transaction. He expressed great anxiety to hear what was said. One had told the first lieutenant 'In my opinion, sir, you have the damned fool on the larboard arm-chest, and the damned villain on the starboard'; another had remarked that after the vessel should have been captured by Mr. Spencer, Cromwell might allow him to live, provided he made himself useful; he would probably make him his secretary. I remarked, 'I do not think this would have suited your temper.'

This effectually aroused him, his countenance assumed a demoniacal expression; he said no more of the innocence of Cromwell. . . .

"I . . . asked him if he had no message to send to his friends; he answered, 'None that they would wish to receive.' When urged still farther to send some words of consolation in so great an affliction, he said, 'Tell them I die wishing them every blessing and happiness; I deserve death for this and many other crimes—there are few crimes that I have not committed; I feel sincerely penitent, and my only fear of death is that my repentance may be too late.' I asked him if there was anyone whom he had injured to whom he could yet make reparation . . . he made no answer, but soon after continued, 'I have wronged many persons, but chiefly my parents,' he said, 'this will kill my poor mother.' I was not before aware that he had a mother; when recovered from the pain of this announcement, I asked him if it would not have been still more dreadful had he succeeded in his attempt, murdered the officers and the greater part of the crew of the vessel, and run that career of crime which with so much satisfaction he had marked out for himself; he replied, after a pause, 'I do not know what would have become of me had I succeeded . . . . I fear,' said he, 'this may injure my father.' I told him it was almost too late to think of that—that had he succeeded in his wishes, it would have injured his father much more—that had it been possible to have taken him home, as I intended to do, it was not in nature that his father should not have interfered to save him—that for those who have friends or money in America there was no punishment for the worst of crimes . . . . 'I will tell you frankly,' he said, 'what I intended to do had I got home—I should have attempted to escape; I had the same project on board the *John Adams* and *Potomac*—it seemed to be a mania with me.' 'Do you not think,' I asked, 'that this is a mania which should be discouraged in the navy?' 'I do, most certainly.' Afterward he said to me, 'But have you not formed an exaggerated estimate of the extent of this conspiracy?' I told him, 'No,' that his systematic efforts to corrupt the crew . . . had been but too successful. I knew that the conspiracy was still extensive—I did not know how extensive . . . . He turned again to say to me, 'But are you not going too far—are you not fast? does the law entirely justify you?' I replied that he had not consulted me in making his arrangements—that his opinion could not be an unprejudiced one—that I had consulted all his brother officers, his messmates included, except the boys, and I placed before him their opinion. He stated that it was just; that he deserved death . . . . He requested that his face might be covered; this was readily granted. . . .

"I now ordered that the other criminals should be consulted as to their wishes in this particular; they joined in the request, and frocks were taken from their bags to cover their heads. Mr. Spencer . . . asked for a bible and prayer book; they were brought, and others ordered to be furnished to his accomplices. 'I am a believer,' he said, 'do you think that repentance at this late hour can be accepted?' . . . He then read in the bible, kneeled down and read in the prayer book . . . . He said, 'I beg your forgiveness for what I have meditated against you.' I gave him my hand, and assured him of my sincere forgiveness; I asked him if I had ever done anything to him to make him seek my life, or whether the hatred he had conceived for me . . . was fostered for the purpose of giving himself some plea of justification. He said, 'It was only a fancy—perhaps there might have been something in your manner which offended me.' . . .

"Mr. Spencer, about this time, sent for Lieut. Gansevoort, and told him that he . . . wished him to bear testimony that he died like a brave man. He then asked me what was to be the signal of the execution. I told him that being desirous to hoist the colors at the moment of execution . . . I had intended to beat the call as for hoisting the colors, then roll off, and at the third roll fire a gun. He asked to be allowed himself to give the word to fire the gun; I acceded to the request, and the drum and fife were dismissed. He asked if the gun was under him; I told him it was next but one to him. He begged that no interval might elapse between giving the word, and firing the gun. I asked if they were firing with the lock and wafer, which had always proved quick and sure, but was told that they had a tube and priming, and were prepared to fire with a match; some delay would have been necessary to have opened the arm-chest, and get out a wafer. I ordered a supply of live coal to be passed aft from the galley, and fresh ones perpetually supplied; then assured him there would be no delay. Time still wearing away in this manner, Small requested leave to address the crew. Mr. Spencer having leave to give the word, was asked if he would consent to the delay. He assented, and Small's face being uncovered, he spoke as follows: 'Shipmates and topmates, take warning by my example; I never was a pirate, I never killed a man; it's for saying that I would do it, that I am about to depart this life; see what a word will do . . . . ' He turned to Mr. Spencer, and said to him, 'I am now ready to die, Mr. Spencer, are you?'

"Cromwell's last words were, 'Tell my wife I die an innocent man; tell Lieut. Morris, I die an innocent man.' But it had been the game of this man to appear innocent, to urge Mr. Spencer on, to furnish him with professional ideas, to bring about a catastrophe, of which Mr. Spencer was to take all the risk, and from which he, Cromwell, was to derive all the benefit. He had taken a great many precautions to appear innocent, but he had not taken enough. I now placed myself on the trunk, in a situation from which my eye could take in everything, I waited for some time, but no word was given. At length Browning saluted me, and said, 'Mr. Spencer says he cannot give the word; he wishes the commander to give the word himself.' The word was accordingly given, and the execution took place."

The narrative continued with a description of bringing down the bodies and laying them out for burial.

"The night had already set in; all the battle-lanterns, and the other lanterns in the vessel, were lighted and distributed among the crew. Collected, with their prayer books, on the booms, in the gangways, and lee-quarter-boat, the service was then read, the responses audibly and devoutly made by the officers and crew, and the bodies consigned to the deep. This office was closed with that prayer, so appropriate to our

situation, appointed to be read in our ships-of-war—
'Preserve us from the dangers of the sea and from the
violence of enemies, that we may be a safeguard unto the
United States of America, and a security for such as pass on
the seas upon their lawful occasions; that the inhabitants of
our land may in peace and quietness serve thee, our God:
and that we may return in safety to enjoy the blessings of the
land with the fruit of our labor, and with a thankful re-
membrance of thy mercies, to praise and glorify thy holy
name, through Jesus Christ, our Lord.' In reading this and
recollecting the uses to which the *Somers* had been destined,
as I now find, before she quitted the United States, I could
not but humbly hope that divine sanction would not be
wanting to the deed of that day."

When Mackenzie's narrative testimony was reported,
comment in public and private, was swift. The New York
Herald said: "As yet we have expressed no opinion on the
conduct of Mackenzie. . . . In relation to the Commander's
narrative . . . the bad taste in its style—the trivial incidents
and horrid execution—the ambitious efforts of fine writing—
and the awful catastrophe at the yard arm—and the strange
jumble of pious ideas, insignificant circumstances, patriotic
sentiments and over-charged figures of speech . . . create a
feeling . . . of horror in the mind. . . . It does not seem to be
written by a human being with the ordinary feelings of
nature. . . . "

And the man who was to be Mackenzie's most formidable
critic, James Fenimore Cooper, was warming up in a letter to
his wife: "Mackenzie's affairs look bad enough. The report is
considered to be the work of a man scarcely *compos mentis.*
I never read a more miserable thing in my life—he has
actually got in one of the prayers he read to his crew. To
crown all he admits he told Spencer that he would not be
hanged if he got in, on account of his father's influence. . . .
In a word, such a medley of folly, conceit, illegality,
feeble-mindedness and fanaticism was never before assembled in a . . . document."

And even Philip Hone, a staunch Mackenzie supporter,

said: "Well would it have been for him if it had never seen
the light. 'Oh that mine enemy should write a book!' was the
vindictive exclamation of some such person as the Secretary
of War. . . . Here is a document ten times longer than was
necessary, written without consultation with any judicious
friend who . . . would have been better able to look at the
consequences, full of public details of trifling circumstances
and irrelevant conversation. . . . Here, instead of a concise,
manly statement . . . we have a long rigmarole story . . . and
conversations with the accused, in one of which he said to
Spencer that he hung him, because if he took him to the
United States he would escape punishment for everybody got
clear who had money and friends."

Wales, Gansevoort, and Mackenzie's written testimony
formed the heart of the defense's case, although many other
witnesses were called. One and all the crew backed the
officers' story of a real and credible danger of mutiny.

But the case for the defense was not entirely watertight.
There was the question of the list of conspirators which had
been found in Spencer's room. Cromwell's name was nowhere on the list, yet he was executed.

On that point Gansevoort testified:

"The next day in the morning (after Spencer's arrest) I
had a conversation with some of the men: the Carpenter's
Mate, Dickerson, and the Gunner's Mate, King. . . . I think the
Carpenter's Mate said, 'that big fellow forward is more
dangerous than the rest: he ought to be confined.' I asked
him whom he meant—and he said Cromwell, the Boatswain's
Mate . . . all other conversations I had with them up to
Cromwell's arrest impressed me with the belief that it was
necessary to have him confined; and after that they
appeared to be relieved. They said that they believed him to
be dangerous."

In contrast to Cromwell, Daniel McKinley's name was
listed as "Certain" among the alleged conspirators, yet he
was not executed. To the Judge Advocate, the problem was:
Did the officers execute Cromwell simply from fear? Did they
spare McKinley because he posed no threat? And if so, did
they not thus ignore the very list that they had used in
condemning Spencer?

Counsel for Mackenzie, on direct examination of Gansevoort, tried to cover this point:

"Had you any conversation with Mr. Spencer with regard to the papers found in the razor case . . . about the name of E. Andrews which appeared in the list of the certain next to his own?"

"Yes, sir: I asked him if that name did not stand for Cromwell; he said no, that it meant Small . . . I said, 'Ah. How is that, when you have Small's name twice on the list?' . . . Mr. Spencer appeared to be surprised and said, 'Ah, I did not know I had written it that way.' "

As Spencer was never shown in defense testimony to have identified Cromwell as the "Andrews" named on the list, however, this "identification" remained conjectural at best. But it could also be conjectured that MacKenzie did not himself believe the list.

Midshipman Perry on cross-examination was asked:

"In your consultation among the officers, was it one of your reasons or theirs for putting Cromwell to death, that he understood navigation and thus by removing him and Small, who were alone, of the suspected portion of the crew, acquainted with navigation, no one could be left capable of taking command, in case of the outbreak of a mutiny?"

"That was one of the small reasons."

The Judge Advocate tried to explore this and other aspects of the defense case, but he was laboring under a heavy and—in retrospect, in any case—astonishing handicap. *All of the crew were still under Mackenzie's command.*

On this point, in a letter dated February 5, 1843, James Fenimore Cooper wrote:

"Why was he left in command of the brig, containing all the witnesses? Every officer should have been taken out of her the instant she arrived, or the men transferred beyond their influence. . . . The world cannot show a parallel to such stupidity, or such corruption. . . . That the Department has favored Mackenzie I take to be indisputable."

In the courtroom, the Judge Advocate angrily announced:

"I am compelled, very reluctantly, to present to the court two incidents. . . . When this case was about being commenced, Midshipman Hays was desired to favor me with an opportunity, by a visit, to ascertain his information. . . . After replying to a few trivial questions, he candidly stated to me that he did not think me entitled, except on the stand, to his information.

"This incident I should never have recalled but for a similar declaration on yesterday, from Midshipman Tillotson. Before the court closed, I sent a messenger for that officer and, on his arrival, desired to know whether he had any objection to afford me, in private, his knowledge of the incidents of the last cruise of the *Somers*. He politely replied he had.

"All the officers and crew of that brig were furnished by the department for witnesses at my selection. With neither have I had any opportunities for conversation.

"My duties to the case compel me to offer these gentlemen, wholly in the dark as to their disposition and acquaintance with facts, except as shown in the record of the Court of Enquiry."

Cut off from pretrial interrogation of the witnesses, the Judge Advocate's questioning was mostly a "fishing expedition." Yet he found some items of interest.

For example, one of the apparent turning points in Mackenzie's decision to execute the three men had been the incident of the broken mast, which had occurred almost immediately after Spencer had been arrested. The Judge Advocate now sought to find out if it was indeed a sinister portent or whether it might have come about through a simple accident. He called Midshipman Hays, who had been the Officer of the Deck that day.

"What order did you give before the mast went?"

"I gave the order to let go the brace."

"Did anyone give a contrary order?"

"Not in my hearing."

"Did you see Mr. O. H. Perry sent for by the Commander immediately after the mast went?"

"He (the Commander) told me to tell Mr. Perry that by his inattention, he had allowed someone to haul on the brace, and carry away the mast."

"Did you hear Mr. O. H. Perry state that he understood the order to be, to haul on the . . . brace?"

"I heard him say so after we arrived in port."

And so at least the possibility of a misunderstood order leading to a broken mast was introduced—although Perry had apparently waited until the ship was in port to tell anyone about it.

That the officers were in a jittery state of tension was illustrated by the next incident. According to Lieutenant Gansevoort, while the mast was being repaired the whole deck crew suddenly rushed aft:

"It was dark at this time. I heard an unusual noise—a rushing on deck, and saw a body of men in each gangway rushing aft toward the quarterdeck; I said to the Commander 'God, I believe they are coming.' I had one of Colt's pistols, which I immediately drew and cocked . . . I jumped on the trunk and ran forward to meet them; as I was going along I sang out to them not to come aft. I told them I would blow out the first man's brains who would put his foot on the quarterdeck."

Again questioning by the Judge Advocate revealed a reasonable alternative to mutiny. Midshipman Rogers had been forward with the men when the mast broke; he had not only ordered them to hurry aft to help repair it, but had begun flogging the slower ones to speed them up. Gansevoort was asked:

"When you ascertained from Mr. Rogers that it was his order that had put the men in motion, did you not order the men forward . . . and did they obey you?"

"They did obey me."

"Did you not afterward express to Commander Mackenzie that you had been under a wrong impression as to the meaning of the men rushing aft at the same time they were obeying Mr. Rogers' order?"

"I think I did."

The next witness, Seaman Daniel McKinley, had been listed on Spencer's list as "certain." McKinley had also missed muster, further raising Mackenzie's suspicions.

"Did you miss muster after the arrest of Mr. Spencer? And if so, state when and why."

"It was after the arrest: I cannot state the date and hour; me and McKee made a bargain . . . to wake one another up when the watches were called. I asked McKee why he did not call me. He told me that the officers would not let him stir; that they were ordered to lie down on the deck, and when he lay down he fell asleep and did not wake up. That was why I missed my muster."

Slowly, the mosaic of incidents which had convinced Mackenzie that a mutiny was under way showed less sinister implications. The Judge Advocate then turned his attention to another point—one that had caused great debate outside the courtroom. Many considered it the most important issue of all. The three men had been executed on December 1; the ship made port on December 4. Why had Mackenzie not kept the prisoners in chains until they reached port, then turned them over to the authorities for a court-martial?

The officers answered this question with unanimity; they felt the mutiny would take place *before* the ship reached port. Spencer's father, outside the court, answered that the three had been in irons for six days before execution, with no shot or scuffle of any kind. Couldn't the officers, he asked, have risked two or three more days? The officers continued to think not. And Mackenzie, in his narrative, had given another reason as well. He said that in any case the port, Saint Thomas, was not American, and he thought it would reflect badly on American prestige if a ship of war should have to ask for help from a foreign navy.

Toward the close of the trial the Judge Advocate introduced another subject, one that had troubled him almost from the beginning of the case. Witnesses had testified that Spencer had dictated to Mackenzie a last message to his parents. Where was that message? Was Mackenzie hiding it? And if so, why?

In search of the answer, he questioned Midshipman Perry:

"Did you not say that you were of the impression that Mr. Spencer did send a written message home?"

"At the time of the execution it was my impression he did

send a message home; the Captain was copying something. I did not see what it was."

This questioning so infuriated Mackenzie that he stood up, approached the Judge Advocate, and angrily asked: "Why do you ask this question about Mr. Spencer's not being able to write in irons? He declined to write."

"Yes, sir," the Judge Advocate replied, "but I am told he afterward dictated to you what to write."

"Yes, he did," Captain Mackenzie answered. "The substance of it is in my report—my official report."

That Mackenzie had included such information only obliquely in his official report instead of delivering it to the court, and had then admitted it so precipitously seemed at least unconventional. The Judge Advocate continued to pursue the subject. His question to McKinley brought this reply:

"While the writing was going on, what was the position of Mr. Spencer and the Commander?"

"Mr. Spencer was sitting at the forward end of the arm-chest and the Commander in front of him on a camp stool. I could not say how long the writing continued; he sat there upward of twenty minutes or half an hour."

Lieutenant Gansevoort and midshipmen Thompson and Perry all testified that it was their impression that Spencer had dictated a letter to his parents. Where was that letter?

Mackenzie was ready with another surprise. He submitted, at long last, "the only memorandum or writing of any description made by me on that day, while in communication with Mr. Spencer." This memorandum, in Mackenzie's handwriting, read in part:

"When asked if he had any message to send; none that they would wish to receive. . . . Many that he had wronged but did not know how reparation could be made to them. Your parents most wronged . . . . himself by saying that he had entertained same idea in *John Adams* and *Potomac*, but had not ripened it into . . . . Do you not think that a mania which should . . . . Certainly. Objected to manner of death; requested to be shot . . . . Instantaneous shotted gun. Arrangements. Conversation about coffin. Beating to call . . . .

No hangmen. You and nothing to do with respects of business and as done in secure and seamanlike manner . . . . strain-hooks moved, tail-blocks well secured. Roll. S. Small stept up. Cromwell overboard, rose, dipping to yardarm."

On this bizarre note, the court-martial came to an end.

There was never any doubt about the Court's findings. From the beginning, the Navy had united behind Mackenzie for the sake of discipline, for this was a day and time when mutinies were a real and terrible threat. Small wooden sailing ships, isolated far out at sea, and with officers only a tiny minority of the crew, were totally at the mercy of any well-managed uprising.

"The court . . . do acquit Commander Alexander Slidell Mackenzie of the charges and specifications preferred by the Secretary of the Navy against him."

Epilogue

Although passions have quieted over the years, the *Somers* mutiny trial is still a matter of considerable controversy. Seasoned sea dogs, mindful of the small ships and cramped conditions of the time, argue that they would have taken the exact same stand as Mackenzie. Others, equally seasoned, snort at the prospect. Another possible angle of the case was revealed some years after the trial with the publication of the autobiography of Thurlow Weed, a prominent New York politician. Weed reported having been told by Guert Gansevoort's cousin that the Lieutenant had twice left the council of officers investigating the possible mutiny to report to Captain Mackenzie "the council's unreadiness to recommend the executions." Each time he was ordered to return and continue deliberations as "the officers had apparently not examined the evidence carefully enough."

Whether this revelation was an accurate report or an attempt by Gansevoort at self-justification is one of the elements that keeps the *Somers* controversy alive.

But controversial or not, it is certainly true that seldom if ever has a court-martial had so many varied repercussions.

It forced, for example, the government to take the first really close look at its system of military—and naval—justice. The result was the first of a long series of major revisions, a series that is still continuing and will continue so long as military justice is considered necessary. Among the regulations that were adopted was a stringent one making it clear that no military man could be put to death—even after a trial—by a local commander without a review of the case . and approval of the sentence by headquarters in Washington. Since that time executions for military crimes have been rare. An incidental result of the trial was to make the government —and the public—aware of the lavish use of flogging by captains at sea. This primitive form of punishment was henceforth abolished.

As military justice became less crude, so did the methods of training. Three years after the trial, and directly because of it, the United States Naval Academy was established at Annapolis, Maryland.

As if these were not enough repercussions for one court-martial, the *Somers* mutiny had one more, and a quite spectacular one: the inspiring of a literary masterpiece. One of America's finest writers, Herman Melville, who was related to Lieutenant Gansevoort, followed the trial closely and passionately. When it was over, he wove the experience into his classic *Billy Budd.* And so, today, more than a century after Mackenzie's death, he still commands a fearful ship. As Captain the Honorable Edward Fairfax Vere, on stage and screen and printed page, again and again he confronts a young midshipman with "the most painful duty that has ever devolved on an American commander."

4

When George Armstrong Custer Rode Out of the West

Prologue

In the late 1860s with the Civil War over, the nation began to turn its attention to the West. Scouts and frontiersmen were followed in turn by settlers in ever-increasing numbers. And as the settlers fanned out across the Plains they began meeting resistance from the Indians, particularly, in the Plains, from the Cheyenne and Sioux. Villages were raided, wagon trains ambushed, Army patrols attacked, and all was reported in the nation's press much embellished with horror stories of mutilation and scalping. (That the Indians were fighting for their own land was discounted; nor was the generous measure of atrocities committed by the settlers given newspaper space.) To meet the threat, Congress in 1867 authorized the Hancock Expedition to eliminate it for all time.

To this force was assigned the impulsive and colorful Brevet Major General George Armstrong Custer who took it into his head to do what no general—on the record, at any rate—had ever done. He decided to ride *out* of the Indian country to see his wife, despite a lack of orders authorizing such a trip. The Army calls it being A.W.O.L. (absent without leave) : the soldiers call it going "over the hill."

George Armstrong Custer was the last—and possibly the most flamboyant—of the dashing and colorful cavalrymen. Galloping into battle with long yellow curls flying and bright red necktie flapping behind, he was the scourge of the Confederacy. He became a hero at Gettysburg and Appomattox and at age twenty-six was the youngest general in the history of the Army.

During the Civil War, Custer had led the Michigan cavalry to victory at such places as Waynesboro, Cedar Creek, and the Chickahominy River, and at Yellow Tavern had joined battle with his equally colorful Confederate counterpart, the fiery J.E.B. Stuart. In that fight Stuart was killed and his force defeated, and the growing Custer legend lengthened a little more.

At the War's end, Custer turned west. In Kansas, Missouri, and the Dakotas, the Cheyenne and Sioux were on the rampage, trying desperately to stop the flood of settlers who were taking over their lands. The conflict was brutal on both sides, with homes burned, livestock carried off, and women and children murdered without mercy. The nation's press clamored for the defeat of the "Red Devils," and when Congress financed the Hancock Expedition, Custer, the "Boy General," eagerly signed up.

His first stop was Fort Riley, Kansas, where he took leave of his beautiful, dark-eyed bride and assumed command of the 7th Cavalry operating as a scouting force throughout the West. According to his orders, the object of his expedition was to hunt out and chastise the Cheyennes. At the end of May, 1867, he was at Fort Hays, Kansas, and was ordered to proceed westward to Fort Wallace, where he would await further instructions.

Custer was not a man who knew how to wait, particularly when he discovered that a cholera epidemic was raging through eastern Kansas, centering around Fort Riley, the location of his bride. As impulsive in love as he was in battle, he disregarded his orders, abandoned his post, and set out with seventy-six men, a few officers, and some fresh horses to see his wife, 275 miles away, much of it through hostile Indian territory.

If he proved anything, he proved that the Wild West was no spot to be A.W.O.L. In the first place there were Indians, none of them friendly. There was also the problem of his own troopers, most of whom were frontiersmen first, soldiers, if at all, second. Once outside of the confines of a fort they were as likely as not to desert at the first opportunity. Not least, there was the Army, not ready to sanction an unauthorized absence from a general any more than a private. The final tally of the escapade: two dead, six wounded, and Custer, five months later, facing a court-martial in Fort Leavenworth, Kansas.

The Court convened on November 8, 1867, with charges that ranged from the trivial to the serious. Absenting himself from his command without proper authority at a time when he was expected to be actively engaged in fighting Indians was one. He was also charged with overworking horses belonging to the government and with expropriating mules and two ambulances for his own use. On the most serious and most professionally damaging level, he was charged with abandoning a detachment that was under attack, with not sending help to the beleaguered detachment, and with failure to pursue the attackers as well as failure to recover and bury the bodies of two men of his command reported killed in the encounter. The final charges accused him of having three of his own men shot down as deserters and then refusing them medical attention, thereby causing the death of one of them.

To these allegations, Custer made no opening statement of defense. Instead, in the tradition of the cavalry, he readied his offense. Outside the court, he told friends he would prove the charges absurd, that instead of taking the expedition on an unauthorized visit to his wife, he had been operating under orders at all times. And as to the Indian attack and the murder of the deserters, he would show that the charges were framed by men who did not know the West, had never commanded cavalry on the Plains in Indian country, and knew so little about the problems of Indian fighting that they were unable to make a cogent case.

The prosecution first set out to prove that Custer had acted against orders. Captain L. B. Weir, the adjutant of General Smith, commanding the district of Upper Arkansas, took the stand. Weir identified the original orders as well as supplementary orders from General Smith that instructed General Custer's command "until further orders" to operate from Fort Wallace.

By returning to Fort Riley, Custer would seem to have been in direct violation of these orders. Moreover, in order to reach Fort Riley, he would have to pass through General Smith's headquarters at Fort Harker—which could only be accomplished with the permission of General Smith. That General was asked to take the stand to clarify matters.

"Did accused receive from you any leave of absence or authority to leave his command during the month of July last?"

"No, sir."

"Did the accused have any authority to march from Fort Wallace to Fort Harker?"

"He had no orders or authority from me."

"As far as you know was there any urgency or demand of public business for the accused to make such a march?"

"None that I know of."

As it turned out, Custer had indeed (at least temporarily) received permission from General Smith to visit his wife. He had materialized suddenly in the middle of the night and waked the general, giving the impression he was not only alone but on leave. As General Smith testified:

"General Custer came to my quarters between two and three at night and I don't know if I asked the question how he came down. It was my impression that he came by stage.

I learned the next morning from my Adjutant General that he came with an escort part of the way, and then I immediately ordered him back to his command."

The prosecution next turned to the trip itself and Custer's conduct of it. It quickly became clear that in their march across the plains there had been a wild and woolly little fight. Master Sergeant James Connelly had been right in the middle of it.

"On the march, what were your particular duties?"

"I was generally in the rear of the column somewhere. I was sent in some cases to lead horses behind and pick up stragglers from the rear."

"Do you know of an attack by the Indians on that march?"

"On the morning of the 17th we were at Castle Rock Station, and about two miles east of there the command halted for about two hours for the men to get coffee. After the halt was over, General Custer told me to take six men and go back after a man named Young, who had his mare. To go back as far as Castle Rock and find him. I did so and found him there. General Custer game me a lead horse to mount, if his horse was played out. I found him at Castle Rock and his horse was unfit for service, and I remounted him. On coming back, when near where the encampment had been where I started from, we were attacked by a party of Indians, and they kept it up for three or four miles. One man got killed and one was wounded, and we were forced to leave him on the field."

"Did you see the wounded man at the time he was wounded?"

"I saw him a short time after. The first time I knew of his being wounded, I was within five or six yards of him to his left, and he called out to me that he was wounded. I rode around to the right of him and asked him where he was wounded. He had his pants inside his boots and the blood was all over his hip. He made no reply but pointed to his hip, and I took it for granted that that was where he was wounded. I rode to the left again and gave the command to halt. At that time two men in front rode along and paid no attention to the command, made their escape, and left me with three men. That was about the hottest of the fighting, and we were forced to leave him on the field. He had not dismounted at that time, and I rode on five or six hundred yards trying to get those men to halt, and when I turned back he had fell or dismounted, I could not tell which."

"Do you know in which part of the attack the other man was killed?"

"He was killed a few minutes before the other man reported to me he was wounded. The Indians were getting closer on our right flank, and the mare Young was riding on appeared to get excited and turned and took Young about 300 yards to the left of the road. Two Indians from the rear thought to cut him off from the detachment which made some divide and there were shots fired at the Indians."

"What effect did those shots have?"

"The Indians who were trying to cut that man off wheeled to the right and rear flank of the detachment."

"Did the Indians fire into the detachment?"

"They had been firing for some time before, but seemed to fire tolerably wild. Just as Young was in the act of getting back on the road, I looked to the rear and saw the man who was killed, and his horse was moving quite slowly. He was six or seven hundred yards in the rear, and was surrounded by six or seven Indians. A few minutes after, there was a shot from a pistol, I judged, and he fell from his saddle. Whether he was wounded before or not I am unable to state."

"After one man was killed and one man wounded and two others had rode off ahead, what did you do then?"

"I rode four or five hundred yards trying to overtake them thinking they had not heard me. But my horse could not overtake them. I fell back to the rear again, and ordered two men whose horses seemed to be better than mine to proceed after the two men, and if they did not halt when they were ordered, to shoot them down."

"Did these two men obey your order?"

"Yes, sir, so far as to halt the men."

"Did you follow them?"

"Yes, sir, at a trot, and sometimes a lope. A great many of

the Indians had fallen to the rear where the man was killed
and stayed there, which left not more than perhaps twenty
on our right flank circling around."

"Did you expect to find the command sooner than you
did?"

"Yes, sir, I expected every ravine I passed to find the
command."

On one point, however, Connelly had been mistaken. After
the command had passed through, Captain A. B. Carpenter,
stationed at Castle Rock, had taken a party to search the
area, and had found the wounded man still alive, but
abandoned for dead by his colleagues. On cross-examination
Connelly was asked about this.

"Did you believe when you left the field that *both* men
were dead?"

"I saw the wounded man a few minutes before he
dismounted and reported to Captain Hamilton that I did not
believe the Indians saw him dismount."

"How do you know the first man was killed?"

"I saw him fall from the saddle."

"Are all men who fall from the saddle necessarily killed?"

"To the best of my knowledge when five or six Indians are
around a man and shots are fired they are usually killed."

The sergeant was dismissed and Captain M. Hamilton,
Custer's second-in-command, was asked what he knew of the
attack.

"About two o'clock . . . Sergeant Connelly reported that he
had been sent back by General Custer. He came into
Donner's Station and reported to me the Indians had
succeeded in attacking. The horse he was riding on was
wounded, and his party was very much demoralized."

"How many were in his party?"

"Six."

"Was a report of the attack made to General Custer?"

"Yes, sir."

"Who made it?"

"I did."

"Were any measures taken for the repulse of the Indians
or any action whatever taken by General Custer for the relief
of the detachment?"

"No, sir. The detachment was all in. I learned afterward that one man had succeeded in secreting himself."

"Was any action taken for the pursuit of the Indians?"

"No, sir."

"Were any measures taken by General Custer to recover the bodies of the men reported wounded or dead?"

"None that I know of, sir."

"How soon after the report reached you did General Custer leave?"

"In about three quarters of an hour or an hour."

"On his way to the east?"

"Yes, sir."

"Was the body of the killed man recovered or buried?"

"Captain Carpenter reported to me that he recovered the wounded man, and that he buried the dead man."

On cross-examination, Custer's defense counsel asked:

"When you reported to General Custer the circumstances related to you by the Sergeant, what answer did he make to you?"

"I don't remember."

"Did he make any answer at all?"

"Not that I remember."

"How did you learn one of the men was wounded?"

"I heard one of the men say he thought one of the men got off."

"Did you report *that* to General Custer?"

"I think he was standing by at the time and heard the remark."

"How near was he to you?"

"Within ten or fifteen feet, either sitting in the door of the house or near it."

"If he was sitting in the house, do you think he could have heard the remark of the man that it was possible one of the men had escaped?"

"Yes, sir."

A member of the court was moved to question why Custer had not even sent someone back for a look. "Were you so well satisfied that both those men were dead that you thought it unnecessary to make any further inquiries?"

"I was satisfied *both* were killed."

"Then why did you make the request of General Custer to make a longer halt at Donner's Station?"

"I thought it was important for the command to stay there if there were any Indians in the neighborhood of the post, and there was some feeling among the men about leaving the post. At that time I thought it would have a bad effect on the morale of the men of the command to leave the post when there had been a fight recently."

Captain Carpenter then took the stand and told of his search for the bodies and his discovery of the wounded man. On cross-examination, he gave the first hint why Custer had not gone back to the spot to fight the Indians.

"Do you not think it would have been injudicious for the accused to have pursued these Indians?"

"It would have been fruitless."

Question by the Court: "What induces you to believe it was fruitless?"

"I do not think the Indians remained in that vicinity after the attack. Any pursuit at that distance would not have resulted in any advantage."

With this testimony, the second part of the prosecution's case was concluded. The Court moved then to the question of the treatment of deserters along the march. According to the charge, Custer had ordered several men shot down without trial and had subsequently denied them medical attention. One man had died. The incident had occurred in daylight during the march from Fort Wallace to Fort Harker. Custer had noticed several of his men, armed with carbines and carrying rations, moving across the plains. The Court called his subsidiary, Lieutenant Cooke.

"On that march were there any desertions from the command?"

"Yes, sir. A great many."

"What orders were given and by whom concerning those deserters?"

"I don't know of any orders except on July 7th when some deserters left by daylight."

"State what orders were given on that occasion."

"To pursue and shoot them down."

"By whom was that order given?"

"By General Custer."

"Were the deserters shot down as a result of that order?"

"Not altogether, I think."

"State what other reasons there were."

"The men were ordered to halt and one of them made a move as if to present his carbine, which I think brought on the shooting."

"Who did he make the motion towards?"

"I think Major Elliott."

"When those deserters were overtaken, did they have carbines with them?"

"Yes, sir, they had three carbines."

"In their hands?"

"Yes, sir."

"How did you come to receive orders to pursue the deserters?"

"I was standing at the headquarters when some of the officers reported to General Custer that there were deserters. He called first for the Officer of the Day, and ordered him to pursue them. Then he ordered the officers standing there, Major Elliott, Lieutenant Custer, the General's brother, and myself as the Officer of the Day was some time getting out."

Lieutenant Tom Custer then took the stand to answer questions from his brother's prosecutor.

"Was the command in camp at that time?"

"Yes, sir. They were resting."

"Were the supposed deserters in sight?"

"Yes, sir. Some of them."

"How many of them were in sight?"

"About six or seven when we started after them."

"Who accompanied you when you went after them?"

"Major Elliott, Lieutenant Cooke, and myself started after them. Lieutenant Cooke caught up with them before I did. I was about one hundred yards from them and could not hear what was said. I saw the men laying down their arms, and Major Elliott and Lieutenant Cooke rode toward them. One of them, I think it was a man named Johnson, ran to get his carbine and a man named Adkins, a scout with the party, ran up to the man and said he would blow his brains out if he attempted to touch his carbine. In the meantime, I saw Major

Elliott and Lieutenant Cooke firing on them. By that time I was with them, myself, and we fired on them."

"State what else occurred."

"There were three of the deserters wounded."

"You say the man Johnson went after his carbine. Did he get it?"

"No, sir, he did not get his hands on it."

"Was he mounted?"

"No, sir, he was dismounted."

"Did he have his carbine at the time he was fired on?"

"I don't think he had."

"Did the supposed deserters have any trial that you know of?"

"No, sir."

"Did you fire on any of those supposed deserters?"

"Yes, sir."

"Were those supposed deserters fired on by order of the accused?"

"Yes, sir."

Major Elliott, who had been the first one to reach the deserters, testified:

"When we got within twenty yards of them, I ordered them to halt, and I think two halted and two did not. I called to them separately to lay down their arms. Three men were armed and one was not. Two of them obeyed and the other—Johnson—broke his carbine as if to shoot me. That was the impression I had. I was riding at a gallop and rode onto him, and whether he threw down his arms just before my horse struck him, I could not tell. It was all done so quickly. I don't know that he intended to shoot me but his actions indicated that."

"Was he shot when you rode him down?"

"I don't know. It all happened in one minute."

With the shooting of the deserters established, the prosecution then examined the charge that Custer had denied them medical assistance. I. J. Coates, surgeon on the expedition, was called.

"When you first saw them did you give them medical attendance?"

"No, sir."

"For what reason did you not?"

"When the wagon first came in the men generally of the command started to the wagon. As I was going to it, I believe General Custer said to me not to go near those men at the time. I stopped there just where I stood. I obeyed the order."

"How long were those men in the wagon before you gave them medical attendance?"

"I suppose two hours."

"What kind of medical attendance did you give them?"

"I administered opiates, and made them comfortable, just as I should have done on the field of battle."

"Did you give them anything else except the opiates?"

"No, sir, in my judgment there was nothing else required."

"Describe Johnson's wound."

"Johnson was wounded in two places. He also had a shot in the side making a flesh wound. He was also wounded in the head, the ball entering in the left temple and coursing out below his jaw, and passing down into his lungs. The same ball entering again in the upper part of the chest."

"Was it a pistol shot, or otherwise?"

"It was a pistol shot."

"How soon after those men were wounded were those wounds dressed at all?"

"I think it was two days after, as well as I recollect."

"During those two days did these men follow the column?"

"Yes, sir, in the wagon."

"Why were those wounded men not carried in the ambulances?"

"At the time those accidents occurred to the men, these ambulances were not there. But in my judgment, the men did better in the wagon going along. The ambulances were very poor. The springs were very weak and all the men who had ridden in them complained that they were very uncomfortable, and I found them so myself, having to ride in them."

"Would it not have been better to have dressed the wounds, than to have delayed it?"

"It was impossible to dress them on account of not having

fresh water. We had no water but in the buffalo wallows. And
it would have been very hurtful to have dressed the wounds
with muddy water. I waited two days till we came to a stream
of fresh water, the first that we came to."

"Isn't it usual to dress shot wounds as soon as possible
with whatever kind of water can be obtained?"

"Sometimes gunshot wounds do not need dressing.
Sometimes they do better by allowing the blood to congeal
on them. That was the case here. The hemorrhages were
contained by the glueing of the clothing to the wound, and
there was no more hemorrhaging after the first hour or so.
The important thing in gunshot wounds is to reverse the
hemorrhage."

"What was the result of the wound received by Johnson?"

"That wound was fatal."

"Did you understand any remark or order of the accused
to be an order not to render medical assistance to the
wounded?"

"No, sir."

"When you reached camp and gave them medical
attendance, who directed you to do so?"

"General Custer."

"In what words did he give the order?"

"As far as I recollect now he said, 'Doctor, my sympathies
are not with these men who are wounded, but I want you to
give them all necessary medical attendance.' "

On cross-examination, Custer's defense counsel elaborated the point.

"Did he direct you to report their condition to him after
your examination?"

"He did. I gave him a complete history of the wounds, and
how they were getting along."

"Did the accused frequently inquire after their condition?"

"Yes, sir, always at night he inquired it—and sometimes
during the march."

"Did you consider any of those men to be mortally
wounded at that time?"

"I did not."

"Did you report that they were not mortally wounded to the accused?"

"I did. And I might say that Johnson, who afterwards died, was the most cheerful at that time."

Question by the Court: "What did you understand General Custer to mean when he directed you not to go near the wagon, and why did you not attend to them immediately when they were brought in?"

This question was objected to by the Judge Advocate as, so he said, he suspected the answer might not be of any benefit to the prosecution. It wasn't. When the court allowed Doctor Coates to answer, he said:

"I had an idea at that time that the objection was made for effect. There had been a great many desertions, some thirty or forty the night previous, and the men were crowding around the wagon, and I had an idea the General wished to make an impression on the men that they would be treated in the severest and harshest manner. I stood back as soon as he gave the order. Soon after the column started and the men were in their proper places I attended to the men."

To counter the surgeon's testimony, the prosecution placed on the stand Lieutenant Henry Jackson, who had been the Officer of the Day when the wounded men were brought in. He testified that the surgeon had *not* visited the men in the first night to administer opiates and make them comfortable. And with this conflicting testimony, the prosecution rested.

The General placed his brother on the stand as his first witness for the defense.

"Were you present at a dinner when the accused and Lieutenant General Sherman, commander of the military division of Missouri, was present?"

"I was."

"Did you hear any conversation between the accused and General Sherman regarding certain orders?"

"Yes, sir."

"State what."

"General Sherman told the accused that he would receive orders from General Augur but not to confine himself to those orders if his judgment led him elsewhere. That if he wished he could go to Denver City, or he could go to Hell if he wanted to. That he could go to any post he wanted to."

On cross-examination Lieutenant Tom Custer was asked:

"What did that conversation between General Sherman and the accused have reference to, particularly?"

"It had reference to his going after the Indians."

"Was there any other conversation or any other orders given by General Sherman at that time as to pursuit of the Indians?"

"I don't remember any other being given."

Lieutenant Cooke was called to testify and confirmed the conversation. Cooke also testified that the General had made an effort during the march to find out if any new orders had been issued to him.

"Did the accused overhaul any stages carrying the mail?"

"Yes, sir."

"With what object?"

"To obtain any orders that might be in reference to his movements. We had not had mail for a month."

"Did he make any inquiries of any trains he met?"

"Yes, sir."

Custer now turned to the incident of the desertion. He put on the stand Quartermaster S. N. Harper, who testified:

"I was bothered by men who were trying to steal stores. One of the men said he was going to desert and that I need not be surprised by it, for there were two thirds of the command going to desert."

"Did he desert that night?"

"Yes, sir."

"Did you report that to the accused?"

"Yes, sir. I told him he must look over my not being ready as I was up all night watching the stores."

"Did you report to the accused that a portion of the command was going to desert?"

"I did—in the morning."

Lieutenant Tom Custer was recalled to testify about the desertions.

"Were there unusual precautions taken the night before the desertions?"

"Yes, sir. I was ordered to put six men and two non-commissioned officers on guard."

"What was the result?"

"Ten men deserted that night."

Master Sergeant Peter MacMahan testified that it was the general talk among the men that they were going to desert. "There were so many deserted, I can't remember the name of any particular one. It took place that day. Some of the men deserted, and they were shot."

"What was the effect of that shooting?"

"It prevented any further desertions."

Custer brought forward no witnesses at all to testify about the incident of the attack by the Indians. He would handle this in his closing defense statement.

Custer presented that closing statement in writing.

"May it please the Court:

"I am charged first with being absent from my command. There are two phases of the journey which must be treated separately. The first from Fort Wallace to Fort Harker, occupying three days. Secondly from Fort Harker to Fort Riley, a distance of seventeen miles, occupying three hours.

"Of the first stage of that journey I can say that I accomplished it on what I believed to be—and had just cause to believe to be—government business. On the second stage, I went with the full knowledge and consent of my immediate commanding officer.

"In forming my division of six companies, I came under the immediate command of Lieutenant General Sherman. On the 17th of June I left the vicinity of Fort MacPherson in pursuance of General Sherman's orders. These are the only orders I acted under from the time I left General Smith to the time I saw that officer again on the 19th of July. I have not been able to produce these orders because they were given to me verbally.

"This, however, is immaterial because I completed the

scout as ordered, prior to receiving other orders which are
here in evidence. The conversation I had with Sherman is
very important because this is the last personal interview I
had with any one of the several commanding officers, and
therefore the last information I had as to what was expected
of me in regard to my movement against the Indians on the
plains.

"The details of the conversation are testified to. The
instructions left my movement almost discretionary with
myself. I was told that I could go to any post. That I could go
to Denver was especially impressed on my mind because
General Hancock was in that area. . . . How in the face of this
direct order and unmistakable authority commanding me to
go two hundred miles . . . how could I be guilty of absence
without leave when I went to Fort Harker, the base of my
supplies and within ten miles of where I was likely to go in
pursuit of Indians?

"Here, gentlemen, the theory of the prosecution is an
absurdity that must be ridden bareback to arrive at any
conclusion unfavorable to myself."

An expansive remark over a glass of brandy by a general
was apparently all that Custer had for justification for his
amazing trip *east* from Indian country. He had not gone to
Denver *or* to Hell—he had gone to his wife. But the
yellow-haired General, perhaps sensing the mood of the
court, now brought General Smith into his defense as
approving the whole trip by some remarks of his own.

After recounting how he had awakened the startled
General, Custer continued: "When I had completed my
report, to which he listened attentively, he said, 'Well, here is
Weir's bed, lie down and take some sleep.'

"I replied to him 'No, General, I would like to go down to
Riley and see my family—how long can you give me?' He
answered 'Hurry back, we shall want you.' . . . He arose at
once and went after Captain Weir to see me to the depot.
General Smith accompanied us out of the door and . . . told
me to remember him to my family at Fort Riley. I left him
and took the cars in the firm confidence . . . that I was going
with his knowledge and consent. Does a Commanding Offi-

cer allow his subordinate to go off in this manner without knowing why and wherefore? ... Did I not go with his consent? For of whom else could I ask permission, since he was the ... senior officer for within more than five hundred miles?

"It is neither probable nor reasonable that if I had come to Harker without leave and under circumstances which justified my arrest and prosecution, General Smith would have allowed me to go off to Riley without making some objection."

In sum, General Sherman had given him verbal permission to go anywhere he wished, and General Smith had consented to such an impression by allowing him to go on to Fort Riley, instead of arresting him on the spot. The fact that apparently no one in the whole West knew that Custer was anywhere except in Indian country was ignored by the cavalryman.

But the General was on firmer ground when he came to the charges concerning the Indian attack and the shooting of deserters. As to the first, he said, "The report as made to me was that Sergeant Connelly had been attacked about eight miles back by a party of forty or fifty Indians. I well knew, and so did everyone else who knows of Indian warfare, that any party I might send back, by the time it reached the scene of the attack, would find no trace of Indians. The latter would not even leave a trail to follow and it would have been the measure of absurdity to have undertaken such an errand. That I was not averse to meet the Indians at that time with my force, if there be any doubt on the subject, may be inferred from the fact . . . that when (Captain Hamilton) recommended a delay on account of . . . the probable presence of Indians in the vicinity, I declined to accede to his suggestion, and mounting my command at once set out upon the march."

As to his failure to go back to find the wounded man, Custer argued that "Captain Hamilton reported to me that both were killed, and until after I was here arraigned I supposed that such was the case."

As to the shooting down of deserters, Custer pleaded necessity. "When those deserters were pointed out to me escaping over the hill, the attention of nearly the whole command was directed toward me to see what I would do. It was well known that . . . there existed a combination for a general escapade from my command."

So Custer turned to his aide, Lieutenant Jackson, and gave the orders to "bring none back alive." In remarks reminiscent of the captain of the *Somers,* Custer said "From all the trustworthy information which had been given me there was manifest in my command a determination to desert which assumed the full proportions of a mutiny. . . . Deeply conscious of what I was taking upon myself and, on the other hand, what I owed to the service and to the men who were well disposed, I did that which under the same circumstances it seemed to me an officer in my position was expected to do."

When the wounded men were brought back, Custer said, that "it is shown by the only witness who can testify to the facts—the Surgeon of the command—that I directly ordered (him) to give them all the attention that was necessary— that I required him to report their condition to me and that I repeatedly inquired after them."

In his concluding remarks, Custer was eloquent: "I have not sought to relieve myself of these Charges and Specifications by reference to any record which I might have made the basis of an appeal were I a forlorn object of compassion. Had I resorted to such a line of defense, however, it would under any circumstance have been only to show that, through six years I have tried honestly and faithfully to devote myself to my country and to all, in my judgment, that was honorable and useful in my profession. I have never been once absent from my command without leave as here charged. I have never wearied or in any way made use of my men for the advancement of my private wishes or interest—as here charged, or severely tasked any living creature, as here charged, except under a sense of duty.

"I have never turned away from our enemy, as here charged, or failed to relieve an imperiled friend, as here charged . . . or, finally, ever saw a man in any strait suffer when by my authority I could relieve him, as here charged.

"So, if I felt guilty of all or one of the Charges or Specifications, it is an era of my life of which I am not conscious."

Custer's reputation was awesome, his eloquence was affecting . . . would it save him now? Behind the scenes, General Sheridan was exerting another pressure on the Army; he badly wanted Custer in the developing Indian Wars.

But the Court had to consider the facts: Custer was supposed to march *west* to fight the Indians, not *east* to his wife, imperiling men in his command for a private mission. They found him guilty on all charges, except the denial of medical attention to the wounded deserters.

"And the court does therefore sentence him, Brevet Major General G. A. Custer . . . to be suspended from rank and command for one year, and to forfeit his pay proper for the same time."

It has been suggested that General Custer was the scapegoat for Congressional complaints arising from the general failure of the Hancock expedition. (One senator charged that "One hundred million dollars has been spent on the Hancock campaign without having accomplished anything.") But, on review of the case, the Judge Advocate General of the Army had a simpler explanation:

"The conclusion unavoidably reached under this branch of the inquiry is that General Custer's anxiety to see his family at Fort Riley overcame his appreciation of the paramount necessity to obey orders which is incumbent on every military officer; and thus the excuses he offers for his acts of insubordination are afterthoughts."

Epilogue

The trial was over, but the Indians were still out on the Plains. Custer, the greatest cavalryman in the Army, was needed in the fight. Almost immediately his good friend General Sheridan, who replaced Hancock in 1867, began petitioning to have Custer returned to active duty. Within ten months Custer was reinstated—and soon was out on the

Plains again. For nine years he would be fighting Indians almost continuously.

In 1876, Custer was attached to an army under General Alfred Howe Terry and assigned to lead an advance party to the junction of the Big Horn and Little Big Horn rivers. An army of Indians under Sitting Bull had been reported there, and Custer's mission was to bar its escape to the east until the main body of Terry's force could be brought up.

Custer arrived at his destination on June 24. His scouts reported an Indian force of 1,200 to 1,500 and impulsive as ever, Custer determined to disregard his orders and attack them himself. Dividing his force he took 224 men and rode directly into the front of an Indian army some 6,000 strong—to annihilation. In a sense he had again gone "over the hill," but this time there was no return.

5

Of Wings—and Cries of Treason

Prologue

Can a member of the armed forces be tried by court-martial for uttering an opinion unappetizing to his military superiors? What jurisdiction does a military court have in such cases? These seem like questions particular to the 1960s and 1970s. Many modern servicemen, planning protest rallies in coffeehouses, might be astonished to learn that it was first raised in 1925 and that their ideological predecessor was a professional soldier who had joined the Army as a private, had risen to the rank of general, and who had been one of America's great heroes in World War I. The fact remains, the court-martial of General William "Billy" Mitchell was the first major "freedom of dissent" case in American military jurisprudence.

The dirigible *Shenandoah*, the most beautiful of the
Navy's lighter-than-air craft, rose gracefully above
the Lakehurst, New Jersey, Naval Air Station, beginning a
goodwill flight over cities, towns, and state fairs in the
Midwest. As the ship took to the air, one man, Zachary
Lansdowne, the *Shenandoah's* commander, did not share in
the satisfaction of the smooth takeoff. He was worried.
Squalls and storms had been reported over the Great Lakes
area, and in 1925 there was no meteorological service to
advise pilots which way storms were moving. Lansdowne,
experienced in dirigibles, knew that it was murder to take
one even *near* a squall. He had protested to his superiors
but had gotten nowhere—in the opinion of the Navy brass
the route of the *Shenandoah* would not cross the path of the
storm. His protests disallowed, Lansdowne had given the
orders and the great helium-filled ship had soared from her
resting place and headed west.

It was, by later accounts, a lovely evening. Down below
people on farms and streets could see the running lights of
the *Shenandoah* passing overhead like a grand constellation. But the *Shenandoah* was not a constellation, it was a
flying machine. And the machine was not perfect. A few
months before she had been partially disabled in an
accident and many of her safety valves had been carried
away. They had not been replaced. Furthermore, one of
her engines, over the bitter objections of her designer,
Jerome Hunsaker, had been removed completely. Yet as
long as the air was smooth, all was serene. Lansdowne
gave final instructions to the lieutenant at the controls and
went to bed.

About three in the morning one of the crewmen on
watch saw lightning to the east. By the time the commander had been called, lightning was flickering on
both sides of the ship and the *Shenandoah* was bucking
stiff headwinds. From their altitude of about 3,000 feet,
Lansdowne directed the ship to 2,000 feet, but even with
engines full ahead, the ship made little headway. Suddenly, the ship rose in the freshening winds, her nose
pointing down. Lansdowne ordered safety valves opened

to bleed off the gas which distended at higher altitudes. But despite the engines, the safety valves, and the frantic efforts of the men at the controls, the ship continued to rise.

The safety level for helium-filled dirigibles was 3,800 feet. Above that the gas expanded so much that a ship could burst. Helplessly the *Shenandoah* rose past that altitude, and even higher. To 5,000 feet. To 6,000 feet, and the center of the squall. Then the ship suddenly dropped like a rock, 3,200 feet in a minute and a half. Lansdowne was prepared; his men emptied water ballast and saved the ship from crashing.

Hearts hammering, the men looked down from the bucking, pitching cabin to the stormswept countryside below. The ship nosed down, then rose again. And suddenly the controls were useless against the strength of the squall. The ship rolled, turned, spun, throwing everyone in the cabin about. Rising once more breathtakingly, the ship, with a terrible noise, suddenly split. Girders tore, the skin pulled apart, and men spilled out to the ground, 6,200 feet below. The ship literally tore in half, the tail section floating in great circles to the earth, with men leaping through holes as the fragments approached the ground. The bow section came down minutes later, bearing a cargo of death. Some men miraculously survived the terrible fall. But not Commander Lansdowne.

In the aftermath of the tragedy, Secretary of the Navy Dwight Wilbur in Washington had soothing words. The accident had proved, he announced, that the nation need fear no attack from enemy aircraft. Flying was simply too hazardous.

In San Antonio, Texas, another high official had a quite different reaction. General William ("Billy") Mitchell, air ace of World War I, apostle of airpower, and gadfly to generals wedded to infantry and admirals infatuated with battleships, had finally had enough. The *Shenandoah* disaster followed closely on another ill-conceived program in which three totally unsuitable craft had been sent on a flight from Los Angeles to Hawaii. All three had crashed, proving to the Navy that airpower was a myth and flying suitable only to stunt men and maniacs. Mitchell had been fighting this attitude for years, and the *Shenandoah* became his Rubicon. He called a press conference and handed out the following release;

"I have been asked from all parts of the country to give my opinion about the reasons for the frightful aeronautical accidents and loss of life, equipment, and treasure that has occurred during the last few days.

"My opinion is as follows: These accidents are the direct result of the incompetency, criminal negligence, and almost treasonable administration of our national defense by the Navy and War Departments."

The words burst on Washington like a star shell and illuminated officers who had hated Mitchell for a long time. Now, at last, he was in their hands. A court-martial was ordered.

Billy Mitchell came from a famous family. His grandfather had founded one of the great banks in the nation; his father had been a U.S. Senator. But it was not banking or law to which the young Mitchell was drawn. He became enchanted with the wooden crates which daring men were attempting to fly and saw in them possibilities so vast they frightened him. When World War I came along, he volunteered to lead America's small group of flying men.

To make certain he got the assignment, Mitchell went to Paris even before America entered the war. He studied the French and English aircraft and worked out possibilities for their use. The Allies had used aircraft merely as observation planes for artillery spotting and intelligence. Mitchell felt they could attack with bombs and machine guns.

General Pershing did not agree, but he was too good a general to pass up new ideas. As Mitchell's constant badgering bothered him, he placed another officer over Mitchell to keep him in line and to exploit whatever good notions he had. And so Mitchell got his chance. In the battle of Saint—Mihiel he sent over waves of aircraft, 1,500 of them, so many they literally "blackened the skies," according to an awed infantryman. Strafing and bombing, they helped to make the battle a stunning success; Pershing graciously gave credit to the airmen.

Mitchell came back from the war a hero. He had been the first American officer under enemy fire, the first to fly over enemy lines, the first to be given a *Croix de Guerre.* He was the very model of the gay, insouciant, reckless pilot, and the American people took him to their hearts. His face became as well-known to them as any movie star's, and he was always referred to as "Billy."

But the war was over—and it had been the war to end all wars. America had not an enemy in sight and no desire to keep millions of men in uniform or spend millions of dollars on defense. When Mitchell arrived in Washington, he found that his fledgling air force, part of the Army, was the first to feel the effects of cutbacks. He soon had just a few pilots and airmen, and only a small scattering of planes, all left over from World War I.

The entrenched powers in the military were the old-line generals and admirals. The generals tolerated him for a time. But the admirals soon developed a bristling feud. What brought it on was Mitchell's brash statement to the public and to Congress that the battleship was useless against air power. The thought that a flimsy wooden crate in the air could challenge a great steel battleship was anathema to any right-thinking admiral.

So an epic test was arranged. Great steel ships, captured from the Germans, were to be moored off Norfolk, Virginia, and attacked by Mitchell's air fleet. Mitchell set to work with a fury. First he needed bombs, bombs bigger than any that had ever been manufactured. He got them designed and built in three months. Then his pilots had to be trained. No aircraft had ever attacked a battleship before. Should you attempt to hit the ship squarely? Or burst the bombs in the water beside her, hoping to open the seams? Mitchell planned both.

For weeks the newspapers heralded the coming test,

and the admirals supplied every delaying tactic and restrictive rule they could muster. But when the day came, and the flimsy little planes staggered into the air with their dangerously heavy loads of bombs, Mitchell won the challenge completely. Every ship was sunk, including the *Ostfriesland*, one of the strongest ships ever built by the Germans and considered almost unsinkable by naval experts.

When the great battleship started to sink at the stern, her bow pointing helplessly toward the skies, some admirals cried openly. They were, all unknowing, watching the future in miniature.

But instead of looking to the future, they turned to a bitter attack on Mitchell. The tests they explained away. After all, the ships had been unarmed and not moving. Antiaircraft guns would have driven the planes off. Nothing had been proved.

But they suffered. And their Army counterparts suffered, too. For Mitchell was the delight of the press. His every statement seemed to make headlines while an opponent would be buried in the back pages. And Mitchell was now carrying his fight for air power to his own superiors. He wanted more aircraft, more trained men, more air bases. He wanted a complete meteorological system set up for the United States. He wanted bombsights, armaments, bombs.

Time and again he went before Congress to plead his case and stir up a storm which usually broke over the head of the Secretary of War. He outlined his vision of the future in chilling terms: cities and manufacturing plants bombed; planes attacking not only infantry but the home front, destroying industrial capacity and the will to fight. He pictured New York City in ruins, skyscrapers tumbling, stone falling to the pavement, sewers bursting, fires spreading.

The War Department had enough problems. It could barely get enough funds to equip its ground troops and

Mitchell was urging them to divert some of these precious funds to his air force. It was absurd. Europe was thousands of miles across the ocean and Asia farther yet. And here, now, Mitchell wanted money to combat a future threat which sounded as likely as an invasion from Mars.

The Secretary of War thought he knew how to deal with the situation. It was in the familiar military tradition, still followed to this day. He transferred Mitchell from his spotlight post in Washington to an outpost—San Antonio, Texas.

Then the two ill-conceived air accidents happened. Mitchell knew his career was on the line but he determined to chance it. He called his press conference, and awaited the summons.

His was to be the most celebrated American court-martial of its day. Beginning in October, 1925, it had the full attention of the press, but the press was divided. Some reporters thought Mitchell a "screwball"; others thought him a visionary held back by crusty, unimaginative generals. But whatever he was, he was fascinating. Handsome, tall, trim, with a ready smile, he was in the image of the American hero. Indeed, his civilian attorney Frank R. Reid told reporters at the trial, "Rome endured as long as there were Romans. America will endure as long as there are Mitchells."

Mitchell was to be brought to trial under the 96th Article of War, known as the "catch-all" provision, which read: "Though not mentioned in these Articles, all disorders and neglects to the prejudice of good order and military discipline, all conduct of a nature to bring discredit upon the military service" would be subject for a court-martial. Under this provision, Mitchell once said, an officer could be tried for tickling a horse.

Mitchell's press statement, if nothing else, had certainly brought "discredit upon the military service," and under the article, the General had no chance. Friends in the service urged him to plead guilty. But Mitchell and his attorney were adamant. They saw one chance. They planned to prove that every one of his statements about the military was true.

The court-martial was held in a converted warehouse in Washington, D.C. In view of the pretrial publicity, the public and the press had expected some sort of indoor coliseum; the choice of a shabby warehouse was seen as a direct slap at Mitchell.

But Mitchell and his attorney, Congressman Reid, could slap back—and they started in fine fettle by challenging the august panel of generals who would hear the case.

The panel, with Major General Charles P. Summerall presiding, comprised four major generals (including Mitchell's boyhood friend Douglas MacArthur) and six brigadier generals. From these eleven officers six would be selected; the Army, anticipating challenges by Mitchell, had chosen extra panelists. They had not anticipated the object of the first challenge: the President of the Court.

General Summerall had commanded the Hawaiian Islands some years earlier, when Mitchell had made a highly publicized inspection trip there. From this inspection Mitchell had made a prediction. In the next war, he warned, the Japanese would attack Pearl Harbor with aircraft and submarines and he predicted that the attack would center on Ford Island. The report was considered so silly it was not even read by most of the Army's hierarchy. Also in that report, Mitchell had delivered a stinging attack on Summerall's defense plans, and now Reid quoted some of Summerall's rebuttal: "The public is being misled by fanciful and irresponsible talk emanating from a source either without experience or whose experience in war is limited to the very narrow field of aviation."

Summerall, furious, told Mitchell's attorney: "I regarded the report as untrue, unfair . . . and ignorant." Later, after he left the panel, he told reporters, "we're enemies, Mitchell and I." Two other generals were chal-

lenged on similar grounds. They departed and the trial
began.

Reid then asked for dismissal on grounds that fore-
shadowed the trials of the 1960s and 1970s—that the court
had no jurisdiction. He argued that the offense was in
the category of the First Amendment, freedom of speech.
But the Army Judge Advocate, Colonel Sherman More-
land, argued that a man who enlisted gave up his civilian
status and its corresponding personal liberties. The court
decided that it did, indeed, have jurisdiction.

In his opening statement, Reid announced that Mitchell
would prove that his statements about the flights to
Hawaii and the *Shenandoah* "were true, as a matter of
fact." In addition, he said, "We will prove by evidence
that Mitchell, after exhausting every usual means to safeguard the aerial defense of the United States, without result, took the only way possible that would cause a
study of true conditions of the national defense to be
made."

In other words, this was to be not a trial of one man
for one offense, but an examination of the whole defense
posture of the United States. The generals on the panel,
who had expected a quick trial, were taken aback,
especially when the defense demanded that seventy-one
witnesses be heard.

The first witnesses were called to establish the fact
of Mitchell's announcement. Newsman A.A.H. Yeager of
the San Antonio *Light* for example testified that on September 5, 1925, he and other reporters had been invited to Mitchell's office where they were handed a mimeographed statement.

These facts were not challenged and the defense began
its parade of witnesses—and immediately established the
theme which was to make this trial memorable: The wars
of the future would be dominated by air power.

The first defense witness to take the stand was Major
General Amos J. Fries, Chief of the Chemical Warfare
Service. His testimony at first seemed irrelevant, and the
prosecution launched a storm of objections.

"I want you to tell us what mustard gas was, how it was used (in World War I) and what its effect is on the occupation of territory."

"It burns the skin . . . goes through clothes as though you had none on. It affects the eyes and lungs likewise. . . ."

"Now tell us what other kinds of chemicals and gases were used?"

"We used pure chlorine . . . released only as a gas on the front lines and allowed to drift with the wind . . . we also used phosgene, a chemical combination of chlorine and carbon monoxide . . . about ten times as poisonous as chlorine."

"Now can you tell us what amount of gas will be necessary to effectively gas an area the size of the *District of Columbia?*"

At last the prosecution grasped the real drift of the questions and objected even more vehemently. To quell the storm the defense counsel nimbly shifted ground—and still made his point.

"So an airplane could carry a ton of this?"

"Airplane bombs would carry gas in the same way as high explosives."

So the defense counsel had neatly started off the trial with a whiff of mustard gas in court, capable of being delivered from airplanes over the District of Columbia, where the trial was being held. While the prosecution was still reeling from this unexpected testimony he brought in a witness from another angle of the case, de-mure—and angry—Mrs. Peggy Lansdowne, widow of the the *Shenandoah's* commander. Mitchell had predicted in his statement that the Navy would try to "whitewash" the *Shenandoah* tragedy. Mrs. Lansdowne had been asked to testify at the hearing into the catastrophe. The day before the hearing the Navy had sent an officer to her with a statement it wished her to read in court as if it were her own statement.

"Have you a copy of this communication?"

"I have not."

"What was done with it?"

"I tore it up."

"Can you state in substance to the court here what was in that communication . . ."

"Irrelevant!" the prosecutor objected, but Reid was now upset.

"Colonel Mitchell in his statement for which he is on trial charged that the Navy would proceed to whitewash the *Shenandoah* accident, and in pursuance of that would do certain things. We expect to show that they absolutely did that by trying to get this witness to give false testimony in regard to the accident."

The court ruled for Reid, and he proceeded:

"Was that statement false?"

"False . . . the main point in which the statement was false was my husband was willing to take the *Shenandoah* anywhere at anytime regardless of weather conditions. It was an insult to his memory to insinuate he would do such a thing. . . . My husband was very much opposed to this flight and protested as vigorously as any officer is allowed to do to his superior."

"Did you finally appear before the *Shenandoah* Board?"

"I did."

"Did you make a statement in regard to it?"

"I did."

She read the statement: "Immediately after the wreck of the *Shenandoah* and the death of my husband, I stated to the newspapers that my husband was ordered by the Navy Department to proceed upon this flight to the midwest in spite of protests made by him to the department, and that the flight was made solely for political purposes. Secretary Wilbur was quoted in the press as saying that my husband had made no protest against going at this time and one of my principal reasons for appearing before the Court is to emphasize the fact that my statement has been substantiated by official correspondence read into the Court record."

Mrs. Lansdowne's testimony was effective. Her husband had been killed in an accident he had foreseen—and the Navy had tried to persuade her to sign a state-

ment denying his warnings. The next day some newspapers called for the resignation of Navy Secretary Wilbur.

Meanwhile in court the bemedaled veteran pilots of
Mitchell's World War I cadre began to take the stand to
prove another part of his argument: the systematic deni-
gration of the air service. Major Carl "Tooey" Spaatz, later
to become one of the great airmen of World War II as commander of the U.S. Strategic Air Forces, now took the stand
to tell—in a nutshell—the story of the tiny air force's
problems in 1925. The total U.S. air power which could
be gotten into the air in case of attack in that year was
twelve to fifteen planes—and even to do that he
would have to use some administrative officers as pilots.

Spaatz went on: "The bulk of equipment in the air service is
very obsolescent or obsolete."

What was holding it up? The Army chiefs who did not
believe in air power were not appropriating any money. The
argument seemed to Spaatz to be reduced *ad absurdum* when
"we tried to get the War Department to appropriate *one
dollar* to rent a field . . . . It required a long time for us to
reach a consummation."

The next defense witness was another major destined to
become a World War II leader, H. H. "Hap" Arnold. He said
that distance as a military factor no longer existed. On
cross-examination, the prosecutor implied that Arnold was
speaking only of war between France and Germany. They
were next-door neighbors; America was thousands of miles
away. Arnold replied, "I think that makes no difference in an
aerial war, where time is annihilated to a few hours."

This was too much for the prosecutor who asked sarcasti-
cally, "Is 3,500 miles of salt water annihilated?"

"Yes, sir, it is today."

Who could believe it in 1925? The prosecutor shrugged
expressively; apparently madmen were appearing as witnesses, to his line of thinking. The court, he was sure, would
agree.

As the trial proceeded, some generals on the panel

became miffed at the defense witnesses' implied comparison between the air and the ground troops. They seemed to be saying that aerial combat was more hazardous. The ground officers didn't like that and one of them asked: "Do you consider service or duty in the air service more dangerous than serving in the line in the infantry, in wartime?"

Arnold countered with the General Staff's own figures that showed twenty-three percent replacements in the air service as against seven percent in the infantry.

After other witnesses were heard, the nation's leading air ace in World War I, Eddie Rickenbacker, approached the stand.

"You have the title of 'ace of aces,' have you not?"

"Correct."

"And for what was that?"

"The greatest number of enemy planes shot down by any American pilot . . . twenty-six planes and balloons."

"Approximately how many hours were you in the air over there?"

"Approximately three hundred."

"How many hours over enemy lines?"

"Approximately three hundred."

"How many hours exposed to enemy antiaircraft fire?"

"Approximately three hundred."

"Were any of your planes ever shot down by antiaircraft fire?"

"No, sir."

This was a point Mitchell dearly wanted to bring out. Most of his superiors in the Army contended that antiaircraft fire would be sufficient to deal with any attack from the air. And on cross-examination, Major Francis Wilby, one of the prosecution attorneys, moved to give increased stress to the Army's contentions.

"Did you ever hear of a German ace by the name of Baron von Richthofen?"

"He was exceptionally good—their best."

"How did he come to his death?"

"My understanding is that he was brought down by machine-gun fire from the ground in trench strafing during the advance on Paris."

"He wasn't as fortunate as you in avoiding machine-gun fire?"

"No, sir."

But Rickenbacker nevertheless had the last word. The prosecutor asked him whether he was aware that in World War I our Twenty-Third Antiaircraft Battery had officially brought down nine planes with only 5,092 shots.

Rickenbacker asked: "Were those all German or some American?"

The exchange evoked bitter smiles from veteran American pilots who had sometimes spent many minutes frantically dodging their own ground fire.

To bolster the testimony about the impotence of antiaircraft fire, the defense now brought witnesses who had particpated in tests the Army had run the previous year. One pilot testified that he had towed a target for an hour without any hits from below. He finally got tired and came down and asked how things were going. The Colonel in charge told him that he had quit long ago. Trying to operate the gun, he said, was like trying to pat his head with one hand and rub his stomach with the other. Other pilots testified to the same results. The antiaircraft guns simply couldn't hit a big target towed slowly across in front of them.

One of Mitchell's more flamboyant witnesses was a congressman who would later become Mayor of New York City, the peppery and outspoken Fiorello La Guardia. La Guardia had a way of creating a sensation wherever he went, and this appearance was to be no exception.

A long-time supporter of Mitchell, La Guardia was convinced that the officers on the panel had been instructed to bring in a guilty verdict, and before appearing in court he told newsmen so in his usual blunt and colorful way. To no one's surprise, his words made headlines and before he appeared in court the papers had put out extra editions.

The members of the court, who had seen the headlines, were not pleased with the witness, who began his testimony with a comic reenactment of some disastrous antiaircraft test at Fort Tilden, New Jersey, in which not a single target had been hit. When he was finished, the prosecutor ignored that issue to hold up a paper proclaiming, over La Guardia's name: "Billy Mitchell is not being tried by a jury of his peers, but by nine beribboned dogrobbers of the General Staff."

"Were you correctly quoted?"

"I did not say *'beribboned,'* " was the answer.

When pressed for an explanation of his remark, La Guardia stated, "I do not think I am called upon to do that, but I'll be glad to do it . . . . From my experience as a member of Congress and from my contact with the General Staff, I am convinced that the training, the background, the experience and the attitude of officers of high rank of the Army are conducive to carrying out the wishes and desires of the General Staff."

Then, looking at a controversial officer on the panel, La Guardia added with a smile, "I want to say that at that time I didn't know that General MacArthur was on this court."

The trial continued week after week. Seemingly every member of the small but elite air fraternity came to lend their support to the man whose career was on the line. Ordinary citizens came, too, including Mitchell's good friend, Will Rogers, who showed up just to sit at the defense table for a few days.

But the real drama of the courtroom was ahead. Billy Mitchell was about to take the stand. Handsome, erect, he strode quietly to the witness chair, and the court was hushed. Reid led him through an account of his war service, and then asked him to describe his troubles during the postwar years; in effect a profusion of recommendations which had been rejected. A radio network, a meteorological service, trained mechanics, all-metal bombers, air units around the world, four-engine bombers, aircraft carriers at sea, airborne torpedoes, "gliding bombs" which could be launched from aircraft at targets miles away.

Every one of these, of course, eventually came into being. But in 1925, and before, Mitchell couldn't get anyone to take them seriously. Now he tried again. He had a vision of the future, and the future was as he saw it. For example, years before the invention of radar, he outlined exactly what was going to come.

"First, you must have listening posts and places in suitable positions for determining the aircraft that are coming, what their numbers are and their position and their probable intentions. . . . Without going into detail, they have to be far enough out so as to enable our own forces to get into the air at any altitude both by day and night, and meet the attack. . . . The scheme must be completely worked out for day and night attack because an attack is not made simply by a ship flying over a place. Feint after feint is made and everything is done to confuse the defense. . . . You might say we have never been able to get a study of a thing like that in this country."

On and on the recommendations went; instruments for flying in bad weather, self-starters for aircraft, bomb-loading machines, variable-pitch and reversible propellors, amphibious planes. And as Mitchell spoke, the generals on the panel could only stare and shake their heads. Two years before Lindbergh piloted his tiny plane across the Atlantic, this acceptance of an era of fleets of sophisticated bombers striking across the world seemed fantastic.

When Mitchell's direct testimony ended, one of the prosecuting attorneys, a brilliant, sarcastic, courtroom veteran, Major Allen Gullion, went immediately to the attack.

Under the whiplash of his questions, all delivered with the contemptuous tone of a sane citizen of 1925 speaking to a mad visionary, Mitchell did not make an effective witness until near the end of the cross-examination.

Gullion's first question startled Mitchell and the court.

"Colonel Mitchell, have you any idea of the estimated wealth of the United States?"

"No."

"The World Almanac, page 754, 1923 edition states that the estimated wealth of the U.S. in 1922 was $302,803, 862,000. Now I would be much obliged to you if you would keep that figure in solution, and the relevancy of questions will appear later." Gullion then went on to quote from Mitchell's criticism of the Pacific Fleet operations of the past summer. Mitchell had predicted an attack on Pearl Harbor by a Pacific power. He had said that mines would be used as part of the attack.

"Would you mind telling us what Pacific power you had in mind?"

"Japan."

Later, he asked, "Do you know of any instance in the World War where one—just one—ship was ever sunk by a mine."

"Yes . . . . The *Audacious*."

"Are you familiar with Corbett?"

"Jim Corbett?"

"No, not Jim Corbett." The assured attorney was momentarily flustered. "Don't think I'm trying to make a hippodrome out of this. I certainly didn't mean Jim Corbett. I have reference to the naval authority Corbett."

"No."

"In his book *Naval Operations of the World War*, Volume I, page 442 he says that the *Audacious* was not sunk that way."

"I have heard others say she was."

"Then you take what you have heard other people say over what is laid down in serious history, do you?"

"I have heard people as serious as anybody could be say that."

Gullion finally got around to his reason for bringing up the figure of the national wealth. Mitchell's criticism had included the prediction that enemy submarines would be assigned to areas all over the Pacific to intercept shipping. Gullion calculated that the Japanese would have to send out 12,500 submarines to adequately cover the Pacific Ocean. Each submarine cost five million dollars. Since a nation would only be able to keep ten percent of its submarines on station at one time, the total cost of such a submarine fleet, according to Gullion's calculations, would be $625 billion. And the wealth of the United States was less than half that.

This mathematical juggling only seemed to amuse Mitchell, but that afternoon he slipped badly. Gullion was questioning one of his prophecies in the report he had submitted after touring the Pacific. Mitchell had said that submarines might some day carry large guns or gas rockets or other missiles, he did not know what but he did know submarines would be a fantastic weapon of the future capable of challenging battleships. Gullion thought this was absurd, and said so. Mitchell said, "That was my opinion."

Gullion: "That was your *opinion?*"

"That was my opinion."

"Is that your opinion now?"

"Yes."

The trap was ready to snap shut—but Gullion seemed almost amazed by his good fortune. For once, he stammered: "Then, any statement—there is no statement of *fact* in your whole paper?"

"The paper is an expression of opinion."

Gullion wanted that to sink in. He repeated, *"There is no statement of fact in your whole paper?"*

"No."

Defense counsel winced, and from then until the end of the cross-examination Gullion would begin every question about the statement with the words: "In this statement which contains not one item of fact you say . . . "

But Mitchell was to make his points, too. When Gullion, quoting from the statement, read: " 'In the development of air power one has to look ahead and not backward . . . . That is why the older services have been psychologically unfit to develop this new arm to the fullest extent practicably . . .' Isn't it a fact that air officers in the development of air power look backward for lessons to guide them?"

Mitchell's answer to this question perhaps summed up the problems of the air service better than any other exchange at the trial: "They have so little to go on in looking backward, they have to look forward in order to meet the conditions in air arms."

Gullion then turned to the heart of Mitchell's criticism. He quoted: "These accidents are the direct result of incompetency, criminal negligence and almost treasonable administration of the national defense by the War and Navy Departments." Gullion looked at Mitchell. "Well, what is treason?"

"There are two definitions of treason, one is that contained in the Constitution. That is, levying war against the United States, or giving aid and comfort to its enemies. The other is to give up or betray; betraying of any trust or confidence; perfidy or breach of faith. I belive that the departments, the system, is almost treasonable . . . in that it does not give a proper place to air power in organizing the defenses of the country, which is vital as an element. That is what I believe. It is a question of the system, and not the individuals, entirely."

Under further questioning, Mitchell elaborated: "I think officers in the air service who are subjected to the command of people who know absolutely nothing about aviation, who come and inspect their outfits without knowing anything about them whatever and ask foolish questions—I think that is repugnant in every way to a man who has given up his life to this duty and is constantly exposed to danger in the air in that way."

After more questions, most of them delivered in sarcastic tones and filled with allusions to "exaggeration," "dreams," and "visions," Mitchell's ordeal was over. But his testimony had overcome all of Gullion's efforts to discredit it in the eyes of the public; newspapers carried Mitchell's philosophy to every corner of America.

The prosecution tried to counter this impression with a range of witnesses varying from dirigible designers to Admiral Richard Byrd, the famous explorer. Reid, too, was a brilliant cross-examiner, and also a master of sarcasm. Finally, his tactics became too much for at least one general on the panel. After one question by Reid, General Edward A. King suddenly burst out "Damned rot!" As a clue to the General's impartial attitude this was revealing. King apologized, but, as Reid told reporters later, "You all know that if this was a civilian court, this case would be thrown out immediately."

Perhaps Mitchell's greatest enemy in the military service was Major General Hugh A. Drum, the Assistant Chief of Staff, G-3 (Operations). Drum was a belligerent, testy witness who thought that aviation as a military factor was next to nonexistent. With a few antiaircraft guns, he could keep any bombing fleet away from a target. If the planes flew high enough to avoid the guns, they would be unable to bomb effectively. When Reid tried to question him, Drum retorted, "Will you tell me what *your* war experience was, and we can judge."

Lieutenant Colonel Lesley J. McNair of the General Staff ridiculed Mitchell's prediction that the oil tanks at Pearl Harbor were vulnerable.

"Would you say that they are noncombustible?"

"I can explain that, but I would prefer not to."

Time and again taking refuge in "confidential" matters, the Colonel did admit that the defenses of Hawaii were not actually in being. But they were planned, and they would take effect when war came.

And so it went. Leaders of the antiaviation group, by far the majority in the military, came forward one by one to counter the testimony of the small clique of men whom Mitchell called "the air fraternity."

As Mitchell said, when he rose to make his closing statement: "The truth of every statement which I have made has been proved by good and sufficient evidence before this court, not by men who gained their knowledge of aviation by staying on the ground . . . but by actual flyers who have gained their knowledge firsthand in war and peace.

"The court has refrained from ruling whether the truth in this case constitutes an absolute defense or not.

"To proceed further with the case would serve no useful purpose.

"I have therefore directed my counsel to entirely close our part of the proceedings without argument."

The court was stunned. In the silence, Gullion jumped to his feet and announced loudly that he did not propose to give up *his* part of the proceeding. He well knew of the country's fascination with Mitchell. But Gullion, who was later to become Judge Advocate General of the Army, knew military justice—and how to win the votes of the officers on the panel. Clutching a newspaper, he pointed to its headline and read, "*The people are behind Mitchell . . . .* Who are the people?" he asked. Then looking at the generals on the board he said, "Are you not *people?* You who served your country in war and risked your lives, are you not people, too? I say that you are the real people, the real citizens and that what you believe is what matters!"

In one of the more obvious appeals to a jury ever heard in a military or a civilian court, Gullion expounded on this argument for ten more minutes, flattering the "distinguished" officers on the panel. But then he turned, almost reluctantly, it seemed, to his main target, Billy Mitchell.

"Is such a man a safe guide? Is he a constructive person or is he a loose-talking imaginative megalomaniac cheered by the adulation of his juniors who see promotion under his banner . . . and intoxicated by the ephemeral applause of the people whose fancy he has for the moment caught?

"Is this man a Moses, fitted to lead the people out of a wilderness which is his creation, only? Is he of the George Washington type, as counsel would have you believe? Is he not rather of the all-too-familiar charlatan and demagogue type—like Alcibiades, Catiline, and except for a decided difference in poise and mental powers in Burr's favor, like Aaron Burr? He is a good flyer, a fair rider, a good shot, flamboyant, self-advertising, wildly imaginative, destructive, never constructive except in wild nonfeasible schemes, never overly careful to the ethics of his method.

"Sirs, we ask the dismissal of the accused for the sake of the Army whose discipline he has endangered and whose fair name he has attempted to discredit . . . we ask it in the name of the American people whose fears he has played upon, whose hysteria he has fomented, whose confidence he has beguiled, and whose faith he has betrayed."

Gullion sat down in the silence of a momentarily stunned courtroom. In that silence, a friend came to Mitchell's side and patted him on the back. Will Rogers was telling Mitchell that the people were with him.

The prosecution rested, and the panel withdrew to consider its verdict. The voting in that panel has never been resolved. One of Mitchell's biographers said that a paper in

MacArthur's handwriting had been found which voted for the dismissal of Mitchell. MacArthur in his own autobiography stated:

"When the verdict was reached, many believed I had betrayed my friend. . . . Nothing could be further from the truth. I did what I could in his behalf."

But when the panel of generals filed back in they read their verdict: Guilty to all charges and specifications.

The sentence: "The accused to be suspended from rank, command, and duty with forfeiture of all pay and allowances for five years."

Billy Mitchell had lost. Within a few months he resigned from the Army and retired to Virginia, cut off from the air service which he had done so much to create.

But the air arm lived on and grew and fulfilled all of Mitchell's predictions. As Reid told reporters immediately after the trial: "They may think they have silenced Mitchell, but his ideas will go marching on, and those who crucified him will be the first to put his aviation suggestions into practice.

"He is a 1925 John Brown."

Epilogue

Although Mitchell's lawyer raised the question of the First Amendment, the court disallowed it, and it would be a long time before it would be raised with success. But another legal irritation to constitutional lawyers was raised with somewhat more success. This was the "catch-all" or "horse-tickling" provision.

The provision, Article 96 of the old Articles of War, now for the first time came under attack in Congress. Fiorello La Guardia submitted a bill at the end of the trial that would drastically reduce the penalties a court-martial could mete out under this article. The bill died, but showed its impact as the provision has been downgraded in revisions of military law and more and more specific offenses have been included instead. (In the Uniform Code of Military Justice, however, the provision is still there, although a revision proposed by Senator Mark Hatfield would eliminate courts-martial under this article.)

But this was a court-martial that was of much greater importance than any legal impact it might have had. It was a court-martial that had the world in attendance. Military men in Germany, France, England, and the Far East took heed of the testimony that had been heard in the courtroom and Mitchell's predictions about the future of air power helped mold their plans. Only in his own country was Mitchell a prophet without honor.

Throughout the Twenties and Thirties, American military men based their appraisal of air power on the statement of French General Ferdinand Foch. Air power, he had said, was "pour le sport." It took the reality of one of Mitchell's most fantastic predictions to wake them—and when the Japanese attacked Pearl Harbor with airplanes and submarines it was almost too late.

6

When the Guns Flamed

Prologue

*"In the course of many wars since
Abraham Lincoln's time, thousands of deserters
had been tried and found guilty. Hundreds of
those deserters had been sentenced to death.*

*But such death sentences—since
the Civil War—had not actually been executed.
Not in the Indian wars; not in the Spanish-
American War; not in the First War; not in
the Second War; not in the Korean War. Despite all the heavy sentences, nobody was shot
to death—and, at least during the Second and
Korean Wars, there were few who believed that
anybody would be shot to death. And this was
because it was widely held that the people of
the United States no longer demanded—indeed,
would no longer tolerate—the extreme penalty
for a citizen who refused to fight. So the
military representatives of the United States*

116

followed a practice of commuting the death sentence, reducing the prison sentences systematically, and releasing the deserters shortly after the wars were over.

This was the practice in every case except one. *No deserter was actually shot except* Private Slovik."

William Bradford Huie
The Execution of Private
Slovik.

Huie was, of course, referring to executions for desertion as the result of court-martial sentences, not to the "General Custer" variety of the last century. But it is a little-known fact that the death penalty in military justice is more rare than in civilian justice. This is so because military review boards tend to scale down sentences awarded by court-martial panels, and almost invariably do so when a non-mandatory death penalty is decreed.

But Slovik faced the firing squad. Why?

August 25, 1944, Omaha Beach, the Allied armies' staging and supply center in Normandy. A small, wiry, dark-haired soldier milled around with several of his companions, awaiting assignment. Private Eddie Slovik was not your normal all-American G.I. A product of reform school with two prison terms on his prewar record, he came to the Army with an attitude illustrated by a statement to a friend while en route to Europe. He would *never*, he averred, fire his rifle.

And so on Omaha Beach he received his assignment: he was to be one of twelve replacements to G Company, 109th Infantry, 28th Division—the division known throughout the European Theater of World War II as the "jinxed division," because of its many casualties. A truck pulled up and the twelve set off to meet their unit in Elbeuf, slightly to the southwest of Rouen. The ride was one of some four to five hours and passed through countryside that looked like the remnants of Hell itself. Everywhere were endless piles of bodies, charred horseflesh, and tangled, twisted wreckage.

What had taken place in the area was a massacre. German troops had been squeezed into an untenable position in the "Falaise Pocket," and had been forced to flee into open ground in broad daylight. Men, trucks, and horse-drawn artillery had jammed onto a single narrow road. They had presented a perfect target for the rockets, machine-gun fire, and bombs of Allied planes. The scene was not a pleasant introduction to combat—particularly for a man with no stomach to fight.

Ahead, in Elbeuf, vicious fighting continued as elite S.S. troops of the German Army fought to hold open a bridge across the Eure River to let the remnants of their units escape. As it approached the battle area, Slovik's truck was forced to stop, and the soldiers were told to continue to their companies on foot. Suddenly artillery shells began dropping among them and the men frantically turned to digging foxholes to avoid the shrapnel. When the shelling ceased, another even more formidable sound began—the rumbling of tanks coming in their direction. This time, however, the men were in luck. The tanks belonged to a Canadian company making its way to the front. Gratefully, the American soldiers clambered out of their foxholes and made their way to Elbeuf to join their units. All except Private John Tankey and Private Eddie Slovik, who remained with the Canadians.

Tankey and Slovik stayed with the Canadians for forty-five days, indulging military protocol only to the extent of sending a letter to their outfit stating that they had become lost. The Canadians cheerfully assimilated them and put them to a variety of chores, including foraging for provisions. They even taught the Canadians how to cook potato pancakes (it required stealing several eggs). While they traveled about in a "blitz buggy" loaned to them by the Canadians and foraged for food in the countryside, their outfit was engaged in bitter fighting. One member received the Congressional Medal of Honor for heroism in the Battle of the Ourq River. A month and a half later, on October 8th, the two men finally reported to 28th Division headquarters, then located at Elsenborn, Belgium. Tankey rejoined his unit and went on to be seriously wounded in the Battle of Hürtgen Forest. No charges of any sort were ever preferred against him. But Slovik seemed to have other ideas. At Elsenborn, after talking to the officer in charge, he suddenly turned and began walking away. The officer told Tankey to stop his friend, but Slovik just pulled away from him.

"I know what I'm doing," he said.

The next morning he appeared at the headquarters of the 112th Infantry Military Government detachment with a green slip of paper on which he had written a confession of desertion. He was placed under arrest, examined by a psychiatrist who found him sane, and ordered to stand ready for a court-martial.

The court-martial of Private Slovik is one of the shortest on record, possibly the briefest of all major courts-martial in American history. It convened at 10 A.M., November 11, 1944, and was over by 11:40 A.M. Nine officers sat in judgment. None of them were combat officers—line officers were too badly needed at the front. These were staff officers who might be expected to be more lenient with an alleged deserter.

The charge against Slovik was violation of the 58th Article of War—desertion to avoid hazardous duty. Specifically he was charged with deserting at Elbeuf when he failed to join his unit, and he was charged with desertion when he walked away from the officer in charge of his unit.

The first witness, Private George F. Thompson, had been with Slovik since they left Fort Meade, Maryland, and had also been assigned to Company G. He described the trip from Omaha Beach.

"Well, we got on the trucks . . . and sometime after that, I don't know how long, probably two or three hours, we stopped at some place which seemed to be more or less a rest camp or something. We dropped our packs off there and got on the trucks again and went to Elbeuf where we again detrucked."

"Was there any action at that place?"

"There was a lot of troop movement and shelling."

"When was the last time you saw Private Slovik?"

"We detrucked and moved along the edge of the city and then we dug in about 11 o'clock that night in an open lot. About 11:30 we moved into the city to join our company. There was a lot of confusion. That's the last time I saw him."

Captain Ralph O. Grotte, the commander of Company G, described his encounter when Slovik suddenly appeared at Grotte's headquarters on October 8th.

"He asked me if he could be tried for being absent without leave. I told him I would find out and placed him in arrest and had him returned to his platoon area, and told him to stay in that area."

An hour later Slovik had surprised Grotte by returning to his headquarters and asking: "If I leave now will it be desertion?"

"What did you tell him?"

"I said it would be. He left me and was not seen in the company after that."

Second Lieutenant Thomas F. Griffin, the Commanding Officer of the Military Government detachment at Rocherath, Belgium, testified about Slovik's next appearance.

"It was on the 9th of October at around eleven o'clock in town, where our headquarters were set up . . . . Private Schmidt, who was cook that day, told me that this Private Slovik had come in earlier that morning and said that he told him he thought we were MPs and wanted to surrender to us. I called the S-1 of the 109th Infantry and told him that we had one of his men who was AWOL and would they send someone to get him."

First Lieutenant Wayne L. Hurd of the 109th Infantry told what happened next.

"At that time I was appointed temporary MP officer . . . I was standing in front of the orderly room at Rocherath, Belgium, when Staff Sergeant Bromberg brought Slovik in . . . Slovik handed me a green slip of paper."

The Lieutenant read the paper—which was Slovik's

confession—and quickly passed it to his Commanding Officer, Colonel Henbest, who "called me down and in Slovik's presence, Slovik signed the slip and then Colonel Henbest signed and also me."

"This happened on or about 11 October 1944?"

"Yes, sir."

"At Rocherath, Belgium?"

"Yes, sir. Everything that appeared on the green slip of paper was made very clear to the defendant."

In the words of one military lawyer commenting on the case well after the fact: "That last volunteered answer was to be the final nail in the coffin. Everything was made clear to Slovik—except that he was being set up as an example."

Slovik's confession, hand-printed in ink, was admitted into evidence without objection.

> I, Pvt. Eddie D. Slovik #36896415 confess to the Desertion of the United States Army. At the time of my Desertion we were in Albuff in France. I came to Albuff as a Replacement. They were shelling the town and we were told to dig in for the night. The following morning they were shelling us again. I was so scared nerves and trembling that at the time the other Replacements moved out I couldn't move. I stayed their in my foxhole till it was quite and I was able to move. I then walked in town. Not seeing any of our troops so I stayed over night at a French hospital. The next morning I turned myself over to the Canadian Provost Corps. After being with them six weeks I was turned over to American M.P. They turned me lose. I told my commanding officer my story. I said that if I had to go out their again I'd run away. He said their was nothing he could do for me so I ran away again AND I'LL RUN AWAY AGAIN IF I HAVE TO GO OUT THEIR.
>
> Signed Pvt. Eddie D. Slovik
> A.S.N. 36896415

The introduction of the confession ended the prosecution's case. Captain Edward Woods, Slovik's defense counsel, stood up.

"The accused understands his rights as a witness and elects to remain silent, but defense requests that the law member advise the accused as to his rights as a witness."

The Law Officer then carefully explained to Slovik his rights as a defendant and suggested he take some time to talk to his counsel about them. After a brief conference, Slovik announced: "I will remain silent."

It was clear from the interchange that the strategy of the trial had not been devised by the defense counsel. The strategy had apparently been based on a simple fact. *At no time since America had entered World War II had anyone been executed for desertion.* And there had been plenty of desertions. It was also clear that Slovik knew this. In the prison stockade, where he lived while awaiting trial, he was surrounded by deserters. He had also seen many of them return from a court-martial bragging that they had been sentenced to twenty years at hard labor. It was common knowledge throughout the stockade that the sentence meant that they were safe for the duration of the War and would certainly be released shortly thereafter.

On these grounds Private Slovik had devised his strategy, and his defense counsel had nothing more to say than, "the defense rests."

In his closing statement the prosecution outlined the unchallenged testimony surrounding Slovik's desertion, particularly emphasizing Slovik's written assertion that if sent back to service he would run away again. The defense had no closing statement. The Court wasted no time in finding Slovik guilty and the record then reads:

"The Court was closed, and upon secret written ballot, all the members present at the time the vote was taken concurring, sentences the accused:

"To be dishonorably discharged from the service, to forfeit all pay and allowances due or to become due, and to be shot to death with musketry."

The drama of the Slovik court-martial is the story of what happened next. The trial record was forwarded for review by superior officers, ending on the desk of General Dwight Eisenhower. What was it that changed it from a routine case of desertion, in which the sentence would be reduced, to a case which ended in the only recorded execution of a deserter in this century?

For practical purposes, the change began when the FBI forwarded Slovik's civilian prison record to Colonel Henry J. Sommer, the Judge Advocate of the 28th Division, and the first person to review the case.

Slovik's civilian record was not known to the court at the time of the trial. The Army, then as now, did not take into account a man's civilian record in a military case. But in the process of review the record was allowed to be consulted to aid in determining whether the sentence should be modified, or clemency awarded. Slovik's civilian record began to tell against him.

He had served two terms in reform school at Ionia, Michigan, and had been in numerous difficulties with the law as an adolescent. His first term resulted from a charge of embezzlement; as a counterman in a drugstore in Detroit, he had been caught pocketing change. He was also charged with stealing candy and cigarettes from the store. The total amount: $59.60. The sentence: six months to ten years. Released on parole, he had gone out one drunken night with friends, stolen a car, and wrecked it. The next day he turned himself in and began his second prison sentence.

Colonel Sommer looked at the record, and decided if there was going to be one test case to stop desertions, Slovik, a man with a known criminal record, should be it. He recommended to General Norman D. Cota, the divisional commander, that the death sentence be approved.

HEADQUARTERS
28th Infantry Division
27 November 1944

In the foregoing case of Private Eddie D. Slovik, 36896415, Company G, 109th Infantry . . . the sentence . . . that the accused be shot to death with musketry is approved and the Record of Trial forwarded for action under Article of War 48.

Signed:
Norman D. Cota

When news of this recommendation reached Slovik, the Private began to realize for the first time that something was going terribly wrong. Most of the deserters of his acquaintance had had their sentences modified immediately. Worrying more and more about it, Slovik decided to write a personal letter to General Eisenhower, who was known throughout the Army for his fairness and generosity with troops. On December 9th, he wrote:

I, Private Eddie D. Slovik, ASN 36896415, was convicted on the 11th day of November year 1944 Armistice Day by General Court Martial to be shot to death for desertion of the United States Army.

The time of my conviction or before my conviction I had no intentions of deserting the army whatsoever. For if I intended too I wouldnt have given or surrendered myself as I did. I have nothing against the United States army whatsoever, I merely wanted a transfer from the line. I asked my CO when I came back if their was a possible chance of my being transferred cause I feared hazardars duty to myself, and because of my nerves. I'll admit I have some awfull bad nerves, which no doubt in my mind we all have. I was refused this transfer.

I must tell you more about my past. I assume you have my records of my past criminal life in my younger stage of life. After being released from jail I was put on a two year parole after spending five years in jail. In them two years I was on parole I got myself a good job cause I was in class 4-F, the army didn't want anything to do with me at the time. So after five months out of jail I decided to get married which I did. I have a swell wife now and a good home. After being married almost a year and a half I learned to stay away from bad company which was the cause of my being in jail. Then the draft came. I didn't have to come to the army when they called me. I could of went back to jail. But I was sick of being locked up all my life so I came to the army. When I went down to the draft board, I was told that the only reason they were taking a chance on me in the army was cause I got married and had a good record after being out of jail almost two years. To my knowledge sir I have a good record in the past two years. I also have a good record as a soldier up to the time I got in this trouble. I tried my best to do what the army wanted me to do till I first ran away or should I say I left the company.

I don't believe I ran away the first time as I stated in my first confession. I came over to France as a replacement, and when the enemy started to shelling us I got scared and nerves that I couldn't move out of my fox hole. I guess I never did give myself the chance to get over my first fear of shelling. The next day their wasn't any American troops around so I turned myself over to the Canadian MPs. They in turn were trying to get in touch with my outfit about me. I guess it must have taken them six weeks to catch up with the American troops. Well sir when I was turned over to my outfit I tried to explain to my CO just what took place, and what had happened to me. Then I asked for a transfer. Which was refused. Then I wrote my confession. I was then told that if I would go back to the line they would distroy my confession, however if I refused to go back on the line they would half to hold it against me which they did.

How can I tell you how humbley sorry I am for the sins Ive committed. I didn't realize at the time what I was doing, or what the word desertion meant. What it is like to be condemned to die. I beg of you deeply and sincerely for the sake of my dear wife and mother back home to have mercy on me. To my knowledge I have a good record since my marriage and as a soldier. I'd like to continue to be a good soldier.

Anxiously awaiting your reply, which I earnestly pray is favorable. God bless you and in your Work for victory:

I remain Yours for Victory
Pvt Eddie D. Slovik

Given a general of Eisenhower's known compassion, this letter might have been effective. But the fact is, the General never read it. Private Slovik's luck was just bad. At the time his letter was reaching the Supreme Commander's headquarters, German troops were stealing through the snowy forest toward Bastogne to begin the Battle of the Bulge. In the turmoil of the battle, the letter never reached the General. But it did receive full attention from his staff Judge Advocate, Brigadier General Edward C. Betts, whose duty it was to advise General Eisenhower on what action to take. Betts assigned the review of the case to Major Frederick J. Bertolet.

Major Bertolet's review, which was forwarded to General Eisenhower, once again referred to Slovik's civilian prison record, a shadow growing ever larger over the accused's hope for survival. Among other points, it emphasized:

"The power to exercise clemency is a trust; it is not to be granted as a matter of course in any class of cases, but its exercise should depend upon the facts and considerations of military discipline. The record of the accused in civil life indicates that between 1932 and 1938 he was convicted five times by the Juvenile Court of Detroit for four offenses of breaking and entering and for one instance of assault and battery. In each case he was placed on parole. In 1937 he was sentenced to six months to ten years for embezzlement, and in 1939 he was again confined for unlawfully driving away an automobile. The report of the FBI attached to the record does not indicate how much time the accused actually served either in the reformatory or in the state prison, but in his own letter requesting clemency accused states that he was in jail five years. These prior offenses are not of sufficient gravity to influence my recommendation in the instant case. However, they indicate a persistent refusal to conform to the rules of society in civilian life, an imperviousness to penal correction and a total lack of appreciation of clemency; these qualities the accused brought with him into his military life. He was obstinately determined not to engage in combat, and on two occasions, the second after express warning as to results, he deserted. He boldly confessed to these offenses and concluded his confession with the statement, 'so I ran away again AND I'LL RUN AWAY AGAIN IF I HAVE TO GO OUT THEIR.' There can be no doubt that he deliberately sought the safety and comparative comfort of the guardhouse. To him, and to those soldiers who may follow his example, if he achieves his end, confinement is neither deterrent not punishment. . . . If the death penalty is ever to be imposed for desertion it should be imposed in this case, not as a punitive measure nor as retribution, but to maintain that discipline upon which alone an army can succeed against the enemy."

On December 23, 1944, this order was issued from Supreme Headquarters:

HEADQUARTERS
European Theater of Operations
United States Army
23 December 1944

In the foregoing case of:

Private Eddie D. Slovik, 36896415
Company G, 109th Infantry

the sentence, as approved, is confirmed. Pursuant to Article of War 50 1/2, the order directing the execution of the sentence is withheld.

Signed:
Dwight D. Eisenhower

Article of War 50 1/2 stated that in a sentence of this severity, the record of the trial must be examined and found "legally sufficient" to support the sentence by the Office of the Judge Advocate General.

The head of the branch office of the Judge Advocate General in Paris was Brigadier General E. C. McNeil. His staff reviewed the case and found that "accused was accorded fully due process of law as provided by the Articles of War." Then General McNeil added his personal comment in an endorsement:

"This is the first death sentence for desertion which has reached me for examination. It is probably the first of the kind in the American Army for over eighty years—there were none in World War I. In this case the extreme penalty of death appears warranted. This soldier had performed no front line duty. He did not intend to. He deserted from his group of fifteen when about to join the infantry company to which he had been assigned. His subsequent conduct shows a deliberate plan to secure trial and incarceration in a safe place. The sentence adjudged was more severe than he had anticipated, but the imposition of a less severe sentence would only have accomplished the accused's purpose of securing his incarceration and consequent freedom from the dangers which so many of our armed forces are required to face daily. His unfavorable civilian record indicates that he is not a worthy subject of clemency."

Private Eddie Slovik's luck had finally run out. On a snow-swept range in the Vosges Mountains in January, 1945, he faced twelve soldiers raising rifles to their shoulders. Then the guns flamed.

Epilogue

Private Slovik did not die for legal immortality, but he may have achieved it, anyway. He was the last person to be executed for a military crime in this country's history, and given the current trend against the death penalty, he may just remain the last.

This does not mean that the death sentence has been abolished in the armed forces. Over the past decades, it has been carried out for such nonmilitary offenses as murder, but even this is rare.

The death sentence is also permitted under the Code's Article 85, pertaining to desertion. "Any person found guilty of desertion or attempted desertion shall be punished, if the offense is committed in time of war, by death or such other punishment as a court-martial may direct." But here the death penalty is only allowed during time of war, and even so is not mandatory. (In effect, therefore, this provision has not applied since the end of World War II.)

No war has been officially declared in Vietnam, but another kind of war has been declared within the military. Hundreds of servicemen have been emulating Private Slovik and deserting. Some have gone to Sweden, others to Canada, Cuba, or other neutral countries. In Private Slovik's war, the practice was to keep recaptured deserters under lock and key (with the exception of Slovik himself) until sometime after the fighting was all over and then release them. What the policy will be upon the close of the conflict in Indochina remains to be seen.

7
Bad Night at Ribbon Creek

Prologue

The United States Marine Corps was founded, according to Corps history, on November 10, 1775. From its beginning it was an elite force.

Over the years its original mission ("landing force and boarding party") has expanded, as has its field of activity. Marine Corps members have fought, as its song says, in Mexico—at the halls of the Montezumas—and at Tripoli, and its members distinguished themselves in France during World War I. The Marines met their greatest challenge, however, in World War II, when they swarmed ashore on island after tropical island in the Pacific, often with frightful losses, always with success.

The unique spirit of the Marine Corps was typified by Marine General Holland "Howlin' Mad" Smith at the Battle of Saipan in 1944, when he relieved from command an Army general whose forces were lagging behind the Marines. When the general protested that his men were being held up by small-arms fire, "Howlin' Mad" Smith retorted, "The *Marines* are never held up by small-arms fire."

During World War II it was considered a special honor to be a Marine. It meant you were tough, that you fought where others drew back, that your entire unit had an *esprit de corps* that would carry the day no matter what the odds. And with these sentiments arose a tradition of training. Marine recruits were subjected to pre-planned brutality to prepare them for the brutality of combat. These Marines were all volunteers and knew what was coming. They suffered through it—and perhaps became better Marines because of it.

World War II ended, the Cold War began, the Korean action started up and sputtered to its half-hearted close, America became involved in Indochina. But it was not like World War II. Many Marine recruits were not looking forward to a life in combat—the wars were smaller, farther away, remote from the realities of life in America—and their motivation began to change. But Marine training did not. Still the shaven-headed Drill Instructors ruled their swampy camps dispensing the same rude form of discipline that had helped to shape them.

Then came the night of April 8, 1956, and another event was added to the legend of the Marine Corps.

Staff Sergeant Matthew C. McKeon, 66581, U. S. Marine Corps, was an unhappy man. A pulled leg muscle caused him constant pain. And Platoon 71, his first platoon as a newly assigned Drill Instructor at Parris Island, South Carolina, pained him even more. It was all in front of him as he emerged from his barracks on Sunday morning, April 8, 1956. Men were lying all over the grass, sleeping, smoking, telling jokes, or just horsing around. They didn't *look* like Marines. They didn't *act* like Marines. But they were all in the Marine Corps and worst of all, they were his platoon.

"Everybody up! Field Day!" he commanded, and the new recruits, mostly eighteen or nineteen years old, scrambled to their feet and made for the barracks to begin scrubbing and cleaning. An angry Matthew McKeon went back to his own barracks to brood over his next move.

By nightfall he had made up his mind. He took an old broomstick and, using it as a crutch, hobbled to the barracks where his unruly platoon lived. Making his way inside, he looked around and coldly snapped, "fall out in two minutes."

Out they piled, pulling on fatigues, and lined up in the dark, sure of one thing—they were going on a dreaded night march. McKeon had already told one of them that he was going to take them into the swamps that night. What he had not told anyone was that he was going straight through the swamps and into Ribbon Creek itself. Ribbon Creek is a treacherous tidal stream. At high tide it has a depth of 12 feet and a width of 200 feet. As McKeon led his men toward the churning, murky stream the tide was high.

"Are there any of you men who can't swim?" he asked. "Yes," came the reply from several recruits. McKeon's response was not intended to encourage. "All recruits who can't swim will drown, and those who can swim will be eaten by sharks."

Across a wide border of black mud, carpeted with swamp grass, McKeon led his men. Above him the moon appeared briefly from behind dark rolling clouds, revealing the edge of the mudbank. McKeon, with his men following, stepped straight into the stream, up to his knees in water. Two steps more and he was up to his waist. He turned upstream, hugging the shoreline, and his line of men turned with him.

But there was a problem. The bottom of the stream was thick, viscous mud. Men sank into it, had trouble pulling their feet out, and the swift current of the stream caused them to lose balance. From ahead McKeon yelled over his shoulder, "Everybody OK?" "No," came the answer. McKeon turned, saw one of the recruits in trouble, and told his mates to help him out. They pulled him free of the muck.

McKeon now turned left into chest-high water some fifteen feet out. Then he turned left again to come back downstream parallel to the column. But by then, in the swirling current, there was no column.

McKeon ordered his men out, telling them to give each other a hand. By this time men were going under, grabbing each other for support, pulling their frightened colleagues under with them. Everyone seemed to be adrift, arms flailing, feet struggling to touch bottom. Strong swimmers tried to help the weak, but even these efforts had tragic results. Tom Hardeman, the platoon's best swimmer, died in his rescue attempts. He was not the only one.

By the time the survivors had crawled out of the stream, six men had died. Rescuers arrived at the scene, but too late. Sergeant McKeon hobbled back to the base and immediate arrest. By morning his name was known far beyond the shores of Ribbon Creek.

As details of the tragedy became known there were reports of Sergeant McKeon slapping his recruits and swigging vodka before taking them out into the swamps. The immediate reaction of the public was rage and disgust. That of the Marine Corps resembled panic. It was widely assumed that a court-martial was inevitable and that it would be less McKeon who was on trial than the Marine Corps itself. And to forestall this, the Commandant of the Corps, General Randolph Pate, appeared before a Congressional committee and quickly disavowed McKeon.

"It is our first military and moral obligation to see that Sergeant McKeon is punished to the full extent allowed by our Uniform Code of Military Justice," he said.

When a Board of Inquiry was convened to examine the incident, it not surprisingly followed the lead given by the Commandant and recommended the Sergeant be tried.

To the Sergeant's defense came a surprising figure: Emile Zola Berman, a brilliant trial attorney. Hawk-nosed, tiny, and bone-frail, Berman was hardly in the Marine image. But he had at least one Marine attribute. He liked stepping into trouble.

And the challenge seemed almost insuperable. If the top officer of the Marine Corps had already indicated in public that the sergeant was wrong, was it likely that a court-martial board of subordinate officers would rule otherwise?

Parris Island in August is hot and uncomfortable. In the

bare, one-story white schoolhouse where the trial convened, only Sergeant McKeon looked cool. His gaunt face betrayed no emotion as his seven attorneys conferred in whispers. The court's Law Officer, Navy Captain Irving Klein, surveyed the scene through gold-rimmed spectacles, nodded, and softly said, "Proceed."

The chief prosecuting officer was Marine Major Charles Sevier, who described himself as "a plain, unspectacular guy trying to do a job." He rose to enumerate the charges against McKeon. They ranged from the relatively minor to the extremely grave. The minor ones charged him with possession of alcoholic beverages in barracks and with drinking in the presence of a recruit. More seriously, he was charged with "oppression" for leading his platoon into water over their heads, with culpable negligence in the deaths of the six men, and with manslaughter.

Sevier's job was more than simply arguing for the conviction of McKeon. It was also to defend the Marine Corps' training techniques, and to do so the Major was forced to prove that McKeon's actions, far from being in accord with official training procedures, actually represented a tragic lapse in such procedures, complicated by McKeon's drinking. To newsmen Sevier said, "I have the greatest sympathy for D. I.'s. They have a terribly tough job. But damn it, we have to try to maintain excellent discipline without brutality."

To establish his case, Sevier began by entering the Marine training regulations into the record. They showed that night marches of any kind were not a part of the training program. Indeed, as recently as 1951 they had been specifically prohibited by a general order posted in the camp. After a witness had testified as to the tide tables of Ribbon Creek, Sevier asked to take the whole court to the site of the tragedy. Beneath the bright hot August sun, the officers of the court were led down the same path the young recruits had taken to stare out over the swift-flowing creek, and decide whether they thought a reasonable man would have led an incompletely trained platoon into this dangerous stream in the dark of night.

Back in the steaming court, Sevier placed on the stand survivors of Platoon 71. One after another they told of their skirmish with death in the turbulent waters. Many of them thought that the Sergeant had been drunk. Private David M. McPherson testified that before calling the march the Sergeant had called him to his room, had slapped him, and had been drinking from a vodka bottle.

The outlook certainly looked bleak for Sergeant McKeon. It appeared that the entire Marine Corps, from the Commandant on down, had lined up to prove his activity in violation of Marine Corps rules and traditions and to show him as a drunkard and a bully as well. But Emile Zola Berman had not yet been heard from.

Berman had been hired by ex-Marines who felt that, despite the statements of General Pate, McKeon had indeed acted in the best Marine tradition. And they believed that most former Marines agreed. So Berman called a press conference. Surrounded by reporters and in the view of the television cameras, Berman boldly invited all Marines and former Marines to express their views on the McKeon case. Within minutes the switchboard at the camp was alight. Calls and telegrams poured in by the hundreds. Their overwhelming verdict: Marine Corps training *must* be tough. In some cases it wasn't tough enough. By and large the Marines were proud of their status as an elite corps and were equally proud of the training techniques that made them that way.

Armed with these reactions, Berman made his second bold move. He went directly to General Randolph Pate and asked him to testify in McKeon's behalf. Never in American military history had a commanding general, in charge of seeing that a case was brought to trial, reversed himself and testified as a defense witness. Pate agreed to do so. Berman then went to another general, known as the toughest general in the Marines, and the only man ever to win five Navy Crosses— an award given only for extraordinary heroism in action against an armed enemy—Lieutenant General Lewis B. "Chesty" Puller. He, too, agreed to testify. Then Berman began his case.

"We shall prove," he said in his rasping voice, "that it is

the mission of this command to produce Marines." The fatal
night march was, he maintained, "part and parcel" of the
training methods that had won for the Marine Corps its
reputation. "Sergeant McKeon," he continued, "was a
dedicated member of the Corps. He wasn't acting out of
sadistic pleasure but was trying to accomplish its purpose—
to make Marines. These methods require no apology, either
by the Marines or Sergeant McKeon."

Berman called to the stand McKeon's noncommissioned
superior, Staff Sergeant Edward A. Huff, a Senior Drill Instructor. Huff testified that night marches were not at all
uncommon, no matter what the Corps might have to say
about them. In fact, he had threatened to take McKeon's
platoon on a night march himself, but had never gotten
around to it. As to McKeon, Huff said he was "an
outstanding D.I. He done his work, he done it well, and he
never seemed to complain. By my figuring he worked 132
hours a week. A good man."

Berman's next witness was Matthew McKeon himself. A
tall, bony man, he marched to the witness chair to be
questioned on his story of what had happened that fateful
night, and the day leading up to it.

Patiently, Berman led the soft-spoken Sergeant through
the story of that day. After his morning confrontation with
the platoon, McKeon testified, he had dozed in the drill
instructor's room until awakened by Staff Sergeant Elwyn B.
Scarborough.

"Sergeant Scarborough asked me if I had anything to
drink and I told him I never kept it around. He said take me
up the road a way and I can get some."

"Did he say whether he wanted a drink?"

"He said he was feeling pretty rough."

"Did you leave the D.I. room with Sergeant Scarborough
and go somewhere?"

"Yes. We went out and got in my car and went up to the
Administration Building . . . Scarborough said stop here . . .
and he got out. I went up a little further and turned around.
Then he got back in my car and he was carrying something
in a bag. It was a bottle."

"Did you return immediately to the D.I. Room in Building 761?"

"Yes, sir."

"Who carried the bag and the bottle?"

"Sergeant Scarborough."

"Did you immediately have a drink?"

"Sergeant Muckler came in before we had a drink."

"Did you order a Field Day?"

"I did."

"Did you speak to Private Langone?"

"Yes, I called him in the room and told him I wanted him to see they turned to for the Field Day."

"Was that bottle in evidence at all when Private Langone was there?"

"No. It was in the possession of Sergeant Scarborough."

"Did there come a time when there was just you and Sergeant Scarborough, with the door closed?"

"Yes, sir."

"Did he have a drink and did he offer you a drink?"

"Yes, sir. I told him I could not take it straight and I went topside to get a Coke."

"Did you know it was a vodka bottle?"

"It looked like gin to me. I knew it was an alcoholic beverage."

"You chased it with a bottle of Coke?"

"Yes, sir."

"Did anyone else come in?"

"Yes, sir. Sergeant Richard J. King. He was squaring away his personal gear."

"During the time he was there, did each of you have another drink?"

"Yes, sir."

"Tell us, is that all of the drink you had out of that vodka bottle in the D.I. room that entire day?"

"Yes, sir."

"Are you customarily a drinker of hard liquor?"

"No, sir. I like a beer."

McKeon then testified that he had gone to the NCO club with his friends, and there had a beer. After lunch, he came back and dozed until time for evening chow. Berman picked up a bottle of vodka three quarters full and showed it to McKeon.

"Could you tell us whether or not this looks like the amount of fluid which was in the bottle (after you had finished drinking) ?"

"Yes, sir."

"Did something occur during chow time which was not in accordance with Sergeant Huff's orders?"

"Yes, sir. I was sitting talking with the other D.I.s and drinking coffee and Private Langone came by and I asked him where he was going and he said he was going for seconds, and I asked him what he had done today to deserve seconds and he gave me some sarcastic remark.

"I stood up to him and said I wanted to see him in my room when we got back to the barracks. Others in the platoon went back for seconds. Sergeant Huff had said they were not to eat seconds.

"I ordered a Field Day because they had ignored the order and had seconds. I felt that by giving Field Days for disciplinary purposes the next time they were told to do something they would do it. That was my way of teaching discipline. I called Private Langone into my room and I told him he had better start swinging and he said he did not want to hit me.

"I said, 'Do you ever hit your Father or Mother?' He said, 'No, sir.' I said, 'Why not?' He said he respected them and I said do you not respect your superiors? He said he did and I said was that respect in the mess hall this evening and I slapped him."

McKeon said he then lectured Private Langone on the need for discipline.

"I asked him to send privates Maloof and Wood in. They were two big men physically. Private Wood came in first. Maloof came in in a sloppy way and I asked him was that the position of attention and he said it was not, and he straightened himself up and I slapped him. It was not my intention to hurt him. It was my way of showing that I did not approve of the things they had done."

McKeon testified that he then called Private MacPherson.

"I spoke to MacPherson regarding the discipline of the platoon and he had the attitude that he was just a recruit himself and he would take care of himself and I slapped him; I told him that Marines as a unit work together, are not individuals, and I told him to sit down and I sat on the rack next to him and I noticed the bottle.

"The bottle was on the other side of the room on the deck by the edge of the table. I got up, walked over, and picked up the bottle. I asked him if he had ever drank vodka and I asked him if he wanted a drink.

"I said that when he could prove himself a man he could have a drink and I put the bottle to my lips. The top was on and no liquid was drunk. This was my way of saying that he had not arrived at a man's estate."

"Was the cap on or off the bottle?"

"The cap was on it and I did not take a single drop. That is the truth.

"I talked with him a little more and he told me that the trouble with the platoon was that it was too easy and I told him that it couldn't be much harder. We've tried everything on you people to teach you discipline, I said, and tonight we are going to try something different. I am going to take you people to the swamps."

"Did you ever hear of any sharks in Parris Island? Did you intend to feed them to the sharks?"

"No, sir. It was just talk. If there were any sharks down there I would not have gone first."

In the stillness of the court McKeon then described the march to the river.

"We went down to the edge of the bank of the river to the right of the shrubbery and about twenty to twenty-five feet away from the drainage ditch. I turned around when we hit water and told them to follow me and make sure everyone got into the water."

McKeon stood next to a map, pointing out the route.

"This area was flooded and we went off the brink. I stepped in mud and then in water and took two or three steps out of the center of the creek. The water was around my knees and mud over my ankles. We took a right, went parallel to the bank about five or six feet from the bank. We went up for approximately thirty feet upstream.

"I broke left, I do not know how many steps I took out; it was more or less like a curve. I started back downstream. Some of the column were still going upstream. There was ten to fifteen feet separating the two lines. The water gradually got higher as we went downstream. When we turned it was about waist high. The highest it got was about my chest.

"I asked if everything was all right, and word came back that it was. There was a little fooling going on behind me and I told them to knock off the fooling. I asked where the nonswimmers were and word came back and I spotted them. I did not want those people wandering out and getting into any trouble.

"I found they were in ranks with people around them. There was not one behind the other. A few of the men wanted to swim across and I told them this was not a swimming lesson; there would be no one going across. There was a light on the water. There was a moon with big black rolling clouds. I told them that if they were caught in combat to keep out of the light, close to the shore-line into the shadows. I asked again where the nonswimmers were and apparently they were all right. I asked where was Leake. He was my problem boy. He was trying all the time, but he did nothing right. Back of the platoon someone said there is Leake and I said bring him up here. Leake came across with two holding him.

"I held up the column and went back. I recall the water was up to their hips. I asked Leake if he was scared. I told him there was nothing to be scared about. But he was petrified and I told the two guys who had him to take him back and watch Leake.

"I was at the front of the column and had took approximately five or six steps when they started to yell and there was a big commotion. It was in the rear and off to my right about thirty feet. I turned around when the yelling started and I saw a group splashing in the water. They seemed to be reaching for something.

"The next thing I gave the command for everybody to get

out of the water and I started out to this area. As it was the quickest way, I swam. It was tough walking. There was a kid looked like he was going the wrong way. He had his back towards me. I pulled him in to ten feet from the beach. He said he was all right.

"The group was almost parallel to me by this time. I started out and saw this boy coming in. I thought he was making it all right and I ignored him as there was a kid who seemed to be floating. I could just see the top of his head. There were about three or four splashing around me. I headed towards this kid and then another man latched on to me. He got a hold of my neck and I tried to break his hold but every time we went down. I told him to keep his head—he was a colored boy. I thought it was Private Wood. He would not leave go, not saying anything. We went down a second time and we seemed to go down further than the first. I tell you, sir, all I was thinking about was getting to the top. The kid let go and that's the last I seen of him."

At this point, for the first time on the stand, McKeon lost his composure. He bowed his head and motioned that he couldn't go on. After a recess, he resumed:

"The second time I came up I did not see anything. I swam around a while and I knew then that I had lost some men. I remember saying 'Oh God, what have I done?'

"I swam in towards the shore and was met by two men. They wanted to go back and start diving for them and I told them it was no use. I knew while I was out there struggling with that boy that there was a current and there was no light and I figured if I did send a detail out there I might lose another one."

"What was your purpose in taking the men on that exercise that night?"

"We had tried other variations of teaching these people discipline but nothing seemed to work and I figured I would take them down to the swamps and show them that way. If they got a little wet and muddy it might put a little more spirit into the platoon and build up their morale and make them different. The main thing was to take them down and the next time they would do as they were told."

The following day on the stand, McKeon faced Major Sevier in cross-examination.

"You testified yesterday on many occasions you would give a man a slap to bring him to the position of attention?"

"Not on many occasions, quite a few times. But I do not remember how many times."

"That was your way of maintaining discipline?"

"No, sir. It was one of the ways. I got other ways."

"Did you set an example of discipline that day when you carried a vodka bottle in there and drank in front of a recruit?"

"I grant you that was a bad gesture."

"You called Private Gerald Langone into your room?"

"Yes, sir"

"Did you call him a Guinea?"

"I may have done so. I am not denying it. I do not recall it."

"Is that the way you enforce discipline?"

"I have heard a lot worse names than that."

"Is that the same man you called in and slapped?"

"Yes, sir."

"Is that the way you teach discipline, by slapping people?"

"I respected my superiors ever since I was able to know the difference between right and wrong and I was slapped many times."

"By your parents?"

"Yes, and by the nuns in school. It was a slap to show I disapproved of what they were doing. It was a proof that we were trying to learn them something and that we are their superiors."

After a few more questions, Sevier excused the witness and there was a short intermission. Outside, during the break, the next witness, General Randolph Pate, spotted McKeon, walked up to him, and shook his hand. Tieless and affable, the man who in April had angrily called McKeon's action "deplorable" now warmly said, "Hello, Sergeant."

The Sergeant stood speechless. The General continued,

"I'm sorry to meet you under these circumstances. I'm here to help you all I can. How are you getting along?"

The Sergeant still said nothing.

"We are after justice, you know, and we know you are, too. My regards to your wife. Is she here now?"

McKeon, rigid, shook his head.

"I'd like to meet her before I go if I get a chance. Good luck to you, boy."

The General, tall with high forehead and reddish hair, then broke off this strange scene and strode into the court.

On the stand he faced the frail little attorney and smiled. The questions began.

"Would you tell us what you profess to be the mission of the Marine Corps?"

"Congress has said that we are the nation's force in readiness and our mission is to be ready at all times for combat. All of the training of Marines is preparation for war and for no other cause at all."

"What would you say was the one most important factor of training?"

"All factors are important, discipline more than anything else, his response to order, his willingness to be a member of a team and sacrifice when necessary."

Berman then changed his approach. "In your official capacity as the Commandant of the United States Marine Corps, had you been permitted to deal with Sergeant McKeon what would have been the action you would have taken?"

The question was a corker. How can a commanding general give an official opinion without it seeming to be an order? Major Sevier saw the pitfall and leaped to his feet to object.

"That question," he said, "goes to the heart of the issue of this case—the issue which the court has been called to decide."

Captain Klein ruled that the objection was sustained. The General was amazed. "But I don't object," he said. "I don't know the law but—"

"Sir, it is I that has an objection," said Major Sevier.

The expression on General Pate's face made many of the courtroom viewers smile. One Marine sitting in the back nudged his neighbor and whispered: "Old Pate may be taking Sevier on a night march!"

Berman tried twice again to get an answer, this time in the guise of an expert witness. Major Sevier objected both times and was upheld on the grounds that the alleged expert witness hadn't heard the evidence. Growing annoyed, Berman tried a fourth time with a lengthy hypothetical question starting out:

"I want you to assume what is the evidence in this case—"

The question droned on for five minutes while General Pate fidgeted. Finally the question ended with: " . . . what action in your opinion, stated with a reasonable degree of accuracy, would you have taken?"

Again Major Sevier objected that this was an invasion of the court. For the first time, Captain Klein disagreed.

"You are assuming that the question will in fact invade the province of the court. This is an opinion that the witness gives based upon his expert knowledge that the court can accept or disregard. The opposing side is in a position also to ask a hypothetical question of the same witness, assuming a state of facts existing in evidence, assuming it to be true, and upon these facts will elicit from the expert his opinion. The court can, and I am certain will, make its findings upon all the evidence and not necessarily upon the opinion of one expert."

Berman had won. The General at last stated his reply.

"It is evident that this D.I. had drunk some vodka and I assume it was against regulations. I think I would take a stripe away from him, for a thing like that is a fairly serious thing when dealing with recruits.

"As to the remaining part of it I suspect I would have transferred him away for stupidity or for lack of judgment. I would probably have written in his record book though, that on no condition was this sergeant to drill recruits again."

Berman had his answer. The General was recommending light punishment indeed, for a trial in which manslaughter was one of the charges. But Captain Klein leaned over his desk and asked some questions which abruptly took the edge off the General's testimony. These questions put into the record that it was General Pate who had reviewed the findings of the Court of Inquiry in the McKeon case and that it was he who had recommended that the court-martial be held.

It was Berman's turn to object, and Captain Klein explained quietly, "I wanted to know whether at a prior time the same expert gave another recommendation to the one he has given as an opinion today."

Following General Pate came General Puller. Tough-faced, barrel-chested, wearing full uniform and eight rows of ribbons, he strode like a bantam cock into the auditorium of the little schoolhouse, settled himself comfortably in the witness chair, crossed his legs, and glowered about the courtroom. Before anyone could ask a question, the General said, in a voice loud enough to scrape the paint off the walls, "If I don't talk loud enough, somebody say something back there."

Not a voice was heard.

Under questioning, Puller expressed his views. "The most important thing in training is discipline. It was not oppression of the recruits to order them out." The march, he maintained, was good military practice.

"The main thing that I have learned here as a recruit that I have remembered all my life is that I was taught the definition of esprit de corps—love for one's own military legion. In my case, the U.S. Marine Corps. It means more than self-preservation, religion, or patriotism."

Puller continued that the night march was a deplorable accident—but he added that he felt one reason American troops did so poorly in Korea was their lack of night training. "Americans are so used to electric lights they're practically night blind," he said. He emphasized that the Marines' only mission is success in battle, and added that if we are to win the next war the nation's youth must get a lot more of the kind of training that McKeon had tried to give Recruit Platoon 71 at Parris Island.

With the recommendations of the two top Marine generals ringing in their ears, with public opinion having changed totally from disgust at one sergeant's bungling to pride in the Marine Corp's tough tradition, the panel of officers retired to consider their verdict. After seven hours they returned. They found McKeon guilty of drinking in barracks and of simple negligence in the death of the six recruits. They found him not guilty of the more serious charges of oppression and manslaughter.

Berman and his associates were elated. Here, they felt, was the clear influence of generals Pate and Puller. Then they heard the sentence.

The rustle of voices dropped to a dead hush in the green-walled auditorium as the tall sergeant snapped to attention. Sweat glistened on the faces of many of the spectators, as they pressed forward to hear. In a soft voice Colonel Edward L. Hutchinson read: "It is my duty to inform you that the court sentences you to be discharged from the service with a bad-conduct discharge, to forfeit $30 a month for nine months, to be confined at hard labor for nine months, and to be reduced in grade to private."

With this stiff sentence it was apparent the court had made up its mind strictly on the facts, and despite the testimony of their own Commandant. They did not believe McKeon had led the famous night march to oppress—or to murder—his troops. But they apparently believed his conduct in training recruits was much farther out of line than did their generals.

Some months later the Secretary of the Navy, Charles S. Thomas, reviewed the case and softened much of the harsh sentence. He removed the bad-conduct discharge, which to a man like McKeon was the major penalty. But he allowed to stand the confinement at hard labor and the reduction to private.

Epilogue

To students of military justice, the case of Sergeant McKeon holds a special fascination. Over the years the most persistent criticism of military law has been the issue of command influence, and in this case that issue was turned inside out.

Critics have pointed out that in the military it is the commander who decides who will be court-martialed and on what charges. This same commander then proceeds to select judge, jurors, prosecutor, and very often defense counsel as well, all from his subordinates. These men are dependent upon the commander for promotions, recommendations, and assignments to duty. Under these circumstances it is a rare court that will act against the wishes of a determined commander.

And that is exactly what this court did! The Commandant of the Marine Corps, no less, had detailed in open court the punishment he felt was called for, and the court simply paid him no attention.

In fact, the fame that the case achieved shows how rare it is for a court to ignore command influence. The Presidio "mutiny" trials, critics say, are more typical. (In those trials, it took three investigations before the commander could find an investigating officer who would recommend the charges of mutiny that he desired.) And the issue is still alive. New revisions of the Uniform Code of Military Justice are before Congress, designed to limit the scope of command influence. There can be little doubt that the major flaws of the system arise from just such influence as was dramatically brought out in the reaction of the President of the United States to the trial, in 1970–71, of Lieutenant William Calley.

In Marine Corps history, the result of the case was a re-examination of training techniques. The Drill Instructor is still a fearsome figure to the Marine recruit. And because of the Indochinese war training is still rigorous, but it will never again be what it was that night on the banks of Ribbon Creek.

8
The Sergeant on the Balcony

Prologue

The American approach to military justice was originally copied from British models. In 1689, with the acceptance by William and Mary of the Bill of Rights, Parliament acquired the power to define the jurisdiction of courts-martial. It proceeded to grant court-martial jurisdiction over mutiny, sedition, and desertion only, further stating that ". . . no man may be forejudged of life or limb or subjected to any kind of punishment by martial law, or in any other manner than by the judgment of his peers and according to the known and established laws of this realm."

Colonial American practice, of course, followed this approach. But Alexander Hamilton, among others, had different ideas. He argued in the Federalist Papers that Congress' power to prescribe rules for the government of the armed forces "ought to exist without limitation, because it is impossible to foresee or define the extent and variety of national exigencies, or the corresponding extent and variety of the means which may be necessary to satisfy them."

American military commanders generally took the Hamiltonian view and beginning with George Washington extended court-martial jurisdiction to a variety of nonmilitary offenses. The general orders of Washington, for example, report the military trial of soldiers for "killing a Cow . . . stealing Fowls . . . and stealing eleven Geese." There were also such cases as that of Sergeant Harris at West Point for "beating a Mr. Williams, an inhabitant living near this garrison," in 1795 and of Private Kelly for "abusing and using violence on Mrs. Crunkhyte, a citizen of the United States," in 1796.

By the time of the Civil War, Congress had agreed to the extended scope of military jurisdiction providing military trials for servicemen accused of such civil offenses as larceny, robbery, burglary, and arson, but the act only applied "in time of war, insurrection, or rebellion." In 1916, on the eve of World War I, the Articles of War were revised to provide military trial, even in peacetime, for all noncapital crimes and offenses by persons "subject to military law." In 1950, the Uniform Code of Military Justice extended this jurisdiction to capital crimes as well.

All of this history was to be re-examined by the Supreme Court. It was to be re-examined because of a trial that at the time seemed nothing if not routine. Rape, after all, is no stranger to the annals of military law. And when a beery sergeant lurched into the hotel room of a teen-age girl in Honolulu, he little knew he was making legal history.

F rom a penthouse balcony of the Reef Hotel in Hawaii, Michaela Scholes gazed down at the serene Pacific before retiring to bed. A pretty, happy fourteen-year-old, she had come with her parents from the mainland for an eagerly anticipated vacation. Now, on this July night, she was taking a final look at the white surf breaking against the beach. Her parents had gone out for the evening and she was alone.

But not quite. On a neighboring balcony two soldiers watched the attractive teen-ager. She turned without seeing them and went back into her room; the soldiers went down to the bar where they mentioned their discovery to a friend, Sergeant James F. O'Callahan.

About an hour or so later a hotel security officer heard a scream, and saw a man rush out onto the Scholes' tenth-floor balcony, hastily donning his trousers. In a superb acrobatic demonstration which in other circumstances would have gained the security officer's admiration, the man swung off the tenth balcony, and descended from balcony to balcony to the ground. When he arrived the security officer was waiting for him and took him back to the Scholes' room where he was identified by the bruised and hysterical young girl as the man who had attempted to rape her.

Sergeant O'Callahan was then taken into custody by the military police, warned of his constitutional rights, and asked to make a confession. He did. Other witnesses were found, including his soldier companions of the evening. It was, the Army felt, a very simple case.

Sergeant O'Callahan was brought to trial at Fort Shafter in the Territory of Hawaii on October 11, 1956. He was charged with assault and battery with intent to commit rape, attempted rape, and housebreaking with intent to commit rape.

In his opening remarks, the Trial Counsel mentioned a point which was to keep the case alive long after most such cases have been settled. "Much of the evidence that will be brought to the attention of the court is by deposition, because some of the prosecution witnesses are no longer within this area."

Specialist Second Class Charles C. Redden then took the stand and testified that on the evening of the 21st of July, he and O'Callahan and another friend, Specialist Third Class William A. Floyd, had gone to Don the Beachcombers, and the Edgewater Hotel. They left O'Callahan at the Edgewater, and went on to the Reef Hotel.

"What did you and Floyd do at the Reef Hotel?"

"We went up to Penthouse Apartment M to check on some female acquaintances that we had known previously."

"What did you do when you got up to Apartment M?"

"We knocked on the door but no one answered. Apparently they weren't home."

"Did you stay up there in the penthouse area for any length of time?"

"We walked down to the terrace and looked down to the ocean a few moments."

"While you were stationed at Penthouse M did you notice any person up there on the balcony?"

"Yes. We saw a girl on the balcony."

"How close were you to this girl?"

"About ten or fifteen feet. It would be hard to say. She was looking out at the ocean like we were. We were in the hallway between Apartments M and N. She was in Apartment N."

"Did you have any conversation with her?"

"No, sir."

Redden and Floyd had then gone for a drink in the cocktail lounge, where they had seen O'Callahan. "He asked us where we had been. We told him we had checked on some previous acquaintances. We told him they weren't home, and somewhere along the line we said we had seen a girl, just in passing."

"During the course of the evening, was the subject of girls discussed between you?"

"Yes, I believe so."

"Did he express any intention or desires along that line?"

"Yes, sir. He made a statement to the effect that he intended to have a woman that night before he went back to the barracks."

"Did he say in what manner he would get her?"

"No, sir. But he did say that he was going to have a woman even if he had to beat one on the head, or something to that effect."

Redden testified that Floyd then left them, and he and O'Callahan had walked out into the lobby and talked for a while. What they were talking about was evident in the testimony: "We mutually agreed to try and pick up the two women who were sitting at the bar."

"And what happened after that?"

"While we were sitting there, Floyd came back and he and an Air Force Lieutenant, I believe, also agreed to pick up these women, and they succeeded."

"And what was O'Callahan's reaction to that?"

"Well, both of us were pretty mad."

"What happened after that?"

"O'Callahan and I walked out into the lobby, and he requested that I take him up to the apartment where I saw this girl. I agreed and took him upstairs on the penthouse elevator."

"After you got off the elevator, where did you go then?"

"We walked out on the terrace between Apartments M and N."

"And at that time did you see the girl?"

"Yes, I did . . . I saw her lying in bed with covers over her face. She was facing the wall so all I could see was her hair. I assumed it was the same girl."

"Where there there any comments made concerning the girl between you and Sergeant O'Callahan?"

"Yes, sir . . . O'Callahan wanted to go in the room, and I didn't go along with this, and I immediately tried to talk him out of it. He tried to convince me that we could go in and have intercourse with the girl and not get caught."

"How did he say this might happen?"

"Well, he said that one of us could hold her, while the other had intercourse with her, sir. I told him that if he went into the room that they could slap a rape charge on him."

O'Callahan, Redden said, decided he would take the chance, and Redden left him there and went back to his car. When O'Callahan did not reappear, he drove off.

On cross-examination, the defense counsel asked: "Did Sergeant O'Callahan's actions on the night in question appear to be usual as to his usual type of conduct?"

"No, sir, they didn't."

"In what way did they differ?"

"Well, he seemed to have lost his power of reasoning. To me he seemed that way. He wouldn't listen to anything. Just didn't seem right that night."

Michaela Scholes, the victim of the attempted rape, had

gone home with her parents to California. Other witnesses who had seen her immediately after the attempted rape had also gone back to the mainland. The Trial Counsel approached the Law Officer's bench: "At this time, prosecution would like to introduce in evidence a series of interrogatories. Prosecution Exhibit I for identification is an interrogatory or deposition of Miss Michaela Scholes. Her address is . . . a distance of more than one hundred miles from this post."

The Law Officer looked at the Defense Counsel and asked if he had an objection.

The Defense Counsel had. "Defense objects to the introduction of the deposition. There has been no showing that the witness is unavailable, nor does the defense believe that it is unreasonable in a case of this nature to have the witness presently in the courtroom in person since she was a victim in the alleged offense. The accused has a right to be confronted by witnesses against him, and the defense objects to the introduction of her testimony by way of deposition."

Trial Counsel added that he also planned to offer depositions from Hugh C. Scott, Robert L. Scott Jr., and Mrs. Barbara C. Cole, all witnesses for the prosecution.

The Defense Counsel said: "Defense believes that the proposed exhibits by the prosecution are objectionable in view of the serious nature of the offense. It is not unreasonable to require the government to produce if not all the witnesses . . . at least the victim in the proposed alleged offense. Although not in point, I cite Valli 21 CMR 186. Defense objects to the introduction of depositions, also, because no showing has been made that the witnesses are not reasonably available."

The Law Officer deferred his decision. "Before hearing argument from the government, I would like to inquire from the defense whether the Defense Counsel was afforded the opportunity to present cross-interrogatories."

"Counsel was afforded that opportunity and objected to the taking of the deposition at that time as well as at this time."

The Trial Counsel then pointed out that "the taking of

depositions are permissible in a case of this nature provided they are within certain conditions, and one of them is if they live more than a hundred miles from the place of trial. The depositions show on their face that the witnesses are residing in a place greater in distance than a hundred miles."

The Law Officer then ruled: "Article 49 (d) (1) provides that depositions are authorized where the witness resides or is beyond the State, Territory, or District in which the court . . . is ordered to sit, or beyond the distance of one hundred miles from the place of trial. I am aware of the Valli case on the matter, where each individual case has to be considered as to the reasonableness of the particular situation. In this particular case, it is the opinion of the Law Officer that the government has not acted unreasonably. . . . The objection is overruled."

With that ruling, the history of military justice turned a corner.

The Trial Counsel read Michaela's interrogatory into the record.

"Did anything unusual happen to you July 21?"

"I woke up and I was struggling with someone. I can't really remember if he said anything then."

"Did you feel someone lying upon you while you were in bed in room 1086 at the Reef Hotel?"

At this point in the reading of the interrogatory, the Defense Counsel objected again. "Leading question."

The Law Officer ruled, "The Manual provides that a wider latitude on leading questions is permitted on depositions. I am going to overrule the objection. You may read the answer."

"He was sitting on me."

"Did this person tell you to keep quiet . . . for he had a knife and would cut your throat, or words to that effect?"

"He said to lay right there and keep your hands where I can see them. He told me he had a knife, but I didn't see it. He said, 'I have a knife and if you move I will kill you'."

At this point, according to the record, the would-be rapist had an untimely urge apparently stronger than lust. He left the terrified girl on the bed while he went to the bathroom. According to Michaela, "He started going to the door that led into my parents' room—it was a suite. As he was walking into the other room he threatened me with the knife. After he went into the other room, I got up, opened the door leading into the hall and ran down the hall and then down to the next floor. Then the gag fell out of my mouth and I started to yell for help and a woman heard me and I went into her room."

"Was this person disguised in any way?"

"Yes, he had a nylon stocking over his head. Well, it was over his face."

"Did you struggle with this individual while he was in bed with you?"

"He was sitting on me, he wasn't in bed. He had both my hands about here (she indicated the forearm). I was then turned on my right side, because the right side of my face was in the pillow, and it was then that he hit me. He struck the left side of my face. I continued struggling a little, and then he hit me down here—my mouth, and I stopped struggling altogether."

"What was your age at the time of this incident?"

"Fourteen."

"Did you receive any injuries as a result of your encounter with this male person?"

"Yes, I received a black eye, and the side of my eye was bruised. The white part of my eye turned red from the pupil on back. It was black and purple and blue. Then on my mouth, as the doctor told me, was a similar bruise inside my mouth. The whole left side of my face was swollen. All over the inside of my mouth, it hurt."

The Trial Counsel then read into the record the depositions of Hugh C. Scott, his brother Robert, and their mother, Mrs. H.M. Cole. They testified that they heard the screams and saw Michaela running towards them. Hugh Scott had stepped out on the balcony and seen O'Callahan climbing down the balconies to the ground.

The next witness was present in person—and placed on the stand. He was Herman Oliviera, the Security Officer at the Reef Hotel. He testified that he had a call from the operator on duty who said a woman was screaming upstairs. He immediately locked all the elevator doors.

Oliviera stationed two men at the entrance to the fire escapes, then rushed outside to watch the balconies—the only other possible escape. "I saw O'Callahan coming down from the eighth or ninth floor, just jumping from ledge to ledge on the side of the building towards the ground."

The Trial Counsel apparently was afraid the court might not believe a man could descend ten stories, jumping from balcony to balcony. His question showed his thoroughness of preparation on this matter.

"Do the balconies have a railing around them?"

"Yes, a railing so you can step on one ledge and can go down to the next, jumping from ledge to side."

"Did you ever have occasion to go from one floor to the other—going from one balcony to the other?"

"Oh yes, I have."

"Have you seen anybody else do it?"

"Oh yes. I saw you do it last night."

Oliviera then testified that he had captured the suspect and taken him back to Michaela Scholes' room. "The girl was very hysterical . . . her arms looking something like they had been bound. Her wrists were all marked up."

"Did he make any statement to you as to what took place in that apartment?"

"Yes. He told me . . . that he was afraid of me because I had picked him up previously as a peeping-tom."

This unexpected glimpse into O'Callahan's background was ordered stricken from the record by the Law Officer. "I wish to instruct the members of the court that it is highly improper and unfair for members of the court to consider that answer in this case. Improper disclosure by the witness."

O'Callahan's confession was then introduced into the record. It read, in part:

"I looked into the next room and saw the girl still sound asleep on her side with her face towards the wall. I then proceeded to the clothes closet and found a man's brown shoe which I took into the latrine and removed the shoe lacing in order to use it to tie the girl's hands with; while in the latrine I saw a coat hanger with a pair of silk panties hanging on them and took them off the hanger to use as a gag. I then proceeded to turn out the light. Doing this, I went into the room where the girl was asleep.

"Upon entering the room I removed my pants and shirt . . . and my shoes. I went to the bed where the girl was sleeping and shook her by the shoulder to arouse her. When the girl looked up she seemed to open her mouth as if to scream, and I hit her two times on the upper left side of her face, and proceeded to shove the gag into her mouth. While shoving the gag into her mouth, she began to struggle, and I put one arm under each knee. The girl then grabbed my wristwatch off my left wrist and I told her to give me that watch back, which she did.

"Upon putting the gag in her mouth I took the shoelace and tied it around her left wrist, and then tied her right wrist to the left one. After tying her arms, I told her I had a knife and if she tried to yell I would cut her throat, and I sat down on the edge of the bed. At this time I had to go to the latrine and I told her that if she moved I would cut her throat, and I went into the next room to urinate. At this time the girl got out of bed and ran out into the hall, screaming. I rushed out of the latrine and put on my pants and shoes, and started going over the railings of all the balconies in an attempt to reach the ground."

"What were your intentions prior to entering the girl's apartment?"

"Rape."

"Did you remove any of the girl's clothing?"

"No."

"Did you touch this girl's private parts?"

"No."

"Were you naked at any time during your attempt?"

"No."

With the introduction of O'Callahan's confession, the prosecution rested. The Defense Counsel stood up. "The defense has no opening statement. The rights of the accused have been explained, and he has elected to remain silent. The defense rests."

O'Callahan had no alibi; he did not contest the introduction
of his confession. His hopes lay outside this court, in the
ladder of judicial review which might find that his rights had
been prejudiced by the physical absence of the key witnesses
against him.

The court found him guilty as charged. The maximum
penalty for these offenses was twenty years at hard labor.
The court sentenced him: "To be dishonorably discharged
from the service, to forfeit all pay and allowances, and to be
confined at hard labor for ten years."

On appeal, O'Callahan's conviction was affirmed by the
Army Board of Review, and, subsequently by the United
States Court of Military Appeals, which took up the matter of
nonconfrontation in these words:

"The substance of the deposition testimony is to the effect
that a man entered a penthouse apartment at the Reef Hotel,
and assaulted the occupant, a fourteen-year-old girl, while
she was in bed. There is an abundance of *other* competent
evidence of the entry and assault to establish the *corpus* of
the offenses charged."

The court then cited Floyd and Redden's testimony of
accompanying the accused to the girl's room, and the
security officer's testimony of watching O'Callahan descend
from the balcony of the victim's apartment, and taking him
to the victim's presence where O'Callahan was identified on
the spot.

"On the record, the accused's guilt was proved beyond a
reasonable doubt by evidence *other* than the depositions,
and the use of the latter was not prejudicial to him. There is,
therefore, no justification whatever to grant extraordinary
relief."

But from his cell in the Lewisburg penitentiary, O'Callahan
had one more string to his bow. He filed a petition for a writ
of *habeas corpus* in the United States District Court for the
Middle District of Pennsylvania, alleging that the court-
martial was without jurisdiction to try him for nonmilitary
offenses committed off post while on leave. He failed in the
District Court; he failed again in the Third Circuit Court of
Appeals. Then his writ came to the Supreme Court.

The Court took it under advisement, and on June 2, 1969,

issued its decision. Justice William O. Douglas wrote the opinion.

Quoting from a previous decision, *Toth v. Quarles*, Douglas said: " 'Conceding in military personnel that high degree of honesty and sense of justice which nearly all of them undoubtedly have, it still remains true that military tribunals have not been and probably never can be constituted in such way that they can have the same kind of qualifications that the Constitution has deemed essential to fair trials of civilians in federal courts.'

"A court-martial is tried, not by a jury of the defendant's peers which must decide unanimously, but by a panel of officers empowered to act by a two-thirds vote. The presiding officer at a court-martial is not a judge whose objectivity and independence are protected by tenure and undiminishable salary and nurtured by the judicial tradition, but by a military law officer. Substantially different rules of evidence and procedure apply in military trials. . . .

"Courts-martial as an institution are singularly inept in dealing with the nice subtleties of constitutional law. . . . A civilian trial is held in an atmosphere conducive to the protection of individual rights, while the military trial is marked by the age-old manifest destiny of retributive justice.

"As recently stated, 'None of the travesties of justice perpetuated under the Uniform Code of Military Justice is really very surprising, for military law has always been and continues to be primarily an instrument of discipline, not justice. . . .'

"The mere fact that petitioner was at the time of his offense and of his court-martial on active duty in the Armed Forces does not automatically dispose of this case . . . the Government invites us to draw the conclusion that once it is established that the accused is a member of the Armed Forces, lack of relationship between the offense and military interests is irrelevant.

"The fact that courts-martial have no jurisdiction over nonsoldiers . . . does not necessarily imply that they have unlimited jurisdiction over soldiers, regardless of the nature of the offenses charged. . . .

"We have concluded that the crime to be under military

jurisdiction must be service-connected . . . lest cases arising in the land and naval forces . . . be expanded to deprive every member of the armed services of the benefits of an indictment by a grand jury and a trial by a jury of his peers.

"In the present case the petitioner was on leave when he committed the crimes with which he is charged. There was no connection—not even the remotest one—between his military duties and the crimes in question. The crimes were not committed on a military post or enclave; nor was the person whom he attacked performing any duties relating to the military. Moreover, Hawaii, the situs of the crime, is not an armed camp under military control, as are some of our far-flung outposts.

"We have accordingly decided that since petitioner's crimes were not service-connected, he could not be tried by court-martial but rather was entitled to trial by the civilian courts."

The Sergeant on the Balcony was free. And military justice would never again be quite the same.

Epilogue

The Supreme Court had begun its curtailment of military jurisdiction in 1955. The case involved a former airman who was accused of murder in Korea, but who had been discharged before his alleged culpability was discovered. The Court held that the constitutional power "to make rules for the government and regulation of the land and naval forces" could not be extended to authorize the military trial of a civilian who was no longer a member of those forces. Two years later the Court further curtailed the military. This time it held unconstitutional the trial of two women accused of murdering their soldier-husbands while "accompanying the armed forces outside the United States."

These cases were similar in that they both dealt with the military's jurisdiction over civilians in peacetime. Where the

O'Callahan case went so much further was in its apparent removal from military jurisdiction of *military* men who were accused of *nonmilitary* offenses. And in at least one proposed revision, nonmilitary offenses would be specifically removed from court-martial jurisdiction.

9

Henderson's Secret

Prologue

Since the "Boston Massacre," when Crispus Attucks fell before British gunfire, Negroes have been involved in all of this nation's wars. But this involvement has been consistently accompanied by humiliation, discrimination, segregation, and other ugly and undemocratic manifestations of the American spirit.

George Washington didn't want any Negro troops at all. When the Continental armies were organized, Negroes were officially barred. This policy was changed following a British proclamation that they would free all slaves who came over to their side. To prevent wholesale desertions, some States began to form Negro companies and other States allowed Negroes to fight side by side with white troops. Lafayette is said to have praised the valor of the Negro soldiers, and a Hessian officer named Schloezer, serving with the British, called them "able-bodied, strong and brave fellows."

Only in the South was there still resistance to the

enlistment of black troops, and it proved costly. More than 50,000 slaves defected to the British.

But the fate of the Negro was unchanged by the war. Captain Mark Starlin of the Virginia Navy was the black commander of the Revolutionary gunboat *Patriot.* Despite a fine war record, he was—at the war's end—re-enslaved by his prewar master.

In the Spanish-American War, Negro troops in the Ninth and Tenth cavalry were with Theodore Roosevelt at Santiago Ridge. So outstanding was their heroism that a Southern officer is reported to have said "the Negroes saved that fight." And Teddy Roosevelt, in a well-meaning but patronizing slur, said, "Well the Ninth and Tenth men are all right. They can drink out of our canteens."

But by World War I nothing had changed. Negro recruits were segregated in the Army, limited to mess service in the Navy, and barred completely from the air service and the Marines. Pressure from the National Association for the Advancement of Colored People caused a small relaxation. Officer training for Negroes was begun at Fort Des Moines, Iowa, and 106 Negro captains and 533 first and second lieutenants were graduated. But elsewhere Jim Crowism was rife. Most army camps were in the South and they were constantly disrupted by riots and disorders and characterized by flagrant discrimination. Yet despite all the trouble and humiliation, black troops fought with distinction along the Western Front in 1918.

World War II came and still there was segregation. But under the aegis of President Franklin Roosevelt, things slowly began to change. By 1940 the War Department made it clear that it would stand for no discrimination in officers candidate schools and announced that Negroes would, for the first time, be trained as pilots. In 1942 the Navy announced opening its ranks to blacks for ratings other than messmen and the Marine Corps began accepting Negroes. And in 1945, the first "integrated" unit was formed in the Army; it was composed of separate white and black platoons under the same command. The unit was broken up after the War and full integration in the armed services began only in

1949, following the recommendations of a committee set up by President Harry S. Truman.

By 1956 this integration was continuing—but so was discrimination. The Navy, the most class conscious of the services, was the prime offender. But if the Navy had racial problems they were kept well hidden until a sailor named Henderson came into the possession of a gun.

D isbursing Clerk Third Class Jimmie Henderson, a twenty-year-old Negro, was a proud man—and with reason. Despite limited schooling and a mediocre rating on his intelligence tests, he had by sheer hard work arrived at a status usually denied members of his race. For more than a century, the U.S. Navy, the most conservative of the services, had automatically assigned Negroes to duty as stewards or cooks—sea-going domestic help. In the late 1940's the Navy, along with the other services, began to change this policy and offer Negroes all types of assignments. Yet in 1957, Henderson could complain with justice that seventy-five percent of the Negroes in the Navy still served as domestics.

In contrast, Henderson had achieved a rating that involved his handling large amounts of money and required some skill in bookkeeping. His department head, Ensign Arthur Lusk Morris, was a young man with liberal political beliefs who once urged Henderson to take a test that would qualify him for college under a special Navy program.

They sailed aboard the USS *Uvalde,* a cargo ship. Henderson got along well with his shipmates, but at some point his relationship with his department head began to deteriorate. He took the test for advancement to Second Class and passed it, but Ensign Morris refused to recommend him for advancement. He said he didn't feel that Henderson was qualified as yet. The first embers of resentment were thus kindled in Henderson's mind.

In the middle of May, 1957, Radio Seaman Raymond

Newell Ross noticed that his watch, which he had left in the shower, had disappeared. He waited a couple of days for it to be returned, then went to the ship's legal officer, who, as it happened, was Ensign Morris. He told Morris that he suspected Henderson, who angrily denied having anything to do with the watch. But a search by Ensign Morris and the chief master-at-arms turned up the watch in Henderson's locker. Henderson was placed on report by Ensign Morris and the chief, tried by a special court-martial, and sentenced to reduction in rate and four months in the brig. The sentence rankled in two ways. Henderson was extremely proud of his rating—and the four months confinement would extend his tour of duty in the Navy beyond his normal release date. The resentment already burning in Henderson flamed up. It exploded early on a May morning in a murderous rampage culminating in a grim, silent, strangely calm Negro with a .45 holding one shipmate hostage on the flying bridge for six and one half hours while below several others lay dead or injured.

On September 23, 1957, Jimmie Henderson listened stolidly in court to the charges against him. They charged him with the premeditated murder of Ensign Arthur L. Morris, with intentionally inflicting grevious bodily harm by shooting Ensign Richard D. Harrison with a .45, with committing assault by hitting Metalsmith Third Class Joseph H. Verbeek on the head and shoulders with a hammer, and with unlawfully detaining Radio Seaman Robert W. Lakey as a hostage. Henderson pleaded not guilty to them all.

The first witness for the prosecution was Chief Hospitalman James D. Mann, a medical corpsman on the *Uvalde.*

"Would you relate to the court the events that occurred?"

"Well at approximately 0610 on the 28th of May I was asleep in the sick bay aboard the *Uvalde.* At that time I was called by the command duty officer of the *Uvalde,* Mr. Van Popering. I got up and dressed, and about the time I was dressed a sailor aboard the *Uvalde* by the name of Verbeek walked into the sick bay—and I observed him to be somewhat dazed and slightly shocked; he had blood on the front of his face and head, and down the front of his clothing. I immediately sent for my Third Class Petty Officer aboard to assist me. I lay Verbeek down on the operating table and commenced working on him."

"Will you describe the wounds for the court?"

"One wound was in the center of the head, one on the left side, and one over the left eye."

"What was the severity of the wounds?"

"Well, the wounds were a gaping type of wound. I was then called to Officers' Country. . . . Upon entering the stateroom I observed Ensign Harrison lying on the lower stateroom bunk . . . he was obviously in great pain. He was rolling from side to side. Upon examining Ensign Harrison I found he had a puncture-type wound, a clean circular-type wound in the lower left arm with the skin creased in. . . . There was another wound on the left side of the abdomen, a rather clean wound, but no other wound."

"Now, Chief, what did you do when you found Ensign Harrison?"

"I first made a splint for his arm."

"Now did you make any further examination?"

"Yes, sir, and I found an object about the size of a bullet or a marble lodged just under the skin of his right side."

"Referring to the splinting of the arm. Did you complete the splinting of the arm?"

"No, sir. I was called to the adjacent stateroom by Ensign Brown. . . . I entered the stateroom and I saw a body lying on the lower bunk of the stateroom. The body was faced up, with the head forward of the ship, and the feet aft of the ship on the lower bunk."

"Now will you describe what you saw there?"

"It had a blanket wrapped around the head and the right hand was clutching this blanket . . . the eyes were closed and the mouth gaping open. I found wounds in the right lower leg and the upper left chest area of the heart."

"Was it the body of anybody you know?"

"Yes, sir, the body was the body of Ensign Arthur Lusk Morris."

"What did you do then?"

"I immediately sent below for a stethoscope to try to detect heartbeats. While the stethoscope was coming up, I

took a flashlight . . . and shined it into the eyes of Ensign
Morris to see if there was any reaction. A normal eye will
contract and dilate when you move the light. There was no
reaction whatsoever to the light. I felt the pulse . . . there was
no pulse beat."

"What did the result of those tests you made indicate to
you, Chief?"

"The results of the tests indicated that he was dead. . . .
Dr. Rein of the Naval Station at Treasure Island came aboard
and certified that he was dead."

Radio Seaman Ross then explained to the court the
incident of the watch which led to Ensign Morris' putting
Henderson on report—and to his special court-martial.

Next, Darrel G. Wright, Ship's Serviceman Third Class
testified to Henderson's growing resentment of the man he
had thought was his friend, Ensign Morris.

"Do you know what billet the accused had on the
Uvalde?"

"Yes, sir. He was a Disbursing Clerk Third Class. He
worked directly in the same office with Ensign Morris."

"Can you describe this office?"

"Yes, sir. It was the disbursing office and ship's store
office and both Mr. Morris and Henderson had their desks in
there, with another storekeeper who kept the ship's store
records."

"How would you characterize the relationship between
Mr. Morris and Henderson?"

"Well, I believe that Henderson was a little behind in his
work at times and Mr. Morris being a fairly new officer aboard
at that time . . . I think he needed some help from Henderson
that Henderson didn't offer him. I know from personal
experience of my own that his baskets were always filled with
travel claims that weren't brought up to date and so on."

Did you ever overhear any conversation between Mr.
Morris and Henderson relative to his merit?"

"Yes, sir, I've heard Mr. Morris tell him to get his work
out."

"Did you ever hear Henderson express a like or dislike for
Ensign Morris?"

"Well, several times in the compartment, especially when

we were at sea or someplace . . . I've heard him say 'I'd like to kill that son of a bitch.' "

The prosecutor asked Wright if he had seen Henderson after the court-martial.

"Yes, sir . . . I believe it was just after I closed the ship's store . . . when I went back to the compartment Jimmie was sitting there by the locker and I come in and sat on the deck and he says: 'Well, I guess you heard what I got?' And I said, 'No, I didn't hear at all.' . . . 'Well,' he said, 'I got busted and four months confinement.' So I sat there and he made the remark that he would get anyone that had anything to do with this court-martial."

"How did he appear?"

"Well, he appeared to me to be quite serious about it, and I made the remark then that I wouldn't say anything myself like that."

The next witness was William B. Harris, a Boiler-Tender Third Class. He testified that he was in a card game with the accused on the 20th of May, after the watch had been recovered but before the trial. "I recall his saying that if he got a court-martial 'I'll kill that bastard.' "

On cross-examination, Henderson's counsel probed for the first time into the area of racial discrimination.

"During the time that you knew Henderson on the *Uvalde* were you ever aware of any discrimination towards anyone on account of race?"

"Well, it was just things that I heard. There was nothing said to me personally."

"Did you hear this from Henderson, or from whom?"

"Not from Henderson. Just from different groups."

"Was there in your opinion discrimination aboard the ship?"

"Well, I didn't really notice it there until the last. And I more or less became aware of it that there was just in my opinion maybe a little bit."

"Was it the enlisted men or the officers?"

"Well, I don't believe it was the enlisted men. I think it had more to do with the officers."

The Trial Counsel was on his feet with an objection.

"At this time I have to object to this line of questioning. It has not been tied to the facts of this case at all. We have just this witness' personal opinion that possibly toward the end of his stay aboard the *Uvalde* there was some discrimination. It hasn't been tied down as to date. It hasn't been tied down as to the individual, Mr. Morris."

But the Law Officer overruled the objection, and the prosecutor took the floor for re-direct examination.

"Did you ever observe any discrimination by Ensign Morris against Henderson?"

"No, I didn't."

"Well, who were these other persons you hear about . . . who in particular?"

"Well, I would say there were more in the Supply Department because they had come more in contact with them . . . nobody told me personally. It was just at chow. We would be talking about different things and that would come up. Just conversation."

Storekeeper Second Class Arthur F. Caban knew Henderson better than most of his shipmates because he worked in the same supply compartment with him and Ensign Morris.

"Did you ever have any conversation with Henderson on the evening after the court-martial?"

"Yes. That evening, there was about five or six of us in the supply compartment and he was sitting up against the bulkhead . . . and he called one of the other men over and he asked him, 'Do you know I tried to buy a gun over in the city?' He said, 'No.' He said, 'Yeah. I tried to buy me a gun but I was too young. And this other man asked him why he wanted a gun? He just said, 'I have my plans.' "

On cross-examination, the defense counsel asked:

"Did you get the impression that he bragged a lot?"

"I'd say he was more proud of what he did than actually bragging."

"Anything about the fact that he was one of the only Negroes not in the stewards' branch?"

"No."

"Were you aware of any racial discrimination aboard the *Uvalde?*"

Once again the Trial Counsel was on his feet, irritated. "Don't ask any questions about racial discrimination."

Law Officer, "Are you objecting?"

Trial Counsel, "Yes, sir, I am."

"State your grounds."

"On the obvious grounds that it goes beyond the scope of direct examination."

"Sustained."

So far the prosecution had painted a picture of a sailor embittered over being held back from advancement by Ensign Morris, now doubly furious because the same officer had brought him to trial. The next witness was the man upon whose head Henderson's anger first broke, Metalsmith Third Class Joseph H. Verbeek.

Verbeek described the *Uvalde* lying dark against the Oakland docks at 3:30 that morning when he awoke to take the watch. The ship was quiet, its officers and men sleeping. Still not fully awake, Verbeek went to the "head," as the bathroom is called aboard ship, and was surprised to find Henderson there, taking a shower.

"What happened then?"

"I went back to the shipfitters shop to make a pot of coffee . . . I heard a knock on the door. I said, 'Come in,' and Henderson was there and he came in. I asked him what he was doing and he said he couldn't sleep because of what he had received at the court-martial that afternoon. He stated that it would be February now before he got discharged from the Navy because he would have to make up his brig time."

"Now what was Henderson doing when he was in the room with you?"

"He was sitting there and he looked very comfortable."

"What happened when you returned from your five o'clock rounds?"

"I returned to the shipfitter's shop and found Henderson there . . . I probably said 'Hi' to him. I know I went by him and into the carpenter's shop."

"What were the lighting conditions in that area?"

"In the shipfitter's shop the lights were out but in the carpenter's shop the lights were on."

"And what did Henderson do?"

"Well, shortly after, he came back in and sat down in the same chair which he was sitting in before."

"How did Henderson appear at that time?"

"He seemed normal to me. He was quiet, and never said anything."

"What happened next?"

"I told him I had to make a report to the quarterdeck."

"So what happened?"

"Prior to leaving, I asked him whether he wanted to listen to more records, and he said yes. So I just walked out of the carpenter's shop into the dimly lighted shipfitter's shop."

"What happened next?"

"I passed through the shipfitter's shop. I got almost to the foot of the ladder, when I was struck from behind with something . . . it was just like somebody turned the lights out for a moment . . . and I was stunned, and I turned around and I saw Henderson with a hammer. He was trying to beat me on the head, and I tried to cover up, and I was trying to push him back to avoid being hit. I kept pushing him back, and he kept hitting me, and the more he hit me, the dizzier I got. . . . I got hit on the head, the shoulder, and the hands, and finally I got so dizzy, I started going down. I put my hands over the back of my head and he kept hitting me . . . and my right hand was broken and my left hand was scarred and swollen up and—"

Verbeek started to cry. After a moment, the prosecutor said:

"Go ahead, please."

"Well, anyhow, all during this time I had no idea what Henderson wanted."

"Was he saying anything to you, Verbeek?"

"Well, at last I started hollering, and he said, 'Shut up, shut up.' And, of course, when I went down I went face first and at that time when I was down, he said, 'Give me the belt.' That was the first idea I had of what he wanted at all. He rolled me to one side and took the belt. He took the pistol and belt and the clips. Then I heard what sounded to me like the inserting of a clip into a pistol. And he also said at that point when he got up, 'Sorry, Verbeek.' "

"What happened then?"

"Henderson went into the carpenter shop and I don't know what he did there. . . . Then he came out of the carpenter's shop and he said, 'You stay laying there.' And then I heard him go up the ladder."

Verbeek stumbled bleeding into the corridor and met a sailor who spread the word to the quarterdeck that Henderson had his gun. Meanwhile Henderson was on his way to Ensign Morris. In stateroom 1015, Morris lay sleeping in the lower bunk. By coincidence, Ensign Richard D. Harrison, who had been Henderson's defense counsel at the court-martial, was occupying the top bunk in the same room. Harrison was the next witness.

"I was awakened on the 28th of May by a light going on in our stateroom. I glanced up, and since the clock was on the bulkhead I noticed it was about 0600. Henderson, when I first saw him, made a statement asking when he would be going to the brig. With this in mind I thought he wanted to speak to me, so I jumped down onto the deck. Soon, thereafter, Henderson raised from behind his right hip a .45 caliber pistol . . . and I moved from this position by natural instinct to a position standing beside a chair.

"Mr. Morris was lying in his bunk. Upon having the weapon come into view, Mr. Morris sat up in bed, his legs hanging over the side. Almost immediately thereafter, Henderson took the gun and started ejecting cartridges from the gun . . . 2 or 3 cartridges. . . . Soon thereafter . . . of course this happened very rapidly . . . one clip was ejected and another shoved in, and with this . . . the gun fired . . . in the direction of the washbasin."

"Then what happened?"

"Without hardly any delay he swung the gun around and fired four more shots. This is the way it was fired: The first shot went off Bang!—Bang Bang Bang Bang! alternating shots between Mr. Morris and myself with the motion of the gun."

"Now the point that we are trying to get at, Mr. Harrison, did this appear to be a deliberate swinging or was this a promiscuous swinging?"

"It appeared to be a *deliberate* swing, yes."

"Prior to this shooting, was there any conversation?"

"Yes, sir. Art and I tried to convince him that, first of all, he was going to be ruining his own life by doing this . . . and second of all that his court-martial sentence that he had received before would be reduced."

"Had you, in fact, talked to the Captain about the sentence?"

"No, we had not."

"Why did you tell him this?"

"Well, we were trying to prevent him from shooting us, and this was a natural instinct to us."

"Where were you wounded?"

"I was shot through the left forearm and the abdomen, with the bullet lodging just beneath the skin on the right side of my body."

Lieutenant (jg) Henry James Sidford was asleep in the next room when the gunfire erupted.

"Mr. Harrison stumbled into my room, holding his stomach in his hands, and said almost in an incredulous voice, 'Henderson shot us.' I helped him into my bed. I could tell he was in quite serious pain. I tried to reassure him."

"What did you do next?"

"I went to the ship's quarterdeck and got arms out for the men."

"Did you yourself pass these weapons out?"

"Yes, sir."

Henderson, meanwhile, had run up to the flying bridge. On the way he met Robert W. Lakey, a Radioman Third Class. Lakey testified:

"When I met Henderson he just said 'Hello.' He said he wanted to talk to me, to tell me something. And I said, 'All right, let's go into the radio room,' but there was someone there, so he said, 'Let's step outside.' Then he wanted to go up to the signal bridge."

"Was there anything said at this time?"

"Yes, sir, Henderson said, 'Lakey, I've done something crazy this morning, I think I killed Mr. Morris.' "

"Did you notice anything in his hand at the time?"

"Yes, sir, he took out a clip and shoved it into the gun, and worked the action to put a bullet into the chamber."

"How long were you with him altogether?"

"Approximately two hours. I said, 'Why did you ever do a crazy thing like that,' and he said, 'Well, I just had to get him.' He said, 'I'm sorry, Lakey, I'm going to have to hold you as a hostage.' I said, 'OK.' "

"Did he say anything else?"

"He said he'd give up his gun when the reporters came."

With a gun pointing at Lakey, Henderson looked over the lip of the flying bridge and saw that men and officers were armed. Guns were pointing at him, but no one could shoot because of the muzzle in Lakey's side. Henderson had already used the gun, and nobody doubted he would use it again. He told Lakey:

"I'm going to get Mr. Cornwall, and the Captain and the Exec and Mr. Sullivan."

"How did he appear?"

"Just like always, real calm and everything."

"Did everyone else have guns around him?"

"Yes, sir."

"How did that make Henderson feel, having all those guns around him?"

"He started feeling a little nervous."

"How did you feel?"

"When I saw *him* get nervous, I got nervous too."

Hour after hour the angry Negro held forth on the bridge. Officers tried to talk him into surrendering the gun. His mother was brought to the ship, and pleaded with him to give up the weapon. Henderson listened to none of them. Then a chaplain came onto the bridge. He talked for four and a half hours, and somehow gained Henderson's confidence. At last Henderson descended into the pilot house, and gave over the gun, after extracting a promise that he could meet with the "press of this country."

The prosecution introduced a confession Henderson had

made at the time of his arrest. It was accepted without challenge by the defense. And the prosecution ended its case.

The defense counsel opened with brief remarks.

"We now know *what* happened. The defense proposes to explain why . . . why, gentlemen, did it happen?

"We will prove that though the accused is said to be legally sane, he was so disturbed emotionally and mentally that he did not and could not on the 28th of May have had the mental capacity of entertaining the required premeditated design to kill."

Lieutenant James F. McAvenia, who had been the head of the Advancement Board when Henderson was turned down for promotion, testified:

"He was not recommended either by his department head or his division officer. They figured he was not adequately equipped to go up for Second Class Disbursing Clerk. By that I mean they thought he did not have the desire to do the best job possible."

"Could there have been racial discrimination involved in this decision?"

"There was no racial discrimination."

"Has the question of racial discrimination towards Henderson ever been mentioned to you?"

"Since the events of the 28th I have talked to practically every Negro boy aboard ship, in addition to some Japanese and Filipinos. I got a complete negativeness."

"Of course, during your inquiry you didn't ask the accused, did you?"

"No, he was not aboard at the time."

Lieutenant Duncan C. McCrea was the Executive Officer and Henderson bore a particular dislike toward him. McCrea testified:

"He was a lousy sailor, constantly being complained about by everybody, even the enlisted men. He would read magazines instead of doing his work."

"He said *you* were two-faced."

"You can't be popular with everyone."

The ship's Captain, Robert O. Beer, was one of the officers

standing close by when the chaplain had talked to Henderson on the bridge.

The Captain testified:

"The chaplain asked Henderson what he was thinking about. Henderson said, 'I was just thinking if I shot and killed the Captain they would shoot me. Then it would be all over.' "

"Now Captain, you said you were leaning over the binnacle. Did you move a little more out of the line of fire?"

"Very definitely."

The arrival of Henderson's mother was described.

"Did he say anything to his mother?"

"Yes, he tried to get her to leave. He asked her, 'What are you doing here?' and she said she was there because she was sent for, and he said, 'Well, momma, go home.' "

"Did she say anything else?"

"Well, at first she tried to get him to put the gun down. And then later, when he went to put it down, she said, 'Don't give it up. They will shoot you.' "

"Then what happened?"

"He didn't put it down."

When Henderson had surrendered his gun he had been taken to the brig at Treasure Island. There the bitterness which had exploded into murder on the ship took a new form. Marine Corps Lieutenant Warren Widdhan was the Guard Officer attached to the brig. He testified for almost an hour about the actions of Henderson as a prisoner. He said that he had kept a log on Henderson because he was such a problem.

"He had no respect for authority. He caused a constant commotion in the brig, kept the other prisoners up all night. There were many times it almost led to a riot. He attacked two guards. He continually beat on his cell with his tray. He defecated in his paper plate, urinated in his cup and threw it into the face of his guard. He stuffed the commode with clothes to make it flood. When we took his clothes away, he stuck his foot down to make it flood.

"He would shout to the other prisoners, especially the blacks, tell them to start kicking the guards. 'Let's start a riot on these white Caucasian bastards.'

"The 4th of September was the red-letter day as far as Henderson was concerned. He threw a paper cup filled with urine at the guard. Tore his pillow up. Tied the cell with his dungarees so no one could get in. Screamed and hammered with his tray all day."

"During this period, did Henderson ever express any feelings as to racial discrimination?"

"Did he! He felt that the white race in Henderson's own words was one of the lowest things that ever walked on earth. Anybody that was white was a white Caucasian son of a bitch, and he wouldn't hesitate to kill you irregardless of race, religion, or sex."

Herman J. Schnurr was the chaplain who had talked Henderson into surrendering.

"When you first went up to him, what did you say?"

"Well, we talked about things that might be considered completely inane."

"How long did you talk to him?"

"About four and a half hours. Since then, some of my colleagues have made some remarks about me being 'gassy.' I seem to have the world's record."

"What were some of the things you talked about?"

"Well, as you probably know, he was extremely proud of his record in the Navy. . . . He received a rating in a category which is extremely difficult to advance in and he was very proud, and justifiably so, of his clean record. And apparently some weeks before the events occurred, he received some treatment which he did not feel was justifiably fair, and he was court-martialed, and he felt it was an injustice that was far more strict than should be meted out to him because of what he had done—and he felt that this young man, Mr. Morris, was the cause of this injustice."

"How did you gain his confidence?"

"I offered him a cigarette and he said he didn't smoke. I

offered him coffee, and he said he didn't drink coffee. I said, 'You don't have any bad habits except shooting people?' We both laughed at that."

"When you asked him about the shooting, what did he say?"

"Well, he expressed disappointment that other people weren't available for shooting. He felt very bitter about the court-martial accusing him of theft when he had handled funds so honestly all along."

"How did he appear when he spoke to you?"

"He was very relaxed. He wasn't as disturbed as I was, to tell you the truth."

"What did he say when you asked him to surrender his gun?"

"He said, 'Look, I shot an officer. That's bad enough, but I'm a colored boy. They're going to push me around.' "

"Did he ever indicate to you that because he shot Mr. Morris he would be a hero and a martyr to the Negro race?"

"Never—until after he was in the brig."

"What did he say in the brig?"

"Well, there he began having the feeling that he was being persecuted because of the race to which he belonged. That he was something of a champion for his people. He used a phrase 'to become a Moses' for his people. He felt that by his case becoming known to many people, it would help members of his race. I think he felt that through the publicity, other people would be deterred from being harsh to people of his race. After he was in the brig, he began to place great importance on the newspapers."

Henderson's mother and father had not brought him up. They had separated and left the little boy to be raised by a relative, Mrs. Bertha H. Lee. She was the next witness.

"Why did Henderson go into the Navy?"

"Well, he was in school, and he was a very smart kid in school. I thought he was a very nice kid, and he was very obedient when he lived with me, at the time he was going to school. The reason why he went into the Navy was to aid his mother. His mother and father were separated at the time. He was living with me and I don't have a husband. I am separated, too.

"He didn't have any money and couldn't afford to go to school. I asked him to go down to welfare and get six dollars a week cause I couldn't afford to send him to school. I didn't want him to go into the Navy. I begged him not to do that. That was one thing I didn't want him to do. He said, 'I don't want to be a burden on you.' "

"Where was his mother and father?"

"Well, they were in Marin City, but I couldn't tell you just where they were."

"Did his mother ever express any interest or appreciation for what you were doing for Jimmie?"

"No, she didn't."

It was time for the accused to testify. Spectators craned their necks to see the quiet, slim young Negro take the stand. After all the evidence of his violent tantrums in the brig, his wild emotional rage which climaxed in the death of one man and the shooting of a bystander, he seemed—as almost all witnesses had testified—"the same as he always was, calm."

"When is your next birthday?"

"Tomorrow."

"How old will you be then?"

"Twenty-one."

"What do you think of your father?"

"I didn't see my father until I was fourteen."

"Who raised you?"

"My aunt and my godmother and my godfather."

"What was your mother doing all this time?"

"Not much of anything."

"What did you think of your mother?"

"Oh, I didn't like my mother. She was loud and she used profanity and she ran around with—you know—some of the worst people."

"Did any incident occur involving your playmates when you were about nine or ten?"

"Yes, sir."

"How old was your playmate?"

"He was about fifteen."

"Was this day or nighttime?"

"Nighttime."

"At the house where you were living?"

"Yes, sir. I was with my brother on the side of the house."

"Where was your mother?"

"With my playmate."

"Where?"

"On the porch."

"Did you know what was going on?"

"Yes, sir. I did."

"Did you tell your mother?"

"There was nothing I could do. It was none of my business."

"Later on did you have any other incidents like this occur with your mother?"

"Yes."

"Are you ashamed of your mother?"

"Yes."

"Did you ever try to do anything to your mother?"

"Yes. I tried to poison her."

"How?"

"With some lye. There were some sweet potatoes on the stove and I put lye into the potatoes."

"What happened?"

"After she started eating, I said I saw a rat run over the stove."

"Then what did she do?"

"She found out it was lye and she wouldn't eat it."

"Why did you put the lye into the sweet potatoes?"

"To kill her. She beat me for something I didn't do."

"Did you ever tell the psychiatrists who examined you anything about this?"

"No, I did not."

"Who was the first person you told about this?"

"You."

"Why?"

"They weren't Negro."

"Why did you tell me?"

"You are a Negro."

"When you were in school where were your parents?"

"My father was in jail."

"Do you know why?"

"He had cut a lady at a party."

"Why did you decide to join the Navy?"

"To get away from them."

"Where was your first duty station?"

"Moffat Field."

"How did you get along?"

"Very good."

"At the time were there any other Negroes in disbursing at Moffat Field?"

"No."

"Well, how did you happen to get into disbursing?"

"Well, my clerking school score was pretty high and I typed fifty words a minute in boot camp and my arithmetic was average, so that's how I got in."

"Were there any other Negroes aboard the *Uvalde* other than stewards or cooks?"

"Well, there were a few deckhands."

"After you got your rate were you pretty proud of your rate?"

"I was."

"Did you ever feel any racial discrimination aboard ship?"

"Yes, several times."

"When?"

"Well, when men didn't make their payment chits right, I tore them up, and the men who resented it most were mostly Caucasians."

Henderson testified that the Executive Officer had made him stand watch, even though the yeomen—like Henderson, a clerical rating—did not have to stand watch.

He testified that he constantly read Negro publications such as *Ebony* and the Pittsburgh *Courier*, and read where a Negro teen-ager, Emmett Till, had been killed by Caucasian teen-agers.

"Do you think this is just the reverse of the Emmett Till situation?"

"Almost."

"There some white men killed a Negro and were acquitted and here you killed a white man so you feel you should be acquitted?"

"That's right. It should be evened up."

"Did you tell this to the doctors?"

"No. It's none of their business."

"What did you think of Mr. Morris?"

The court buzzed at Henderson's answer.

"I liked him."

"What did he think of you?"

"He thought I was a pretty smart guy."

"Why do you think that?"

"Well, when I took my high school test, he gave it to me, and he recommended me to take the college test to be an officer."

"And did he recommend you?"

"He said he would if I took the test, but I didn't."

"Mr. Morris was one of the few men who took an interest in you?"

"Yes, he was."

"Why do you think Mr. Morris didn't recommend you for the advancement in rating?"

"I didn't care too much for the officers."

"Which one?"

"None of them."

Now the defense counsel moved to the events which led to the murder. Henderson told how he had found the watch in the shower.

"Did you know whose watch it was at that time?"

"No."

"Why did you take this watch?"

"Because I found it."

"Losers weepers, finders keepers?"

"That's correct. I'm a gambler."

Henderson said that he tried to sell it, but the prospective buyer wouldn't take it because he thought the guy who owned it would spot it on him.

"Why do you think Mr. Morris placed you on report?"

"Prior to this incident, Mr. Morris lost one hundred dollars due to his own fault, and I laughed at him, and I thought he was trying to get back at me by putting me on report."

As a result of that report, Henderson testified, he was court-martialed—and he determined to kill every officer on the three-man court. He told of his hammering attack on Verbeek to get the gun. Then, as the court listened intently, he told his own story of the murder.

He told how, on the way through Officer's Country, he stopped first at the Executive Officer's room.

"Why?"

"To kill him."

But the Executive Officer wasn't in, so Henderson went down the dark silent corridor to Ensign Morris' room and turned on the light, waking Morris and Ensign Harrison.

"Mr. Morris asked me what I wanted. I flashed the gun and said, 'Just this.' I said as you know the court-martial was too much. He began to tell me that the Captain would reduce the sentence. Mr. Harrison said I would do nothing but ruin my life. I said I had already ruined it."

"Why?"

"I had already hit Verbeek."

Henderson said that he went to fire the gun, but it jammed. He stood there in front of them, carefully took the clip out, then took the other clip out of his pocket and put it in.

"Where was Mr. Harrison at this time?"

"He was there, just yelling."

"What was he yelling?"

" 'Don't do this!' "

"What did you do?"

"Well, it surprised me that they didn't try to take the gun. Then I walked forward, and I saw myself in the mirror which is on the left, and then I just pointed the gun at Mr. Morris and he began to plead and then he kept lying that the Captain was going to do this and that and so I got pretty angry."

"What did you want Mr. Morris to say?"

"Well, he could at least have tried to take the gun."

"Then what happened?"

"Well, he kept on lying and then the gun went off."

"How did it go off?"

"Accidental."

"Then what happened?"

"Well, I was getting pretty nervous, and shaky at him lying."

"Why?"

"Well, he was the cause of it. He wrote me up!"

"What happened then?"

"The gun went off, and Mr. Morris kicked his legs up in the bunk, and that's when I shot him two times. I saw the bullets hit him, and by this time I turned to Mr. Harrison and I shot him twice and I said, 'You, too.' "

Silence in the court, as the story sank in, then the Defense Counsel asked gently, "Do you think you're crazy?"

"No, I'm not. I've proven it."

"How have you proven it?"

"By taking that test they gave me."

But Henderson went on to say that he had not cooperated with the psychiatrists, other than the test. "They wanted to know too much about my personal life."

The Defense Counsel now held a sheaf of letters in his hand which Henderson had written from the brig. He read the first:

" 'Mom, I want you to tell the NAACP to get in contact with the President. This is the first time in naval history that a Negro has had his chance to speak his piece, and you can be proud of me and say that my baby is running the whole United States Navy and he is going to win with God on his side.'

"What did you mean by asking the NAACP to get in touch with the President?"

"I was going to talk to Ike, and I was going to tell him what was on my mind . . . the situation in the south."

"Why do you think God is on your side?"

"Because I did what I was going to do and I didn't lie about it."

"Have you talked this over with God?"

"Well, I read the Bible, Lieutenant."

"What do you see in the Bible?"

"Quite a few things."

"What, in particular?"

"Don't kill a man."

The Defense Counsel now read another of Henderson's letters.

" 'Mom, what do my race think? Tell them to come to the court-martial and they will hear the story of their times. . . . Mom, don't you know I've got a secret I've not told no one—DIG— the Navy is trying to hide something but I know what it is . . . you know it, also.' "

"Racial prejudice?"

"Yes, sir."

"Is this the secret you haven't told anybody?"

"Yes."

A letter to his aunt was read by the Defense Counsel.

" 'This will be the funniest court-martial in U.S. Navy history. I do know I will be a symbol to my race and go down in Negro history.' "

"What is so 'funny' about this court-martial?"

"Before you came in I was going to defend *myself*."

"Why will you be a symbol for your race?"

"To stand up for what is right. I put my life at stake over a thirty dollar watch, and I had a chance to run away, but I didn't."

"How is the Navy prejudiced?"

"Well, in the Navy three-fourths of the Negroes are stewards. There are only one-fourth with decent jobs."

"You don't think a steward or cook is a decent job?"

"No. It is a menial job."

"But you were a disbursing clerk?"

"Yes, and they resented me . . . because they couldn't tell me anything."

"Why?"

"They didn't know my job."

"What do you think of yourself, Jimmie?"

"I'm a man."

"Why?"

"I proved it."

"How?"

"Well, Lieutenant, when I came into the Navy I was the

only colored guy out of about 150, and they thought I was going to be a Steward because my GCT was only thirty-two, but I did not. I could do anything they could. I could box better, and I could do basketball better, do a little bit of everything better than they could."

Henderson left the stand, and the Defense Counsel took the floor in summation to tell once again the story of a boy, uncared for by his parents, born with black skin, who had gone wild on a ship and murdered his white superiors.

Why? the Defense Counsel wanted to know. Why? Shouldn't the court look deeper than the facts to find a motive, and treat this boy more leniently than the facts might warrant?

The court listened intensely, but did not agree.

Its verdict, announced to a hushed audience: "The accused to be put to death."

Now began the last act. Henderson's lawyers knew that no death sentence had been carried out in the Navy in more than a century.

But Henderson *wanted* to die. He wanted to be a martyr. When a Navy Clemency Board visited the prisoner in his cell, they found him talking to a psychiatrist. Henderson wouldn't even talk to them. Instead he told his psychiatrist in a loud voice:

"Tell them to keep their cotton-picking hands off my death sentence!"

Epilogue

Like many dreams in Henderson's unfortunate life, this last wish did not come true. The President of the United States must approve any death sentence adjudged by the military courts. President Eisenhower—the man whose signature condemned Private Slovik—this time took no action on the case before he left office. Incoming President John F. Kennedy read the record of the trial—and commuted the sentence from death to life imprisonment.

But what Henderson had called a "secret" was becoming no longer so. In the late 1950s and into the Sixties, integration became more and more real, as new rates and officer billets were opened to Negroes. The pressures of the war in Indochina and the resulting need for manpower cracked the situation wide open. In 1965 even the most conservative of the services, the Navy, was producing recruiting films aimed directly at the Negro showing how complete integration was both aboard ship and ashore.

And, in fact, black men enlisted and *re-enlisted* in record numbers during the Indochinese War. Negro leaders at home complained that casualties among Negroes were at a disproportionate rate. Even so, in 1966, 66.5 percent of the Negro men in the Army re-enlisted.

Why? Langston Hughes and Milton Meltzer in *A Pictorial History of the Negro in America* advance these reasons:

> "Many blacks were in the Army because they could not find jobs in the civilian economy. . . . Further, military pay was steady and certain. In short, there was security in the Army that was not likely to be duplicated in civilian life. Since World War II, military segregation had virtually been eliminated in the Army, and had been reduced in the other services and at civilian facilities servicing the military. The Army became a means of *escaping* segregation and discrimination."

There is still discrimination in the services—the comparative lack of high-ranking Negro officers is an indication—but on balance it seems that Henderson may have gotten one unspoken wish. His secret is out.

10

The American Mayor of Saigon

Prologue

Benedict Arnold's court-martial, almost two hundred years ago, established the precedent that American military commanders cannot profit financially from their command. But traditions die hard, and opportunities are constantly presented. Yet, had this been just another court-martial for financial chicanery, then Captain Archie C. Kuntze's trial would have had no historical importance. Instead this was a trial which focused for the first time on another problem in military administration: the influence of civilians *within* and *above* the military.

Civilian control over the military is written into the Constitution by the designation of the President as Commander in Chief and by giving the Congress the right to declare a war and the responsibility for its financing. Yet in practice, military affairs have been decided by military men. When Secretary of Defense Robert McNamara took office in 1960, with the civilian aids whom the press soon termed his

"Whiz Kids," he wanted to change all that and bring the military under the effective control of officials who had been elected or appointed to high civilian office.

In the Kuntze case, this control became a major issue.

Saigon in 1964 was a violent, teeming city bursting with thousands of American troops, civil servants, and agents, as the American effort expanded following the Tonkin Gulf Resolution. Men and supplies converged on Saigon, choked the docks and the warehouses, the barracks and the hotels.

Almost everyone who came to Saigon at that time had to deal with a hearty, personable, handsome Navy Captain named Archie Kuntze. His official title was Chief of Headquarters Support Activity, Saigon. His unofficial title: "The American Mayor of Saigon."

Kuntze's first and most important duty was to keep supplies moving to the front lines, and he did this well enough to earn a "well done" from the Chief of Naval Operations, who called his job the "most important of any Captain in the Navy." But it was his subsidiary duties that earned him the unofficial title of "Mayor." He was quick to show up at any fire with his military fire department; bombings and protests and outbreaks of any kind brought him to the scene at once with military police. If you needed a hotel room . . . a doctor . . . food . . . he was the man to ask. All the necessities of life, as well as the luxuries, flowed through the hands of this ebullient Captain. In 1964 he was making it big. He was doing his job and he was becoming known as a key man in a messy war.

And then a lovely Chinese girl caught the eye of the Captain. Her name was Jannie Suen and she was not only beautiful, she was intelligent, witty, and fluent in English, French, Chinese, and Vietnamese.

Jannie had dated one after another of the young American officers who were pouring into Saigon, but now her attentions fastened on Captain Kuntze, whose estranged wife was back in the United States. By May, 1965, she began to spend most of her time at 74 Hong Thak Tu, the villa of Captain Kuntze—although she kept an apartment of her own. In Kuntze's words, she was his "hostess." In fact, she presided for Kuntze at dinners and official functions, and in a manner that delighted his guests. Others were less delighted. Some of General William Westmoreland's aides, already jealous of Kuntze's power, saw Kuntze's relationship with the lovely girl as an opportunity to torpedo the influential Captain.

They noticed, for example, that shortly after Kuntze was assigned the responsibility for procuring liquor for all of the military clubs in Vietnam, Jannie went to work for one of the leading liquor dealers in Saigon. Coincidence? Perhaps. But word of other "favors" began to be heard. Jannie's father was a tailor. Cloth and clothing materials were in short supply in Vietnam. Most of it had to be imported, and Jannie's father could not afford the heavy import duty. But the Saigon government exempted from the duty the personal effects of U.S. military personnel, and did not bother to inspect U.S. military aircraft. Kuntze had two such aircraft at his disposal, and soon expensive bolts of cloth were being brought in by himself, and by his assistants and friends. The conclusions were easy to draw.

All this time ships were pulling up to the docks, aircraft were landing at the airport, and Kuntze was doing his usual superb job of receiving and funneling the vital supplies smoothly through the chaotic port to the front.

Meanwhile, the cloth Kuntze brought illegally into Vietnam was purchased by Jannie in a complicated bookkeeping procedure, ending up with the Captain showing large amounts of cash in his own records. The crucial question, as one of the lawyers at the subsequent investigation was to remark in private, was where did this cash come from? Was it indeed "repayment" from Jannie? Or did it represent some sort of extensive black-market activity?

Rumors fed on rumors, and not only in American circles. The Vietnamese government began keeping a careful eye on their pretty little citizen. One night in early January, 1966, Vietnamese Intelligence was informed that a shipment of cloth was due to arrive at the Saigon airport from Bangkok, addressed to Captain Kuntze. By the time Kuntze's Vietnamese chauffeur delivered the goods to Jannie's apartment, agents were already on the scene. The shipment was seized, and Jannie was arrested.

General Westmoreland's Provost Marshal quickly investigated and soon found that checks to the amount of $16,000 had flowed into Kuntze's bank account. An official board of inquiry was set up, and Kuntze was called to account for himself. His testimony added to the deepening suspicion about his activities. He could not, for example, remember from whom he had won several thousand dollars at dice. He could not remember the name of an Air Force officer to whom he had sold a $200 set of golf clubs. Most amazing of all, to the officers on the board, he testified that he had paid for some $4,600 worth of clothing and jewelry for Jannie Suen—but could not tell what clothes she had bought on a shopping junket through Thailand and Hong Kong.

At one point, Kuntze produced a personal check as evidence of a loan to one of his former aides, Yeoman James Parks, which was, he said, repaid in cash and converted into one of several Treasury checks the investigators had discovered. Parks, on duty in Norway, was visited by government agents. He denied the whole transaction.

But the Captain did make some points in his defense. It was his contention that his guilt, if any, was simply in avoiding currency regulations in his transactions with Jannie Suen. After all, hadn't she paid him back for each transaction? And the man who was known as the "Mayor of Saigon" could easily point out that every day in almost every plane that landed in Saigon one military man or another was breaking these regulations. It was a way of life in Saigon—a way of life in any war.

Was Captain Kuntze merely aiding his beautiful friend avoid customs, or was he, in fact, deeply involved in black-market operations? Navy legal officers who came to the scene to aid the investigation tended to believe the former; they could find no evidence of any widespread black-marketing activities.

And Jannie Suen, the one witness who might have cleared it all up, had disappeared.

The Board of Inquiry recommended only a reprimand, but some civilian aides of Defense Secretary Robert McNamara visiting Saigon heard about it and termed it a "whitewash." Official action quickly followed. Kuntze was ordered to stand trial at Treasure Island, California, on November 2, 1966.

Most of the charges were based on currency violations, of which this is typical:

"In that Captain Archie C. Kuntze, U.S. Navy . . . did, at Headquarters Support Activity, Saigon, Republic of Vietnam, on or about 13 August 1965, with intent to deceive, make to Lieutenant Douglas R. Beane, Supply Corps, U.S. Navy, an official statement, to wit: that a U.S. Treasury check, in the amount of $850.83 to be received as a result of the proposed 'Exchange for Cash' transaction, would be used by the payee, the said Archie C. Kuntze, for an *official* purpose, which statement as to purpose was wholly false and was then known by the said Archie C. Kuntze to be false."

There were dozens of such checks involved. In addition the transaction with Parks resulted in a perjury charge. And finally, there were charges relating to his association with Jannie Suen, charging that he did "wrongfully and dishonorably permit Jannie Suen, an unmarried Chinese National female, about twenty-six years of age . . . to reside openly and notoriously in his official quarters."

No war in this century has been as unpopular with Americans as the war in Indochina, and the atmosphere at the Kuntze trial reflected this. Newspapers opposing the war seized on Captain Kuntze as a symbol of a war in which billions of dollars in aid and equipment were pouring into a tiny agricultural country. In such a situation, financial corruption was inevitable, the news stories implied.

In effect, Kuntze had already been convicted in the national press as the trial began. But in real life he still had a fighting chance. He had two advantages. One was an enduring feeling of many officers in the Navy that he was being sacrificed to pressure from the top; that he might, indeed, be guilty of minor infractions of currency regulations, but then, so were a host of others.

Kuntze's second advantage was a superb defense attorney, Captain Dan Flynn, a Navy legal officer who, as one newspaper said, "conceals a brilliant talent for salvaging ruined careers beneath a 'down home' facade." Flynn came out of retirement to take the case.

Civilian lawyers such as Samuel Liebowitz, Melvin Belli, Louis Nizer, and F. Lee Bailey become famous in America. Military legal officers often pursue their whole careers in obscurity. Flynn is one example. Captain Joseph Ross, the prosecutor at the trial, subsequently the head of Military Justice in the Navy Department, is another. The importance the Navy attached to this case was shown by their assigning him prosecutor.

In a memo to the author, Ross gives an insight into military legal practice. This is how it was as Kuntze's trial began:

The Courtroom at Treasure Island is not an imposing one. Like other military courtrooms, it bears little resemblance to those which we are accustomed to seeing in civilian life: dignified, impressive, with the Judge's bench raised and the center of attraction, and with the jury box unobtrusively off to one side. Military courts reflect the preeminent role held by the court members as the triers of both the law and the facts—at least until the role of Law Officer was created under the Uniform Code of Military Justice in 1951. Even then, the exact dimensions of that role were not clear, and most military courtrooms continued to look as before: in center stage was found a long, raised bench behind which the members—usually five to nine officers—sat. The Law Officer was relegated more often than not to a table on one side of the room.

The courtroom at Treasure Island is a compromise between those of the Civil Courts and the traditional military forums. The Law Officer's bench is raised and located at one corner of the front of the courtroom. The court members occupy an L-shaped bench at the other corner, with the President of the court (the Jury foreman) in the center of the "L."

At nine o'clock on the morning of the 2nd of November, the much-heralded trial of Captain Archie Kuntze got under way in that courtroom.

After the initial formalities, Dan Flynn, the Defense Counsel, slowly took to his feet and commenced the *voir dire*, the process of questioning the members to determine whether or not challenges should be exercised against them. It also serves a purpose of establishing a rapport between the counsel and the members. Dan Flynn was a master of the 'voir dire.' By the time he had completed it he had established no challenges, but his manner had the members eating out of his hand.

What Captain Ross was referring to may be seen in Flynn's first words to the court members during voir-dire proceedings:

"Gentlemen of the court, I consider this, along with other Navy lawyers who try courts-martial cases, one of the most delicate procedures in the court-martial trials—that is voir diring the court. If I've ever known what the literal meaning of 'voir dire' is, I've long since forgotten. . . . Now, sometimes I go from my regular duties to sit as a member of the court. When I was first voir dired, I was somewhat offended by it. I thought that if I was put on the appointing order, that that certified me as qualified. But as I got older and as I got more experienced with being asked questions, I realized that I, too, had certain feelings, prejudices, and phobias that were not in tune with the case I was appointed on. As one convening authority said to us court members—he said, 'I don't certify you for *everything* when I put you on the court.' "

Immediately after the voir dire was completed, Flynn dropped his first bombshell:

"Mr. Law Officer, the defense now moves for an order for a change of venue in this trial from Treasure Island, California, to Saigon, Vietnam, on the ground that the defense does not have a fair opportunity to develop and present a defense on Treasure Island . . . to eighteen offenses alleged to have been committed in Saigon. And, on the further ground that the defense does not have a fair opportunity to obtain information on Treasure Island . . . that may be of assistance in cross-examining . . . government witnesses testifying to . . . offenses that allegedly were committed in Saigon."

As Captain Ross rose to his feet to answer this motion he was aware that the trial had been moved from Saigon simply because it was too "hot" there. In that small city were hundreds of correspondents eager to make any indiscretion of an American military officer into a major scandal. Not only the Navy, the State Department as well was anxious to keep this trial from the publicity glare of Saigon. And Ross did not think that the result was unfair to the defendant. On the contrary, he felt Kuntze had a better chance for an impartial trial away from the Saigon atmosphere. And, as he pointed out, most of the witnesses the defense wanted were Vietnamese civilians. Even in Saigon, the Navy would have no power to subpoena them. As for the military witnesses, the government had joined in a motion to allow Flynn to go to Vietnam and take depositions from all the witnesses there, as well as to fly in military witnesses to Treasure Island.

Flynn had an angry rejoinder to that, and brought in the element that one newspaper called "the James Bond touch."

"Now he talks about a trip to Vietnam for the defense counsel. I don't know whether the Convening Authority would grant it or not and neither does he. But here is the trouble with that. If you have looked over this record of the board of investigation you will find that it is infested with ONI agents, CID agents, Counter Intelligence agents, and every other kind of an agent who travels through the dark world of intrigue. If we went to Vietnam without a court and we found some witnesses . . . our witnesses would be destroyed— not physically—but from a standpoint of testimonial help between the time we left Vietnam and the time that we got back. I never have been on a case in my life where there has been so much of this business with agents and the likes of them—Vietnamese, American, and otherwise."

The Law Officer denied the request for the change of venue, accepting the government's position that the defendant could have as fair a trial in Treasure Island as in Saigon. He ruled that prosecution and defense "stood on the same feet" as to availability of witnesses, especially the nonmilitary witnesses for whom there was no compulsory subpoena.

The trial began.

Captain Ross in his opening statement spoke of a "continuous thread running through all of the charges." The charges, Ross said, fell into four categories, all connected. The first category charged the accused with abusing his office by importing certain amounts of cloth into Saigon on government aircraft, in violation of regulations. The second category concerned currency transactions by which Kuntze exchanged the Vietnamese piastres he received from Jannie into American treasury checks. "Such transactions are authorized only for official purposes," said Captain Ross, "and we will show that these transactions were not for official purposes." The third category was the perjury charge on Kuntze's testimony about a personal loan to Yeoman Parks.

"Finally the fourth category of offenses . . . which I will call 'the relationship with Jannie Suen' category, alleges certain misconduct concerning a young lady by that name. This completes the thread, because this information that we will provide you . . . will show the accused's motive in importing all the cloth. So we come to the closed circle."

Flynn then rose to make his statement:

"We are going to talk about a case that happened a long time ago, 7,000 miles away, in a strange land. I don't know the feeling of those witnesses who will testify, but when I come back from those ports—and I'm sure you must have had the same experience—those days seem like a dream to me. They don't seem real. You will remember Yokosuka in her boom days, Sasebo, Subic, Marseilles, Naples—the ports of history. The port that now is on the tip of everybody's tongue, the boom port of the world, is Saigon, Vietnam, and it has been since the day that Captain Kuntze arrived to take over his duties. That is the world these witnesses live in. It was an unreal world. That is what they will be testifying about. Whether it will affect their testimony, I don't know, but I think it behooves all of us who consider their testimony to observe it closely.

"Jannie Suen is going to be in this case from about the first witness to the last. I think the evidence will show—and the prosecution will not disagree that it will show—that she is a Chinese girl. Those of you who have served in that part of the world, in the Orient—and I know that practically all of you have—will remember that a Chinese woman is not known for her stupidity. I want you to analyze the testimony regarding Jannie Suen and see what part she played in this case, to see if she was active, a thinking woman, or if she was just an ordinary girl that we all hope our daughters might be.

"I think the evidence will show in this case that Captain Kuntze was a leader, that he was a flamboyant leader, as most of this type of individuals are. They have to inspire people to follow them. I think the evidence will show he is a man that could say 'No,' whether it was to a seaman, a soldier, or the generals he dealt with, or, for that matter, Mrs. Westmoreland, herself, and I think the evidence will show that he said 'No' to a lot more generals than he ever did to seamen, because they knew better than to ask. I think this evidence will show that that type of an individual begets some hard feeling. 'No, is a bad word. I've never liked it myself.'"

The first witness was Yeoman First Class James F. Parks. Parks was a vital witness for the prosecution. From his transaction with Kuntze flowed the important charge of perjury, and in his position as the "Captain's Writer" (as the Captain's confidential clerk is called) he knew more about the Captain's activities than almost anyone else.

"Parks, during the course of your tour at Saigon, did you have occasion to leave the country at any time?"

"Yes, sir. I did. In March I went to Hong Kong for four days . . . and in August I went to Bangkok, Thailand, for three days."

"Now referring to your visit to Bangkok . . . did you have any discussion with Captain Kuntze about that trip before leaving?"

"Yes, sir. Captain Kuntze was going to Bangkok . . . but he could not go because of official visitors coming into town, so I went in his place . . . the Captain asked me to pick up several items in Bangkok for him."

"What kind of items did he ask you to pick up?"

"A set of earrings, three yards of Thai silk, and cloth."

"What kind of cloth did he ask you to pick up?"

"It was black muslin cloth, I believe, and he gave me a swatch of the material. I'm not sure of the yardage, but I think it was around 250 to 300 yards. I'm not sure of that."

"Now, did you discuss with Captain Kuntze paying for these items you were to purchase?"

"Yes, sir. On 12 August 1965, Captain Kuntze wrote me a check for $770.00."

This was the check that Kuntze had declared was a personal loan.

Further direct examination brought out that Parks on his trip to Bangkok, in addition to the cloth, had bought jewelry that Kuntze had requested: gold earrings enclosing a sapphire. He brought the silk and the earrings back to Saigon in his suitcase on the military airplane. Also aboard was a huge bolt of cloth ordered by the Captain. But the girl on the receiving end apparently was not satisfied.

"Now, did you have any further discussion with the accused at a later date concerning this matter?"

"The next day, which was Tuesday, the Captain mentioned that the Thai silk was not the right color."

"Did he say *why* it was not the right color?"

"Yes, sir. He said that Jannie Suen said the cloth was not the right color."

"Parks, I take it you know who Jannie Suen is?"

"Yes, sir."

"Who was she?"

"She was known in Saigon, sir, as the Captain's girl friend."

"Did you ever see this young lady?"

"Yes, sir. Many times."

"Where, for example?"

"I saw Miss Suen in the Headquarters compound. She came to the Captain's office . . . I talked to her on the phone many times, and I saw her in the Captain's car."

When Parks had been interrogated in Norway, he had made a somewhat sensational statement to the Office of Naval Information (ONI). On cross-examination the Defense Counsel asked about it, even though the statement seemed damaging to his client.

"Now, as the Captain's Writer, of course, you were close to him?"

"Yes, sir."

"And as time went on, Jannie Suen became more prominent?"

"Yes, sir, that's correct."

"And that did not set well with you?"

"No, sir."

"Would you agree with me that she was a sort of a fly in the ointment?"

"Yes, sir, I definitely agree with that."

"All your time with the Captain, did you—have you ever known him to lie to an officer or an enlisted man?"

"Never, sir."

"Square with the sailors and square with the officers?"

"Yes, sir."

"On 23 May 1966 you made a statement in Oslo, Norway, did you not?"

"Yes, sir, I did."

"And who did you give that statement to?"

"Mr. Schwab, I believe, is his name, ONI, London."

"All right. Let's go down here to the sentence where you state: 'I believe the earrings I bought were for the Captain's wife who was in Wisconsin'—did you say that?"

"Yes, sir. I did."

"Now was that your impression or how did you arrive at that?"

"That was strictly an impression, sir, because the Captain went to the States on 15 September and I thought, probably, he wanted the earrings to take back to his wife."

"All right. To go further—'and the silk and the black cloth were for the Captain's girl friend—Jannie Suen.' "

"Yes, sir."

"Is that another impression or assumption or what?"

"I would say it was an assumption, sir."

Parks statement to the ONI had continued:

"Jannie Suen lived with the Captain at his residence the entire time, I would say, except when he had official visitors from outside Saigon. Jannie Suen seemed to have complete run of the Captain's house, and visited him sometimes if we were working late at the Captain's office. He gave Jannie Suen complete charge of his house and official vehicle. She used to take her relatives and friends to the tailor or sewing shop in downtown Saigon, to the Saigon zoo, or other personal errands.

"Another thing that caused criticism of the Captain was that he used to take his girl friend to the U.S. Navy Exchange after closing hours, usually after 1700."

Flynn went phrase by phrase through this statement, asking Parks where he got his information. Again and again it turned out to be hearsay. Then Flynn took another angle.

"Now this fellow Schwab that took your statement, was he an ONI agent?"

"Yes, sir, he was from London, England."

"I want you to tell the court how long your conversation was with this fellow—this ONI fellow."

"I spent approximately four hours with Mr. Schwab."

"Was he nice to you? Was he insistent? How did he handle it?"

"Well, he was nice, sir, but when he first started talking to me he started questioning me about my blackmarket activities."

Flynn glanced at the court as this information came through. He followed, smoothly as ever:

"Well, I'm not going to ask you about your blackmarket

activities, but did he *scare* you? Did he try to trick you or how do you feel he handled it?"

"He didn't try to trick me but I was, naturally, scared."

"And then he swung off and talked to you about whatever your duty was in Bangkok—and then did he swing around to Captain Kuntze?"

"Yes, sir."

"And you were kind of relieved when he got off your back and got on Captain Kuntze's?"

"Yes, sir. Anybody would."

Charles R. Walston, crew chief of one of Kuntze's planes took the stand to back up Parks' testimony about the trip to Bangkok in which he had bought cloth and other items for the Captain. Walston had taken him to a shop he knew. He testified that the cloth was on board his aircraft when they returned to Saigon, addressed for delivery to Kuntze.

On cross-examination, Flynn only had a few questions:

"Was it unusual when you came back from a trip to a port such as Bangkok to have large numbers of packages on board?"

"No, sir. It wasn't unusual."

"Would you say, rather, that it was the usual thing for all of the people to bring back packages?"

"Yes, sir."

Witness after witness was called to testify about various shopping trips on behalf of the Captain. Lieutenant Colonel Arthur D. Simon testified he met Kuntze with Jannie Suen when he was stationed in Bangkok. "Jannie had been doing some shopping—she had been to Bangkok for a few days and went on to Hong Kong and Taipei and then came back." About three weeks after the visit, three packages were mysteriously delivered to Simon's apartment "with just a note that they were for Captain Kuntze." Simon met a lieutenant who was flying back to Saigon, and asked him to bring the packages to Kuntze. The lieutenant, Robert L. Doak, testified that he did just that.

The next witness plunged the court into mystery. His name was Charles M. Foster, a civilian accountant formerly a lieutenant (jg) in the Navy. He appeared with a civilian attorney watching nervously nearby. On direct examination he said that he had accompanied a friend named Martiny on a shopping trip in Bangkok. The friend did not have the cash to pay for cloth, and Foster had supplied it. The cloth had eventually been sent to Kuntze, and Foster had received a check for the amount of money he had advanced.

But Foster did not testify that Kuntze had told him to buy the cloth, and in fact did not testify as to any conversation at all, either before or after the event, with the accused. This brought Flynn to his feet, objecting to the testimony.

"Where is the connection? He says he received a check from Captain Kuntze, but he cannot testify that it was for cloth that Mr. Martiny bought. He cannot testify, and he does not, that Captain Kuntze sent Mr. Martiny to Bangkok for cloth, and he cannot show this beautiful chain of circumstances that the prosecutor described. This is . . . a most vicious type of evidence known to law."

The objection was overruled. Flynn now directed his fire at the witness.

"Did you come into this courtroom today with an attorney who is now sitting in the courtroom, Mr. Long, of Oakland, California?"

"Yes, sir."

"Mr. Foster, you are reluctant to testify about certain aspects of this case, is that right?"

"Yes, sir."

"Those aspects concern the accused's relationship with a young lady by the name of Jannie Suen, is that right?"

"Yes, sir."

"Will you explain why you are reluctant to testify about those matters?"

"I consider Captain Kuntze a personal friend and I would just as soon not testify about that."

Suddenly, Flynn requested a recess to talk to the civilian attorney. Five minutes later, the court reconvened, and Flynn said:

"Mr. Law Officer, I have had a conference with Mr. David Long, the attorney for this witness now on the stand. Mr. Long is satisfied that this witness, a young officer, does not understand the waters in which we may be in. I have agreed with him that there are certain matters which we would not go into, for one reason or another they might be privileged . . . I have no further questions."

The court—and the press—were stunned. What were the certain "privileged" matters? Blackmail? Sex? One court member wanted at least one puzzling fact cleared up:

"Did you tell Captain Kuntze, either verbally or in writing, how much to make out the check for?"

"No, sir. I did not."

"Do you know of your own personal knowledge how Captain Kuntze knew the amount for which to make out the check?"

"No, sir. I don't."

With this, the reluctant—and mysterious—witness was excused.

Those "waters in which we may be in" referred to by Flynn—along with the disappearance of Jannie Suen—were a mystery which hung over this case from beginning to end. What Foster knew of Kuntze's relationship with Miss Suen was never to be told in court.

The next witness was Lieutenant Colonel Jasper C. Vance, Captain Kuntze's Provost Marshal.

"Now, I will direct your attention, with respect to your acquaintance with Miss Suen, to the month of January, 1966. Now, were you informed by the accused that something had happened to Miss Suen about that time?"

"Yes, sir. Captain Kuntze called me at my quarters at around 1900 hours in the evening and asked if I was aware of a raid that the Military Police or the CID might have pulled on Miss Suen's quarters. I told him that I knew nothing about it and said I would check into it to see what I could find out."

"Did he say what had happened to Miss Suen?"

"Yes, he said that the raid had been pulled on her quarters and that she had been arrested by the Vietnamese police, sir. I . . . went to Captain Kuntze's quarters."

"All right. At his quarters did you have a conversation concerning cloth?"

"Yes, sir, cloth was mentioned there. Captain Kuntze showed me a bolt of material or cloth and the bolt was wrapped and in a closet and said that he had been informed by Jannie Suen's brother that some materials of a similar type had been taken from her quarters."

"Did the accused relate that to the cloth that he had mentioned that they had taken from Miss Suen?"

"Indirectly I got the impression this was part of some material they might have taken from the house."

On cross-examination, Flynn asked:

"Now did Captain Kuntze say to you, Colonel, 'Jasper'—or whatever he called you—'Go get the girl out of jail?' What did he say?"

"Absolutely not. Captain Kuntze was, naturally, concerned but he only asked that I find out what happened. At no time did he ask that I use influence to get her out of jail."

The next witness was to testify as to the mechanics of currency exchange which Kuntze had used. He was Lieutenant Gerald H. Young, Supply Corps., USN.

"Would you have knowledge of the transaction in the disbursing field known as 'exchange for cash' transactions?"

"It's a matter of exchanging currency of one type or another for a U.S. Treasury check."

"Directing your attention to August, 1965, what transaction, if any, in regard to exchange for cash check transactions did you consummate with Captain Kuntze?"

"On one or two occasions currency was brought to my office with a request for ex-cash checks."

"What conversations did you have with Captain Kuntze regarding these transactions?"

"My conversation with Captain Kuntze was to verify between him and myself that these were of an official nature—these exchanges."

"And what did you tell him . . . concerning the requirements that had to be met?"

"I did not go into detail. I merely confirmed between us that it was of an official nature."

Young's assistant, Lieutenant Beane, had handled most of the currency transactions with Captain Kuntze. Young verified Beane's signature on many checks which were shown to him by the prosecutor. Typical was one for $850.83.

"Would you describe generally the circumstances surrounding the issuance of this check?"

"On this date the piastres came to my office . . . I was
away . . . Mr. Beane, my assistant, was in the office—and he
wanted me to be sure it was of an official nature and
hesitated to take action on it himself. He waited until I
returned. When I returned I reaffirmed it was of an official
nature and we went ahead and issued the check."

"And how did you affirm this officiality?"

"By going to my next senior up the line, Commander
Tvieta."

"What directions did he give you?"

"He assured me that he had knowledge of it being of an
official nature and said to go ahead and issue the check and
said, 'I recommend it.' "

On cross-examination, Flynn elicited a fact that made
headlines the next day.

"How were you fixed for office help there? Did you have
enough or did you figure you lacked some help?"

"Officewise we were pretty short."

"How about facilities where you kept your money?"

"No, sir, not too good."

"What did you use?"

"For quite some time I had to use an icebox . . . to store
about half of my funds in."

"How much did you have in the icebox?"

"At one time I had in excess of 23 million dollars in the icebox."

"Then if somebody had opened that icebox to get
something like a cold beer, he would have been surprised,
wouldn't he?"

The audience was laughing as Young replied.

"I would have been surprised, too."

Flynn had made his point. In a wartime center like Saigon
where millions of dollars were kept in an icebox for
storage—cold cash indeed—minor currency irregularities
could well be expected to be part of everyday business.

The prosecutor next called Captain Kuntze's steward to
testify as to his relationship with Miss Suen.

"How did you know Miss Suen? How did you become acquainted with her?"

"Well, she came to the Captain's quarters."

"Do you know what date this was approximately?"

"Last May, 1965 . . . .She began staying there often."

"Did she take her meals there?"

"Yes, sir."

"Are you aware if she kept any clothes there?"

"Yes, she kept some clothes there."

"About how many times a week would she stay at the quarters overnight?"

"Four to five days a week."

"Do you know if Miss Suen had her laundry done in the house?"

"Yes, some of her laundry was done by the house laundry-woman."

"On what occasions, if any, did you see the Captain's automobile pick up Miss Suen on the morning after she had stayed at the Captain's house?"

"Four to five days a week."

On cross-examination Flynn tried to cast this relationship in a different light.

"You said that she had some clothes there hanging in one or another of the closets. Would they be clothes that she might wear for dinner or some affair that the Captain was having?"

"Yes, sir."

"Now as to the car picking her up . . . if the Captain was sending her on some business . . . you would have no way of knowing that?"

"No, sir."

"Now the laundry lady, I understand did some of Jannie's laundry; is that right?"

"Yes, sir."

"And I don't suppose you went and looked at this woman's laundry to find out what it was. You are not that kind of a man, are you?"

"No, sir."

"So, for all that you know, it could have been some of the

garments that she wore at the dinners or some of those affairs that the Captain had."

Captain Ross returned for re-direct examination.

"Chief Captain Flynn asked you if those clothes would be party clothes. Would there also be everyday clothes in her possession there in the quarters?"

"Yes, sir."

Flynn was stung. "Now just a minute. This is leading and I think on direct examination we should follow the rules of evidence."

The Law Officer asked, "Will you rephrase your question, Counsel?"

"I think we will just drop it, Captain."

The prosecution next placed witnesses on the stand to show that Kuntze had had Armed Forces Identification and Privilege cards issued to Jannie, giving her the privilege, among others, of buying goods at the duty-free military post exchanges. Not being an employee, she was not entitled to such privileges.

Commander Joseph N. Malnerich had been Captain Kuntze's Executive Officer. He testified that while the Captain was on leave in the States, he had had to reprimand Jannie Suen for using the official car to take her relatives around Saigon.

He also testified that on a later date when he had been about to return to the United States, the Captain had asked him to take $1,000 in military payment scrip to a bank in the U.S. and exchange it for a bank draft. This was not an illegal act, but on cross-examination it opened up an insight into the Captain's domestic problems, as his romance with Jannie Suen grew.

"Did he, at that time, discuss with you attorney's fees or matters relating to a divorce that was then pending?"

"Yes, sir: he indicated that the reason that he wanted to use this procedure—was that he wanted a draft from a U.S. bank that he could use to pay some lawyer's fees. I think it was his wife's attorney. The reason was that he preferred not to have the existence of this bank account known."

"Because of the pending litigation?"

"Yes, sir."

The prosecution moved to introduce the Captain's previous testimony at the Board of Inquiry by stipulation, and it was accepted. This testimony gave a revealing insight into life in Saigon as it was led by a top government official. Politics, CIA agents, women all entered the Captain's testimony.

Most of the money, according to Kuntze, came from:

1) Repayments by Vietnamese and other foreign officials for items he had purchased for them in the big post exchange in Saigon. He bought radios and fans and other items for Vietnamese officials because he had found an "anti-American feeling" in Saigon, and he thought "doing small favors for the Vietnamese was in the best interest of the United States."

2) In addition, during his tour of duty, he had imported more than $3,000 worth of liquor from Hong Kong for these people, who would pay him on arrival.

3) The shadowy area of espionage was barely touched on in his testimony, but it appeared that at one point a CIA agent had approached him, and asked him to change piasters to American money. From that point on, he had habitually done this for espionage agents when they were in a jam and couldn't get money through regular channels.

Kuntze's testimony on the rest of the money was less clear. He said he won a lot of it gambling at dice games, but couldn't remember with whom he had gambled. As to his dealings with Jannie Suen, whom he described as his "official hostess . . . with whom I have contemplated matrimony" he said he once financed a shopping spree for thousands of dollars, but didn't pay attention to what she bought. Anyway, he testified, she had repaid him. It was in the records.

It was in this testimony that Kuntze said that the check he had given Parks was a "personal loan," and, according to the prosecution, perjured himself.

The prosecution rested, having shown a steady flow of

cloth through illegal channels, having introduced testimony that Kuntze was living "notoriously" with Jannie Suen, and that he had, according to Parks, committed perjury.

It had not made any allegation that Kuntze had engaged in widespread blackmarket activities, other than the currency exchange, although the press seemed to take it for granted. As prosecutor Ross told the court members, "I'm accepting the accused's explanation that he did it for Jannie."

But the implication was there that Kuntze, a brilliant naval officer with an assured career and promising future, had been involved in far more than currency exchange. If not, why had he perjured himself in his testimony before the Court of Inquiry? Why had he lied about the transaction with Parks, as Parks had testified?

Defense Counsel Flynn called as his first witness, Yeoman Third Class Stephen B. Howell, who testified that he had worked with Parks in Saigon, and knew him well.

"Did you, on those occasions, ever talk to Parks?"

"Yes, sir."

"Did you go to his office?"

"Yes, sir, on many occasions."

"Now during this time did you form an opinion of Parks as to his honesty and integrity relating to the spoken word in the matter of official duties?"

Prosecutor Ross, realizing that Flynn was attempting to destroy Parks' credibility objected: "This is irrelevant." The Law Officer overruled him, and the witness continued.

"Yes, sir."

"What was that opinion?"

"Low, sir."

"Now, would you believe Parks under oath on a matter of official duty?"

"No, sir."

Personnelman First Class Frederick G. Baldaro testified that his opinion of Parks' integrity was low, also. Chief Yeoman James R. McComb added some detail. He also believed that Parks' integrity was low, and for a reason.

"Parks, I feel, was an opportunist and if it made him look better, I wouldn't believe him under oath, if it would put him in a better light."

Having cast a shadow over Parks' testimony, Flynn now called a series of character witnesses for Kuntze. Commander Porter Eugene Clemens, and Commander Charles E. Johnson had served under Kuntze in Saigon. What was their opinion of the Captain? "Of the highest." Lieutenant Tom Whitus said that the Captain's honesty and integrity was "above reproach." Next Flynn introduced a witness he knew would impress the court. Captain Samuel T. Orme of the Bureau of Naval Personnel. Flynn wanted to know what the Navy, as represented by the Bureau, thought of Captain Kuntze before these events took place.

Flynn asked him, "where Captain Kuntze stands in comparison to other officers of the Navy as regards his record as a combat naval officer."

"I'd place him well within the top 10%."

And now Flynn pressed on to show the court—officers all—what Captain Kuntze had ahead of him if this trial didn't shatter it.

"Now before the trouble broke, can you tell us what his next assignment was, if you know."

"He was under orders to the National War College, if we could have gotten him back in time. Failing that, he would have gone to a major command, probably a cruiser."

For Navy men, attendance at the War College is one basic preliminary to a rise to admiral's rank, and command of a large ship is another. Flynn knew enough to let this testimony sink in "with no further questions."

The next witness was to bring the whole Vietnam war into this crowded courtroom. He was Brigadier General John D. Crowley, who had been Kuntze's immediate boss in Saigon. After a few questions establishing his official relationship with Kuntze, Flynn asked the General if he had brought some slides, as he had requested. The General said yes, a screen was placed, and the General stood up with a pointer. The General's narration began with the period of 1965, when only 20,000 American advisers were in the country. Then came the fantastic buildup. Kuntze was right in the middle of it.

"As the tonnage started to pile in, we ran out of

warehouse space. My estimate is that in February of 1965 we probably had about 60,000 square feet of warehouse space for 50,000 tons a month, and that increased to 300,000 tons a month.

"As things went on a little more, the shipping from the States started to pour in. Here we were one undeveloped port and, mind you, we didn't run this port. We were guests—we had to use the pier on permission of the port director.

"We had no Army truck companies to speak of at this stage and you had to rent trucks . . . this again, came under Captain Kuntze and he had to go out and contract for trucks. . . . We soon ran out of that 60,000 square feet of warehouse space. . . . Just getting the land itself was a tremendous problem. It was Captain Kuntze's organization that had to go out and rent the land. He not only had to rent the land, it had to be filled in, have a hard top put on it, and then fence it in.

"Everybody in this stage was in a rush to ship and we needed it. General Westmoreland had made a big decision. He felt he had to have some ground combat troops in Vietnam to keep the country from being severed. There was a real threat from Qui Nhon through An Khe, up to Pleiku and up through the mountains. We thought the VC were going to cut the country in two. . . . We hadn't gotten trucks along Highway 19 from Qui Nhon to Pleiku for three months. That's when we had to airlift. So, everybody was shipping things in a hurry."

As slide after slide flickered into life on the screen, the General detailed Kuntze's incredibly complicated duties as the man in charge of a primitive port swollen with troops and equipment and merchandise and newsmen and foreign officials. "All of the many, many requirements there took a lot of drive, ingenuity, and a lot of courage."

Next came an even more emphatic endorsement from the man calculated to know Kuntze's official performance best, his immediate Naval superior, Rear Admiral Jack P. Monroe, Commander of the U.S. Naval Forces, Philippines.

"The Headquarters Support Activity, I will say, probably had one of the most complex jobs that I have ever been connected with, and General Crowley, I am sure, must have explained to you the wide variety of responsibilities that they had with the rapidly escalating war, the rapidly escalating personnel that they had to support. With all this environment and the fact that Captain Kuntze had to have intimate and detailed knowledge of this very complex situation at all times, you would expect that there would be certain problems arising, which certainly did, particularly when he was dealing with two or three services at a time. But I think, of every command that I have ever had in my entire forty-four years in the Navy, I have never been more proud of a job that has been done by any of them than I was of the Headquarters Support Activity, Saigon. They did a magnificent job in an outstanding manner."

"Admiral Monroe, if you had command again would you have any qualms about having Captain Kuntze assigned to your staff or to any job under your command?"

"I would be very happy to have Captain Kuntze under my command."

The Admiral turned and looked fully at the officers on the board.

"For the benefit of the court, I would like to say that when I first heard of this investigation being called I simply couldn't believe it. It is one of the most unbelievable things that I have ever heard of—this brilliant officer who has done this outstanding job. I just couldn't believe that these circumstances could occur. I had looked forward to Captain Kuntze going far in the Navy and certainly attaining flag rank and I certainly liked having him serve under me and I still would at any time."

"No further questions."

With the Admiral's words still ringing in the court, the defense rested.

Prosecutor Ross began his closing remarks.

"We heard a lot about the magnificent job of the accused there as the Commanding Officer of HEDSUPPACT, Saigon, and that is not disputed by the government. We heard Admiral Monroe yesterday express his disbelief at this turn of events and, of course, it is hard to believe that this officer would do the things that we have charged him with doing. But . . . nevertheless he did them.

"An examination by the court of . . . his testimony before the board of investigation last spring, is going to show the court that he did very, very many incredible things. Why did he do these things? That's what the court is going to have to consider. That's one of the questions.

"And another question you will have to ultimately come to grips with is this: is this accused, because of his position as a commanding officer of a very large command—the largest shore command in the Navy—is he above the law? Because, essentially, that's what his defense is . . . that he made the law for himself. You have to decide that—whether he's above it."

The prosecutor went through the outline of the evidence he had produced: numerous trips by Kuntze and subordinates to obtain cloth illegally, and numerous times he had transferred piasters into U.S. Treasury checks, claiming it was official business when it was not.

As to the charge of perjury, "the government submits that there is more than ample corroboration in this case. One very large piece of evidence that you have on the table before you is a check. Oh, that check. What a mistake that was, gentlemen, for the accused to bring that forward. . . . A loan? Ridioulous.

"You have to decide whether last Thursday when this man Parks was sitting here on this witness stand, did he commit deliberate, willful perjury, or last May when Captain Kuntze sat in a similar chair, did *he* commit deliberate, willful perjury? . . . hard as that decision is to make concerning a fellow officer, a fellow senior officer, the government has to ask you to perform your duties and make that decision, unpleasant as it is."

Finally, gingerly, the prosecutor moved to the question of the girl who haunted the case, Jannie Suen. "Gentlemen, like it or not, we have to talk about the final category of offenses charged against the accused. We have to talk about Miss Suen residing in the Captain's quarters; we have to talk about allowing her to use the official vehicle; and we have to talk about the ID card.

"I don't know what an official hostess is, but I know that

this accused did not have an employee named Jannie Suen, and I know that there was nothing official about his relationship with her, and I am confident that the court will so find.

"So, gentlemen, I think we come to a complete circle. . . . Look at the whole picture; the picture of importation; the picture of exchange for cash; the picture of falsely testifying; and finally the motive for all of this, the woman. What a pity, gentlemen. It is a crying shame that an officer that we had expected so much from could have done this for a woman."

The case was drawing to an end. The evidence, as presented by the prosecution, was indisputable that Kuntze had engaged in illegal currency transactions, most of them for a woman. But Captain Flynn, snowy-haired and serene, began his summation confidentally. He started out softly and informally, taking the court into his confidence.

"I was in Great Lakes in September when I got the call in this case. I received a phone call and was asked if I could take it. I guess I was one of the few people in the world that morning who hadn't heard of Captain Kuntze. I had never heard of him and I didn't know him. So I asked who the trial counsel was. I always like to know who's the trial counsel as he is the fellow who always gives me trouble in the courtroom. Well, they said it was Captain Joe Ross and, of course, that was most discouraging. And all I can say today is thank God that Captain Joe Ross' case isn't as good as his argument."

A few moments later the President of the Court suddenly interrupted: "Mr. Law Officer . . . do you feel there would be any objection to Captain Flynn sitting down?"

The Law Officer replied: "Not if he so desires."

Flynn smiled. "Thank you, Mr. President and Mr. Law Officer. I'm not much of a talker on my feet, but I am worse on my . . . ."

The officers on the board laughed. Flynn had them entranced. And he got right to the point: the testimony of Parks.

"The first thing that interested me in this case, gentlemen, was the statement of Parks. . . . One of the pleasures, I think, we have all had in the Navy is observing the sailor-men. I always call him a sailor; that is what he comes into the Navy to be and that is what he likes to be called. But he lives in a world in his own group all by themselves. We may observe it, but we can't get in.

"He is an interesting, colorful figure. He is popular the world over because of it. . . . These men have certain codes, they are unwritten but they are strong and they are old. One of their codes is that they will only talk about their commanding officers in two ways; they either say he is wonderful and a good, kind man—or they will tell how tough he is . . . but on personal matters regarding the commanding officer, an outsider learns nothing. . . . As a defense counsel, I have never yet gotten anything from an enlisted man on his commanding officer.

"Now let's come back to Parks. I'm not here to abuse Parks. I would never abuse an enlisted man at any time and above all places, not in a public courtroom.

"But I think you will recall his testimony when he said the ONI approached him in Oslo, Norway, and charged him with blackmarketing. . . . He said that he was upset and worried.

"Now why would that agent go to Oslo, Norway, and why would he charge Parks with blackmarketing? Nobody was interested in Parks' blackmarketing. The reason was to put Parks on the defensive . . . and give him a road to follow down that would release Parks from the predicament that he thought he was in."

Flynn was also angry at the length of the "pleadings"— the charges and specifications against Kuntze.

"Look at this one on Jannie Suen. It says, 'did wrongfully and dishonorably permit Jannie Suen, an unmarried Chinese female'—Now, what in God's world has 'Chinese female' got to do with that offense? If it was an Australian, would that make any difference? . . . No, but this is put in there as it has an aroma of mystery about it and adds spice to the case and makes it a little worse. . . . And then it says that she is about twenty-six years old. I wonder if she was thirty-six if, whoever drew up this epistle, he would have put it in. Well, I thought about it. If she was forty-six, would they have put it in? Well, I

doubt if they would have. . . . It doesn't make any difference
whether she is Chinese, or whether she is twenty-six years
old, but you know how this gives the case a little twist. It is a
little meanness that we hadn't ought to be using in these old
Navy courts. . . .

"Now, up until the time that General Crowley testified in
here, I had the impression that . . . Headquarters Support
Activity, Saigon consisted of the Captain's vehicle, his
quarters, a couple of C-47s and a little compound. I think
we've got a different picture now of what that . . . Activity
was doing—what it was—what the Captain's job was, and
how he carried it out. Here I stand in this courtroom,
pleading for him. I couldn't command a base; I couldn't
command a ship; I couldn't act as a gunnery officer—I doubt
if I could stand a watch. Yet here we are, trying to make out
in this case that he came into this investigation out there in
Saigon and tried to lie to that commission on a $600 check,
or $700 or whatever it was. . . . My God, he could have sold a
truck and settled it that way!"

Flynn discussed the character witnesses he had placed on
the stand, and what good character meant. "Now, good
character gets a premium the world over among all men. . . .
It takes a long time to acquire good character. It is the
aggregate, or happening—the doing, the doing, the doing
upon doing, throughout the years, whether it's paying our
bills, whether it's being neat; whether it's doing this or
that—it takes a long time to attain. . . . Habit is the
strongest force known to man. Captain Kuntze, of course,
has his habits just like all of us. He has driven me crazy day
after day; when we come down to this courtroom I'm nervous
. . . we're wondering what Captain Ross has for us in the next
session, and just about five minutes to the hour—whatever
time the court may meet, we have to go through a ritual.
Captain Kuntze gets out that cussed clothes brush and we've
all got to get brushed. That's habit. The other night we had
an appointment with him to talk over something important at
10 o'clock. He wasn't there. Where was he? Over in Alameda
at the Alameda County Jail bailing out one of his rambunc-
tious young sailors who went over there and got into trouble

and called him up. Habit—habit of twenty-four years. We've got a pea coat out there in our office. I don't know who it belongs to—one of these young fellows, I suppose, that left here—and that's been a great concern to the Captain. He's been on the telephone trying to find out who that pea coat belongs to. My God, frankly, I couldn't care less and I'm glad it wasn't something else. But, that is the force of habit. That is why we brought in the character evidence."

As to Kuntze's damaging testimony at the Board of Investigation, Flynn said that the Captain naively had gone into the session with the Board without adequate preparation or adequate legal counsel. And here he added a word about the techniques of military justice.

"Captain Kuntze had counsel, but there's something wrong with our counsel system in this Navy. . . . If in San Francisco tonight one of the hoodlums gets into trouble, his friends all come around and get him the best counsel that they can get. . . . But in the Navy we can have the finest officer get accused and who does he get as counsel? He gets a legal officer and to him, legal officers are all the same. But the legal officer assigned to him may be a claims officer but an investigation comes, and he becomes a counsel in . . . a *criminal* proceeding.

"Now the medical officers have it better organized. You go up to the hospital and if you have a surgical problem, they don't send you to a dermatologist . . . they get a doctor who handles that type of work.

"At the Board of Investigation," said Flynn, "Captain Kuntze was sitting there testifying and he was immersed in checks and they were apparently falling all over the floor—he was knee-deep in checks. He was permitted to testify with his counsel at his side, about the Parks check and they didn't even have it in the courtroom! . . . I think it was a shame to let him testify about those things without having them in front of him."

As to Kuntze's currency transactions, Flynn implied that it was part of Kuntze's job to get along with the Vietnamese. He recalled his own days as a staff legal officer in the Philippines. "If the Chief of Police at Olongapo, Zambales, the liberty town for Subic Bay, wants a case of liquor . . . I'm going to keep that Chief of Police satisfied. . . . That's the way it works. I suppose that in doing that I violated many regulations. The further out you go in the Pacific, the thicker the layers of regulations. I never have time to look them up. I don't know—we've got a job to do; we get it done the best way we can."

So it was with Captain Kuntze, said Flynn. Most of the currency transactions which were the bulk of the case against him had been for favors to the Vietnamese. He needed to do those favors to get his job done. And now Flynn moved to the point which had been troubling him most of all.

"I am just about to close. I suppose I've talked too long already and I know there are things I forgot to say and will forget that I wished I had said. . . . But before doing this, have you ever asked yourselves, as I have, 'My God. Is this really true, this trial?' "

Flynn's voice rose for the first time.

"All this commotion from what we've heard in this courtroom. I think that you know and have felt and we all know that senior officers of the armed forces of our country have been deprecated within the last few years. We have felt the trim and firm, smug hand of authority from above. We can't do anything about it. And I have sat here day after day with divided responsibility, trying not to say anything against the government—and, as I say, when I talk about the government in this case, I'm not talking about the U.S. Navy. . . . I'm talking about that long arm in the civilian sleeve that has reached down and pushed this case into this courtroom. I don't know what good this case will do them except to make an example out of Captain Kuntze—make an example out of him by trial, and of course, it reflects on all. And he's the type of an officer, of course, who is the object of that kind of an attack. It gets a certain amount of publicity, a certain amount of color. But I'm going to ask you, gentlemen, if you had control of this case, would you send it to this courtroom on these charges? The Navy has been made to dance a jig here on Treasure Island and every other Main

Street in this United States and throughout the Pacific, but I think it ought to stop here. I ask you to call a halt to this kind of business.

"The prosecution asks you, in effect, to convict Captain Kuntze on this type of evidence, whatever it is you want to call it, that you wouldn't hang a yellow dog on, and send that record, and that man, to an unmarked military grave. On the other hand, my request to this court is to let's pick ourselves up and brush ourselves off and say, 'This has gone far enough.' We've put on the show; the fun has been had by whoever wanted it. And I will tell you, gentlemen, that there has never been a case like this in the United States Navy, and you know it and I know it, and we will never see it again."

Headlines in the newspapers the next day said: "Navy Lets Kuntze Off Easy." The court convicted Kuntze on three relatively minor charges of misconduct: permitting Jannie Suen to live with him "openly and notoriously," allowing her to use a U.S. government car, and importing 250 yards of cloth by government plane "an amount in excess of his demonstrable need."

Immediately after announcing its verdict, the court reconvened to hear defense arguments of mitigation before retiring to arrive at Kuntze's sentence. Captain Flynn had an announcement to make.

While Captain Kuntze wiped at his eyes with a hankerchief, Flynn said to a hushed court, "Captain Kuntze knows he is at the end of the road in the Navy and he will submit a request for immediate retirement if he is not dismissed and struck off the rolls. He earned his retirement at Guadalcanal, at Savo, at New Georgia, at Bougainville, and off Okinawa. He made the long trek from Guadalcanal almost to Japan. He earned it along the shores of Korea. He earned it in Vietnam."

The court retired for an hour to deliberate. When it returned it was with a sentence which amounted to almost a complete vindication: an official reprimand and loss of 100 points on the Navy's promotion list.

The puzzle of this efficient officer whose career had seemed so bright ended in a trial which hinted at many things. Newspapers had implied vast blackmarketing activities, but none of the implied charges were proved. Hundreds of millions of dollars had passed through Kuntze's office, money in such profusion that twenty-three million dollars in cash had been stored in an icebox—yet no proof was ever found that Captain had made one penny of profit.

Except for those currency transactions? And except for a beautiful Oriental girl who could have confirmed Kuntze's story but never showed up?

Epilogue

Military men have long chafed at being controlled by civilians, but it took Captain Flynn to bring into a court-martial the memorable phrase the "long arm in the civilian sleeve." The arm was to have a longer reach than he had bargained for.

Time and again in the socially tense 1960s and 1970s, the long arm would reach down to modify harsh court-martial sentences or cancel impending courts-martial. Two outstanding examples are the Pueblo incident and the San Francisco Presidio "mutiny."

When Commander Lloyd C. Bucher surrendered his ship to the North Koreans without a fight, infuriated Navy admirals dearly wanted to put him on trial and have his hide for such un-Navylike conduct. But pressure from the top, inspired in large measure by public outcry, forced them to forego their trial. Bucher was simply reassigned.

In the San Francisco Presidio "mutiny" the courts-martial actually took place, to the intense embarrassment of officials in Washington. The accused were prisoners in the Presidio stockade, protesting such grievances as primitive sanitation facilities. On October 14, 1968, they had refused an order by an officer to move from a grassy spot inside the stockade fence, and had sung "We Shall Overcome." For these acts they were rounded up by military police and taken into the main stockade building. There was no resistance, no violence. The whole affair was over in an hour. The officer designated to investigate the incident decided that what had taken place was not a mutiny. But the commanding officer overruled him and had the incident reinvestigated until he got the recommendation he wanted—that on charges of mutiny, the prisoners be tried individually. A fantastic series of sentences was handed out.

In years past these sentences might have stood. But in 1969 civilians had entered the picture. Congressmen brought pressure on the Defense Department. And the "long arm in the civilian sleeve," in this case the arm of Army Secretary Stanley Resor, reached out dramatically.

The first of the Presidio courts-martial brought in a sentence of *fifteen years* at hard labor. Ordinarily the trial record would have been reviewed by the local commanding officer, then worked its leisurely way through channels to Washington to the board of review. In this case, on Resor's orders, the trial record was flown *on the day it was completed* to Resor's office, and reviewed that same day by Judge Advocate General Kenneth Hodson who, after reviewing the ponderous trial record for all of half an hour, cut the sentence to two years. It was the first time that a court-martial had been reviewed so quickly.

One after another, the sentences handed out by the military in San Francisco were reduced in Washington until the courts in the later cases began handing out sentences of three to fifteen *months* instead of three to fifteen *years*.

As these cases show, civilians more and more were influencing military justice. And the Presidio trial showed that until the Uniform Code of Military Justice is revised to lessen the role of the commanding officer, such civilian influence will be very much needed. Dan Flynn to the contrary.

11
Levy—and the Green Berets

Prologue

In the 1960s a new phenomenon began to appear at military bases everywhere: GI dissent. Military justice had always been presumed to have authority over servicemen in uniform, and even civilian legal experts agreed that an army could not operate if every individual followed the dictates of his conscience instead of the bark of a sergeant. An order to "take the hill" might be followed by days of debate as to whether that hill was worth taking.

It took one of the most unpopular wars in American history—the war in Indochina—to break this tradition and lead the nation's military into a legal path the end of which is not yet clear. In the public mind the first great trial for dissent was that of Captain Howard Brett Levy in 1967. But even before Levy, another Army officer, Lieutenant Henry H. Howe, Jr., had sounded the first note—and had paid a high price for it.

Lieutenant Howe in 1965 had marched in a protest parade in El Paso, Texas, carrying a sign that read on one side, "End Johnson's Fascist Aggression in Vietnam," and on the other, "Let's Have More than a Choice between Petty Ignorant Fascists in 1968."

At almost the same time as the El Paso march, the first great antiwar demonstration was boiling in the streets of Washington, D.C. The immediate reaction by both President Lyndon B. Johnson and the military authorities was outrage and the wrath of the military fell upon Lieutenant Howe. He was tried under a rarely invoked article in the Code of Military Justice, Article 88:

"Any commissioned officer who uses contemptuous words against the President . . . shall be punished as a court-martial may direct."

Howe was convicted and sentenced to two years at hard labor (later reduced to one year) and a dishonorable discharge from the Army. But his conviction did not stifle antiwar dissent. In 1967 Captain Levy arrived at Fort Jackson, South Carolina. His convictions ran even deeper than did those of Lieutenant Howe. Howe, in a radio interview, had said that if ordered, he would have gone to Vietnam to fight. Even though he dissented over the war, he would have obeyed orders. Levy made no such compromise.

The court-martial of Howard Levy opened on May 10, 1967, in Fort Jackson, South Carolina, in sweltering weather. On the panel of officers were ten combat veterans, each of whom affirmed that he held no prejudice against "an officer of Jewish extraction from New York who has deep feelings about civil rights." Asked whether they were members of the John Birch Society or any "like or similar organization" they all said "No."

Mayor Boyd D. Parsons, Sr., had been wounded in Vietnam while trying to rescue two soldiers who had blundered into a minefield, and consequently wore an eye patch. He joined the others in saying he could fairly judge a man who opposed the war in Vietnam.

Perhaps sensitive to the implication that Levy was being discriminated against as a Jew, the Army had assigned a Jewish officer, Captain Richard M. Shusterman, to handle the prosecution.

Levy was tried on five charges, one of which was that he had refused to train Green Beret medics. The others were that he had uttered or written statements "to promote disloyalty and disaffection" among the troops, "intended to impair loyalty, morale, and discipline," and "to the prejudice of good order and discipline in the armed forces" and that he had acted with "conduct unbecoming to an officer."

Once the members of the court-martial had been sworn in, the Law Officer, Colonel Earl V. Brown, excused them for two days—he anticipated a series of defense motions to dismiss the charges, and he was not disappointed. The motions were made by a large, rumpled Southerner, Charles Morgan, Jr., assigned to the case by the American Civil Liberties Union.

Morgan began by arguing that the trial was a travesty and a farce and should be dropped before it began. It came about, he said, as a result of a "witch hunt to rid the post of an unorthodox thinker." The Captain's superiors were plotting to put him in prison for several years because he was, in their own words, "a pinko."

Morgan had other grievances. The press, he said, had been excluded from the pretrial hearings, an effort by the Army to cover up the trial as much as possible. And he had asked that the Commander of the Green Berets be brought to the U.S. to testify and the Army had refused.

Morgan said, "From the beginning of this case I have been shocked to discover the handicaps under which the defense is forced to operate in a military court-martial proceeding. Repeatedly, I have been denied access to witnesses and perhaps, more importantly, to the complete G-2 dossier compiled on Captain Levy which has been made available to military lawyers subject to your command but not to civilian counsel."

But Morgan aimed his heaviest fire at the very system of

military justice, claiming that it deprived *all* servicemen of the right of free speech.

The prosecution had stated that while servicemen had "freedom to think," they did not have the "absolute right to speak freely." This had brought from Morgan an impassioned argument. "Men fight only for what they believe in, for ideas and ideals, and that's what this case is all about.

"What is the clear and present danger of one little Army Captain, a dermatologist at Fort Jackson, saying the United States should not be in Vietnam? I don't say that the statements are true, but who told Levy he couldn't say so?

"This isn't the case of a mutineer or a deserter as the Army has tried to make it. It's the case of a young doctor.

"They're prosecuting a man for saying it's wrong for the United States to be in Vietnam. What's so wrong about that? U.S. Senators say that. We have sergeants going out and speaking for the use of mustard gas in Vietnam. Why can't we have a man speaking against it? I don't think you can prosecute a man for making statements like this."

The prosecution, in rebuttal, said they were not denying the Captain's freedom to speak or think, but they were denying his right to attempt to influence others in his way of thinking.

The Law Officer then denied Morgan's motions, and the trial began.

The major witness against Levy was his commanding officer, Colonel Henry F. Fancy, a thin, tall New Hampshireman. Speaking in a soft monotone, often staring down at the floor, the laconic New Englander told his story in halting answers to questions by the prosecution.

"Sir, during the beginning of October, 1966 did you have an occasion to reevaluate more intensely the training or lack of training of Special Forces aidmen assigned to the dermatology clinic for training?"

"In early October I did evaluate Special Forces aidmen training in more detail."

"What was the occasion for your reevaluation?"

"I was visited in early October by a Military Intelligence agent who asked certain questions about Captain Levy which stimulated me to look further into his dermatology training."

"What was the result of your reevaluation at that time?"

"It indicated that training was not being carried out."

"What action did you take?"

"I decided to give Captain Levy a direct order to accomplish the training. I personally administered the order to Captain Levy. . . .

"I called Captain Levy to my office and he presented himself. I asked him to sit down and I told him that I had the mission of conducting Phase II training of Special Forces aidmen and that this training included . . . ten hours of training in basic dermatology. That he was my chief and only dermatologist, that I expected him to carry out this training. . . . He then stated that he felt that giving such training to the Special Forces aidmen was like giving candy to babies. That he did not approve of the use to which it was put."

"Did he have any further response at that time?"

"He said that in his opinion Special Forces aidmen were thieves and liars, and that he had noticed certain missing items from his clinic. I told him that these were matters which should be reported for investigation."

"What else transpired, if anything, before Captain Levy left your office?"

"I mentioned again that I had this mission which I took seriously, namely, to train these Special Forces aidmen . . . and asked him if he understood this and he did . . . and he stood and told me that he did not feel he could ethically conduct this training because it was against his principles, or words to that effect."

"Sir, did you give this order solely to punish Captain Levy for past dereliction?"

"Absolutely not."

The prosecution had touched on a point of special interest to the defense. In the pretrial hearing Morgan had stated that the disobeyal of the training order was mere window dressing for the Army's major complaint against the doctor—his civil rights activities.

On cross-examination, he went to the point.

"When did you first discover that his file was flagged?"

"I was told by my Executive Officer when I came here that there was a continuing check on Levy . . . the reason was a continuing National Agency check."

Morgan then asked if Colonel Chester Davis had not, in discussing Levy, called Levy a "pinko."

"I don't recall."

"And at that time you became aware of the file being flagged, and the fact that he hadn't joined the Officers Club, and what else do you recall, if anything?"

"I became aware of the fact that there had been a problem after he arrived at the hospital with the Officers Club, but I wasn't aware of the details. I knew he had not become a member, as a result of that conversation. I was told that he found it difficult to comply with certain customs of the service, such as proper wear of the uniform, and trimming of hair, and such general things."

"Now you issued an order for him to train Special Forces aidmen, did you ever issue him an order not to speak about certain given subjects?"

"No. I never issued such an order."

"Never thought of it, did you?"

"Yes, I did."

"But you didn't issue it."

"No, sir."

"Now after you gave him the order, and after you discovered that he hadn't obeyed it, what did you do with respect to Dr. Levy?"

"I carried out the end-of-term critique, and found out that training had not been carried out. I consulted with the Staff Judge Advocate about this matter."

The Colonel went on to testify that, at first, he was going to handle the situation with a simple administrative reprimand, permitted under Article 15 of the Code of Military Justice. But then he got a call from G-2, the Intelligence Division. They wanted him to see Levy's intelligence dossier.

The Colonel then continued, "The personnel from G-2 brought the record to my office and I read it, and felt that it contained information which might have a bearing in the case, and I called the Judge Advocate and asked that he review it, also. . . . I then went to the JA's office and discussed the G-2 dossier with them."

"And what was your next step?"

"I felt, as a result of this review, that the dossier did contain sworn statements which added to the case, and I decided that the court-martial proceedings would be more appropriate than an Article 15 proceeding."

The Defense Counsel had claimed throughout the pretrial hearings that he was operating in the blind because he did not know exactly what was in the G-2 dossier, a dossier vital to the trial because Fancy admitted he had decided to elevate the charges against Levy after reading it.

The Army had compromised by releasing some of the dossier to Morgan, and showing the complete dossier to the military counsel assigned to Levy, Captain Charles M. Sanders, Jr.

But Morgan felt that he was still operating under an unfair restriction. He asked Fancy:

"You read the entire dossier, did you not?"

"I read it rapidly, and certain parts of it more completely."

"And that dossier contained information that Dr. Levy had been to eight meetings of a political organization—or an organization in New York—where they had some lectures?"

"It contained that type of information, and sworn statements."

The meetings Morgan was referring to were a "Militant Labor Forum," a weekly lecture series in New York sponsored by the Socialist Workers Party (Captain Levy, in an interview, had described this party as a "silly Trotskyite group") where three radical Negroes—Daniel Watts, editor of *Liberation*, the late Malcolm X, and Jesse Gray—had spoken.

Morgan's voice was ironic as he asked:

"It wasn't until February that you discovered that he *wasn't* a Communist, was it? February of this year?"

The implication was that—based on the flimsy material in the dossier—Fancy had suspected Levy of being a member of the Communist Party—much more than "a pinko." But the quiet Colonel surprised Morgan with his answer.

"I have to my knowledge not discovered *that* yet."

"I thought you said recently he got a clearance."

"I thought I had a clearance, but I have been sub-sequently told that I have not had a clearance on him."

Morgan now moved to another subject. Under the Geneva Convention, medical corpsmen must be clearly differentiated from combat personnel.

"Do you know that the Green Beret aidmen were trained in combat patrolling, contrary to the Geneva Convention?"

"My knowledge of the Geneva Convention is very slight."

"Do you concede that Dr. Levy taught medical personnel, doctors, nurses, and medical corpsmen, but would not teach only one small select category—and that was ten or so Special Forces aidmen?"

"I concede that Dr. Levy taught the others."

"You say that Dr. Levy told you teaching Green Berets was like giving candy to babies?"

"Yes, sir."

"That was a strange statement. What did you interpret that to mean?"

"I had heard that he had said that before, and had never been able to completely understand what he meant by it, but I gathered that he meant it was something dangerous that he was giving to them."

"Now you're familiar with the fact that Dr. Levy applied for a conscientious-objector status to get out of the service, are you not?"

"Yes, I am."

"And you are familiar with the fact that he was recom-mended for that by the chaplains on this base . . . and also by a psychiatrist . . . and you are the only person that recom-mended that he not be given conscientious-objector status?"

"I believe I disapproved that request."

Colonel Fancy stepped down from the stand, and was succeeded by a stubby, pleasant-faced sergeant named Debevion Landing, who had worked under Captain Levy. In a slow, Southern drawl the Sergeant said that at one time he had intended to demonstrate to the Green Berets how to give a skin sensitivity test. In this test a minute amount of penicillin is injected to determine whether the patient is allergic to the drug.

Landing said that Captain Levy had threatened to punish him if he attempted to teach the Green Berets that test. But on cross-examination, Morgan brought out another angle.

"If an unskilled Green Beret aidman administered the skin sensitivity test improperly, couldn't the results be fatal?"

"Yes, sir."

Landing then went on to testify that he had overheard the Captain denounce the Vietnam war to enlisted men:

"He told a Negro soldier that if he (the Captain) was a Negro, he wouldn't go to Vietnam."

Another of Levy's aides, Sergeant Ronald E. Novak, testified that the Captain went even farther in his denunciation of the war. He told some Green Berets that he hoped some harm would come to them when they went to Vietnam.

"Then he turned to me and said, 'They think I'm kidding, but I'm serious.' "

The officer who had succeeded Captain Levy as staff dermatologist was Captain Ivan Mauer. His testimony was to give the first hint of yet another dimension of the case: the debate among medical men as to whether they should follow their own ethical rules when in the military, or subvert them to the exigencies of warfare.

On direct examination, the prosecutor asked:

"Dr. Mauer, assume for the purpose of this question that Special Forces aidmen coming to Fort Jackson . . . would you comply with an order of your superior commander to train them in basic elements of your specialty?"

"Yes, sir."

But on cross-examination, Morgan brought out *why* the doctor would train the Green Berets.

"As far as you know, Special Forces aidmen are *medical* personnel, correct?"

"That's correct."

"But if you understood that they were primarily combat troops . . . would you train them?"

"No, I wouldn't."

To teach medicine to men who are trained to kill, Mauer

testified, would be in direct conflict with the Hippocratic
Oath and the basic philosphy of medicine: "To attempt to
heal all men regardless of partisan or sectarian activity."

The prosecution produced ten Green Berets to whom Levy
had made alleged seditious remarks. Each of them testified
that Levy had told them the Green Berets was a barbarous
outfit, and that they should refuse to go to Vietnam.

On cross-examination Morgan brought out time and again
that each of these so-called medical aidmen received much
training in light and heavy weapons. His point, vital to the
defense, was that these men were primarily combat troops,
and only secondarily medical corpsmen—and that was why
Levy refused to train them.

Richard W. Gillum, a Green Berets medic, was so anxious
to deliver his testimony he was almost breathless.

"I think the court will be interested in a remark by Dr.
Levy. He compared the Special Forces to Nazi SS Troops. He
compared President Johnson to Adolf Hitler in sending us
over to Vietnam."

On cross-examination, Gillum conceded that he had had
combat training even though he was a medic.

"Did you carry arms on patrol?"

"Yes. I wouldn't want to go out there and have Luke the
Gook shoot at me and not have something to shoot back."

Negro Private First Class Eddie Cordy bolstered the
government's contention that Levy was subverting the
morale of the troops. He testified that—after talking to
Levy—he had made two attempts to get out of the Army.

"I considered him like a friend. Everything he said made
me think."

It was during the testimony of these Green Berets that a
legal argument broke out that was to send the case
careening in a new direction—to the astonishment of the
defense. It began innocently enough when one of the Green
Berets testified that he had been trained to use the 105-mm.
howitzer. Morgan asked him: "Describe the purpose for the
record of what the 105 howitzer does."

The prosecutor objected. Angrily Morgan replied: "The
man testified that Dr. Levy told him that Special Forces were

killers of women and children. I'm trying to demonstrate
what the 105 howitzer does."

He asked for a ruling: "Is the truth or falsity of Captain
Levy's statements relevant?"

The Law Officer said that he would reserve a ruling on that
point. He would think about it overnight.

The prosecution rested its case after Sergeant Geoffrey
Hancock, Jr., a white soldier married to a Negro girl testified
that he had received a letter from Captain Levy while he was
in Okinawa. The letter said, in part:

" . . . Geoffrey, who are you fighting for? Do you know?
Have you thought about it? Your real battle is back here in
the United States, but why must I fight it for you? The same
people who suppress Negroes and poor whites here are doing
it all over again all over the world and you're helping them.
Why? . . . A dead woman is a dead woman in Alabama and
Vietnam. To destroy a child's life in Vietnam equals a
destroyed life in Harlem. For what cause? Democracy, Diem,
Trujillo, Batista, Chiang Kai Shek, Franco, Tshombe . . .
Bullshit?

"I would hasten to remind you, despite your obvious
courage and enthusiasm, Vietnam is not our country, and
you are not a Vietnamese. At least the Vietcong have that on
their side."

After this testimony, the court recessed, and prepared to
hear the defense.

May 17 was a hectic day in court. It began normally
enough with the counsel's opening statement for the
defense. It was a strong one. Morgan stated that Dr. Levy's
utterances and letters were informal, private communications, and as such were protected by the First Amendment.

On the charge of disobeying an order, he would show that
the order was "unlawful" and that Dr. Levy could not obey
such an order as a medical man sworn to uphold the Hippocratic Oath.

"But someone in Special Forces decided to get Levy and
thus initiated the court action," said Morgan.

Various character witnesses took the stand to testify that
Levy was a loyal American. But the highpoint of the morning

was the appearance of dignified, bespectacled, sixty-year-old Seymour Levy, the father of the defendant.

Mr. Levy came to the witness stand clutching a small American flag, a Bible, and a framed copy of the Gettysburg Address. These items had been in his son's bedroom ever since he was a child, Mr. Levy testified. 'He was always surrounded by things of a patriotic or Jewish nature.

"The Gettysburg Address hung fifteen years in the foyer, a literal loyalty nook, so to speak, where there was also a picture of the White House which I received from our then Congressman."

Mr. Levy added, "I brought him up as a loyal Jewish American. He always was a loyal Jewish American. And he is now."

"Why do you say that?"

"I know my son. Perhaps he is stubborn in his convictions. But he follows his convictions and he has the guts to do it. I wish I had."

"Do you share his opposition to the Vietnam war?"

"Yes, sir."

"Do you feel the opponents of the war have the right to express their opinion?"

"I feel this country is in sad shape if I couldn't express my opinion."

Mr. Levy told of his son's earlier more conservative political convictions. During his residency at Bellevue Hospital, "he came in contact with the unfortunate downtrodden Puerto Rican and colored people. He felt they were victims of constant discrimination and deprivation, and that the circumstances in which they lived were completely un-American.

"I agreed these things existed and that not much was being done about it. I tried to be philosophical, telling him people don't like change and prefer the status quo."

The generation gap of the 1960s became visible when the elder Levy concluded: "When he argued against that attitude, I told him I was old and tired and didn't want any more challenges."

Mr. Levy's testimony left the audience moved—the

defense was building its case smoothly—when disaster struck. In an out-of-court hearing the Law Officer announced he was about to give his ruling on the defense counsel's question of the day before: whether the truth or falsity of Levy's statements about the Green Berets was relevant.

As the two lawyers huddled near his desk, the Law Officer began to explain his reasoning. What soon became apparent to both lawyers was that the judge had gone far deeper into the question than they had anticipated.

"The subjective belief of a person in the military that a command is illegal or improper is no defense to a charge of disobedience to an order. If an individual in the military is accorded the right to determine whether any particular order offends his own ethical and philosophical standards, then the Army would soon become a debating society rather than an effective fighting force. An honestly held subjective belief of the illegality of an order may be received, however, in extenuation of the offense of unlawful disobedience.

"My research on the Nuremberg trials . . . has evolved a rule that a soldier may disobey an order demanding that he commit war crimes or genocide or something of that nature."

Morgan then added: "How far back are you required to go to determine within your own conscience whether or not your own talents are being used to perpetrate war crimes?"

"I think there comes a time," replied the Law Officer, "where your training itself should not be given over to that purpose. In other words, if there is an objectively true directive that these aidmen were to be trained to commit *war crimes*, then I think a doctor would be morally bound to *refuse* to give his aid and comfort and training to those individuals."

With these quiet words, American jurisprudence entered a new era. For the first time in a court, the Nuremberg principles would be accepted as a standard. To Morgan, it was a bombshell which was exploding spontaneously in the middle of a trial in which he had never expected it to be considered. He was asked to furnish in a few days witnesses and evidence not only of random atrocities committed by the

Green Berets, but to prove that a pattern of such atrocities existed as part of the policy or practice of the Special Forces.

But the defense was to have yet another surprise. The next day offers to testify began pouring in from all over the nation. Morgan realized that the situation was beginning to get completely out of hand. He issued a statement:

"Captain Levy never accused this nation of war crimes, crimes against humanity, or genocide. He made certain statements referrable to Special Forces.

"Captain Levy is a loyal American. As such, he made no blanket condemnation of overall policies of the United States.

"We intend not to offer evidence which generally castigates the United States policy or relates to the legal question of wars of aggression.

"Whatever testimony will be offered in court tomorrow will relate to land warfare in South Vietnam and to the role of Special Forces in that."

Morgan was given a recess of six days in which to find his witnesses, and discover what proof he could to support the allegation of war crimes.

On May 23, the court reconvened. The first order of business was an out-of-court hearing, which was to become known in legal circles as the "Little Nuremberg Trial." The first witness was a surprise: Robin Moore, author of the best-selling book *Green Berets*, and considered the leading promoter of that force's legend, came to testify about the men he had celebrated.

"With respect to Special Forces aidmen, are they combat troops?"

"Yes, everyone I met was."

"Now, regarding prisoners, do you take prisoners in guerilla warfare?"

"Well, it depends. Sometimes you do—it depends on the exigencies of the situation. The VC, they kill everybody they get their hands on, Vietnamese and Americans alike. I have seen both happen.

"Do we sometimes destroy villages?"

"When necessary, yes."

"What is an assassination team?"

"Well, it's a team trained to hit targets, a target being the term generally used for an individual to be assassinated for political reasons, or whatever."

"Special Forces train them, don't they?"

"I know of an instance where Special Forces are giving this advice. Thank God they are, because the Vietnamese do a pretty botched-up job of it, left to their own devices. It is a necessity of winning a war."

Moore denied any knowledge of brutality by the Special Forces. If there was any brutality, any crimes against humanity, they were committed by the South Vietnamese, Moore testified. But Moore did admit to one fact: the mutilation of enemy dead. The Green Berets, he testified, paid a $10 bounty for ears clipped off the heads of slain Vietcong. This money was reputed to be supplied by the Central Intelligence Agency. A Vietnamese chief had told the Americans that the Montagnards, the mountain tribes of Vietnam, were exaggerating their claims of enemy dead. The bounty system required each Montagnard to bring in the right ear of a victim in order to claim his money.

Donald Duncan, formerly a master sergeant in the Green Berets, testified that he had once been in charge of four Vietcong prisoners, and had got a radio message "to get rid of them."

"The order meant shoot 'em or stick a knife into 'em."

Duncan had delivered the prisoners to the American camp unharmed and an American major had berated him. "You know, we almost told you over the phone to do them in."

Duncan told the major that he couldn't kill anyone with his hands bound, helpless, and the major replied: "You wouldn't have had to do it. All you had to do was turn them over to the Vietnamese."

The third and final witness in the "Little Nuremberg Trial" was a psychiatrist, Peter G. Bourne. He testified of acts of brutality by the South Vietnamese which he had seen. His commanding officer had ordered him not to file a report on it. "Don't rock the boat."

In sum, the testimony of the three witnesses added up to one conclusion: there had been brutality in the Vietnam war, but it was committed by the Vietnamese. In the words of Robin Moore, "Brutality is a way of life over there."

The "Little Nuremberg Trial" was over, but it would have reverberations in the years to come. Colonel Brown's ruling that a soldier has a duty to disobey orders to commit war crimes or atrocities would become an issue in the courts-martial surrounding the Mylai massacre charges. But in this case, even the defense was relieved. The intrusion of an unexpected and unwanted issue was over, and the trial could resume its course. Morgan was anxious to get back as quickly as possible to his main contention—that the Captain's adherence to the Hippocratic Oath and his own professional ethics forbade his obeying the orders to train the Green Berets.

To the stand came four of the most august medical men in this country. Foremost among them was the world-famous pediatrician—and widely-publicized opponent of the war in Indochina—Dr. Benjamin M. Spock, later to be tried—and acquitted—for his own views.

"Would you be willing to train medical personnel to serve in Vietnam if you understood they were to be used first as combat soldiers, and secondarily as medics, and if you understood that the medical personnel were subject to orders of the team commander on whether to treat or abandon patients."

"It would raise grave ethical questions. I could easily decide it was not ethically in accordance with my medical beliefs."

Dr. Spock went on to testify that his own opposition to the Vietnam war would have no bearing on his decision; it would be based solely on medical ethics.

Harvard Professor Jean Mayer was even more emphatic. He would have no part in the training of combat aidmen. He felt that aidmen were under the supervision of a political power, rather than a medical doctor. He admitted that sometimes in warfare the caring for the sick might have to be accomplished by paramedical personnel; but it should only be done under the supervision of a qualified doctor. "The key word is supervision; no aidman should perform a medical act without it.

"There is damage to the image of medicine when done by other than those in the healing art," Mayer testified.

Dr. Victor W. Sidel, a professor of preventive medicine, also from Harvard, added his opinion that the "blurring of the distinction between the medic and the combat soldier is worrisome." He was also worried that the practice of bad medicine in an undeveloped country might lead to "long-term damage."

Dr. Louis asagna of Johns Hopkins University said that the whole idea was a distortion of ethics. The Geneva Convention stated clearly, he emphasized, that soldiers and medics must be differentiated.

Evidence of possible pressure outside the courtroom was brought in by the testimony of Captain Ernest Preston Porter, an eye specialist on the base. He said he would plead the Fifth Amendment if he were asked whether he would be willing to instruct the Green Berets in anything beyond basic first-aid treatment. He told the court that he had been intimidated by the news of what had happened to another doctor who had testified at the trial, Captain Ivan Mauer, who had said he would refuse to teach medicine to men who were trained to kill. As a result of this testimony, Porter testified, Mauer was on his way to Vietnam.

"This is the kind of news that makes one hesitate," said Porter.

The Law Officer wanted to hear more about this veiled charge. "Why were you hesitant to come forward? Didn't you think the truth would help us all?"

"Yes, but I might end up the goat," replied Porter, nervously. Captain Porter went on to give a revealing glimpse into the problems of teaching combat soldiers to be medical men.

He said that many of the Green Berets were high-school dropouts, so lacking in intelligence that it was obvious they could never acquire the medical judgment necessary for the treatment of eye diseases. They had too little education to permit their handling of delicate optical equipment.

After the announcement of Levy's impending court-martial had been published, Porter had been ordered to instruct the aidmen in the various eye diseases: conjunctivitis, blepharitis, cataract, and glaucoma.

Porter said that the aidmen could never be able to make an adequate diagnosis of an eye disease, based on a few hours of training at an Army camp. But the cautious Porter, aware of Dr. Mauer's sudden transfer, was careful to say in his final words: "I haven't said I wouldn't teach *first aid.* I have no objection to training anyone in first aid."

Morgan had brought distinguished medical authorities to the stand to support Levy's defense of medical ethics—and had even shown, in the case of Porter, that Army doctors can be pressured into not adhering to their medical ethics. Now he brought some witnesses to contend the Army's charge that Levy's words had promoted disloyalty and disaffection.

Morgan had complained repeatedly during the trial that the key words in the charge "disloyal and disaffection" were legally incomprehensible. That they were, at least, confusing was illustrated in one of the dialogues with a defense witness:

"He (Levy) never made you disloyal, did he?"

"No."

"He never made you disaffect, did he?"

"What does disaffect mean?"

"I don't know." (Much laughter in the court.)

The Law Officer interjected, "Mr. Morgan, if you don't know the questions, don't ask 'em."

"I don't know the meaning of the word disaffection."

"Well, don't use it in questions then."

"May I have instructions from the court as to the meaning of the word?"

"You should have asked for it before you asked the question."

"I asked you for it the other day."

"It's not a proper legal proceeding to put questions and then come back with a quick retort that you don't know the meaning of the words you asked in the question."

"Colonel, I'm trying to get from you . . . the legal definition of disaffection."

"I told you I'd give a legal definition at the end of the trial."

"If I don't know the definition, I don't know how to proceed."

But nonetheless he did proceed. Captain David J. Travis, a Negro based in Vietnam as an assistant operations officer in the First Infantry, said that he disagreed with Dr. Levy on Vietnam. Yet he remained a good friend of his. He had heard Levy's opinions about the Vietnam war, but it was possible to disagree on politics, and still remain friends. Travis said that he knew no one who had been made disloyal by Captain Levy.

The letter to Sergeant Hancock in Vietnam, which had been cited in the charges against Levy, was explained by another witness, William J. Treanor of Pelham, New York. Treanor was a student at the Foreign Service School at Georgetown University. He said that it was he, himself, who had instigated the letter from Captain Levy to the Sergeant.

But the most impressive witness in regard to free speech was the Jewish chaplain of the base, Rabbi Joseph H. Feinstein. "Dr. Levy," the Rabbi said, "is a man of conscience who is anything but disloyal to his country."

Rabbi Feinstein told the court that Levy was a "sincere" man who had given many reasons for refusing to teach the Green Berets, among them his doubt that the aidmen were sophisticated enough to use the medical knowledge.

"Now regarding discussion and debate, did Dr. Levy discuss that with you at that time?"

"Discuss what?"

"Free speech."

"Well, this is something that he and I have spoken about in the sense that he was exercising his right of free speech, and there were people that were not happy about it."

This brought an objection from the prosecutor and a ruling by the Law Officer: "We are not concerned with this witness' beliefs and ideas."

Morgan retorted: "The First Amendment of the Constitution, of course, provides for free speech, and one of the substantial questions here is—is a man that is dedicated to that principle, and who exercises that right, not a good American simply because he does."

But the Law Officer ruled: "We don't want the witness to decide how far the First Amendment goes. He is not an expert on Constitutional law, I'm sure."

Morgan shrugged, and turned to the witness: "Have you ever known of any enlisted man or any other officer or anyone else to your knowledge that became disloyal because of Dr. Levy and his statements?"

"No."

"How about anyone who became *disaffectionate?*"

"No."

The defense rested, and the opposing lawyers prepared to deliver their summations to the court.

This first trial in the antiwar courts-martial of the late 1960s was coming to a climax. It was a case of so many conflicting currents that the issues tended to blur. Among the swiftly-running currents were: medical ethics, anti-Semitism, Nuremberg principles, and, perhaps most importantly, the right to free speech of a military man.

Defense counsel Morgan stood up, rumpled—and now more discomfited than ever. The air-conditioning in the little clapboard building had broken down. But as perspiration beaded his forehead, Morgan attacked all four issues with vigor and enthusiasm.

Had Dr. Levy subverted any soldiers at all? Ridiculous! "If he's a subversive, he's a pretty ineffective subversive," he said. "Trying to make Levy look sinister is about as rational as selling snow cones in the Supreme Court of the United States."

Morgan pointed out that Levy had been in contact with 12,500 patients on the Army base. The Army had only been able to produce thirteen men to whom Levy was alleged to have made disloyal remarks. "Thirteen witnesses produced out of 12,500 is pretty ludicrous for a pattern of subversion."

Morgan went on to suggest a different motive for the current court-martial: prejudice on two levels . . . against a

Jewish officer out of anti-Semitic feelings, and against an individualist who refused to join the Officers Club, and didn't like to salute.

In support of this reasoning, Morgan reminded the court of Colonel Fancy's testimony. The Colonel had said that he at first was going to handle Levy's case with a simple administrative reprimand. But then someone in the Army decided to try Captain Levy as a subversive, purely on the basis of words, political beliefs, and opinions. And the case had snowballed into a major trial, becoming a landmark case in military justice.

Levy had never denied that he disobeyed the order to train Green Berets, but the order itself was illegal, Morgan said. It was illegal because it was issued solely for punishment. Fancy knew perfectly well that the Captain would disobey it because of his medical ethics, as any doctor should.

Looking over at the defendant, a slim man with a wispy mustache, Morgan reminded the court of a similar case in history: the Dreyfus case.

Captain Alfred Dreyfus had been falsely accused of spying by anti-Semitic fellow officers in the French Army and sentenced to Devil's Island. When the frame-up was exposed the confidence of the people in the entire military establishment was shaken. Two governments fell as a result of the case, Morgan reminded the court.

And then Morgan looked to the future. He said that a guilty verdict for Captain Levy would bestow martyrdom and perhaps make the Army dermatologist the focus for a new peace movement. "Sometimes," he said, "martyrs are made by inadvertence, and around them develop movements that shake the world."

Ten combat officers on the panel stirred uncomfortably as the defense counsel finished his speech. They were more happy to get back to reality, military orders and disobedience, in the closing words of the prosecution. Captain Levy, said Shusterman, had willfully and defiantly disobeyed a lawful order to train Green Beret medical aidmen.

In addition, he had tried to "crush the spirit" of enlisted

men with violent criticism of the Vietnam war. His remarks were "a calculated effort to undermine morale."

"The Government holds he is guilty of all charges and specifications."

The panel of officers retired for six hours of deliberation. At 7:55 P.M. on June 2, 1967, they filed back into the court. Law Officer Brown ordered Captain Levy to approach the court.

The Captain, usually cocky and self-assured, was now tense and pallid. Colonel Basking, the President of the Court, read off the five charges and said, "We find you guilty" under each charge. The court, however, had lightened two of the charges finding Captain Levy guilty of "culpable negligence" instead of "intent to impair and interfere with the performance of duty of a member of the armed forces."

In the courtroom his mother, Mrs. Sadie Levy, said bitterly to a reporter, "Don't console me, it wasn't anything we didn't expect."

The next day, Levy stood for sentencing. The maximum penalty was eleven years. Levy was sentenced to three years, and dismissed from the service.

The Levy case was over but, as Morgan had predicted, the Army had created a martyr—and spawned a revolution.

Epilogue

Levy went to prison. A few months later, Air Force Captain Dale Noyd was convicted of refusing to train airmen who were bound for Vietnam and he, too, went to prison. But the dissent they symbolized refused to disappear. On the contrary, it began mushrooming. Underground newspapers flourished on military bases. Just outside the bases coffee-houses sprang up, where soldiers met to exchange information and advice on desertion routes to Canada and other countries, on ways to harass the services, and on methods of expressing their dissent in sober or spectacular fashion.

One culmination came in 1968, at Fort Ord, California.

Two young privates, Ken Stolte and Daniel Amick, distributed a pamphlet which read, in part:

"WE PROTEST

"We protest the war in Vietnam. We know the war will never bring peace. . . . If you want to fight for peace, stop killing people. . . . The Communist paranoia that we possess does not justify what we are doing to the country of Vietnam and its people. . . ."

At the inevitable court-martial their defense counsel, Francis Heisler, a civilian attorney assigned to the case by the American Civil Liberties Union, summed up the mental conflict that young men must face when called upon to fight a war with which they disagreed:

"You will hear from the prosecution, of course, that such an important right as freedom of speech cannot cover, as it was said by Justice Holmes, the right to shout 'fire!' in a crowded theater. Justice Holmes . . . made a mistake because he did not put in his opinion anything about what happens when there *is* a fire in the theater. Does one have the right to keep quiet about it? . . . There comes a time when silence becomes a crime. Silence in the position of these accused would have been a crime against the nation, against the enemy, and against themselves.

"The fact is that these young people . . . are telling us—sometimes using the wrong methods—that what you older people did to us is not in line with the destiny of mankind. They are rejecting our standards. They are rejecting our false thinkings, and they say, we are going to start over again and we are going back to the concepts which were so gloriously expressed . . . when Sam Adams, and Jefferson, and Madison wrote that leaflet for which *they* were called disloyal by the British Empire.

"Stolte and Amick may have been the loyal ones, and those who are not standing up are the disloyal ones."

The court listened to Mr. Heisler and then sentenced the accused to three years at hard labor. But nonetheless the message was beginning to come through. On September 12, 1969, the Pentagon issued new guidelines for its commanding officers instructing them how to handle dissent among their troops, and requiring them "to impose only such minimum restraints as are necessary to enable the Army to perform its mission."

Under the new guidelines a commander could not prevent the distribution of a publication simply because he did not like its contents, could not prevent his men from going to a coffeehouse or joining a "servicemen's union."

The new guidelines further warned that "severe disciplinary action in response to a relatively insignificant manifestation of dissent can have a counter-productive effect on other members of the command" and concluded, "It is important to recognize that the question of soldier dissent is linked with the constitutional right of free speech."

The impact of the Levy case on freedom to dissent may in the long run, however, become secondary to its reverberation in another legal dimension. For the first time in a Federal court the Nuremberg principles had been invoked.

It is a precedent that is gaining momentum. It began when one noncommissioned officer and six officers of the same Green Berets that Levy had denounced were arrested on a charge of the murder of a Vietnamese national. The case was dropped at the insistence of the Central Intelligence Agency, fearing that their secret files might be forced open in a trial. Had this occurred before Levy's trial he might have won acquittal then and there.

In 1970 the issue exploded again. This time it began in a tiny Vietnamese village named Mylai.

12

Operation Mylai

Prologue

For almost a thousand years men have tried to control the excesses of war, not only for the purposes of knightly chivalry, but for practical reasons: Indiscriminate killings demoralize your own army, turn friendly civilians into enemy partisans, and endanger captured soldiers.

Many people think that the laws of war began with Nuremberg, and it is true that the proceedings at Nuremberg solidified in spectacular fashion many of the laws of the past. But, in fact, in this country the laws of war were first codified in 1863—and were used against, among others, Confederate Captain Henry Wirz, who was hanged in 1865 for his treatment of Union prisoners in the Andersonville, Georgia, prison camp, where nearly 14,000 men died. And in 1902, in an incident very similar to that at Mylai, Brigadier General Jacob Hurd Smith was brought to trial and convicted of the massacre of Philippine civilians

246

during an antiguerilla campaign. (He was reprimanded by President Theodore Roosevelt and retired from the Army.)

International agreements such as the Hague and Geneva Conventions were both ratified into U.S. law by the Senate. And today the U.S. Army Field Manual 27-10 (*The Law of Land Warfare*) requires that "belligerents refrain from employing any kind or degree of violence which is not actually necessary for military purposes, and that they conduct hostilities with regard for the principles of humanity and chivalry."

The contribution of the Nuremberg Trials was the affirmation of the principle that blind obedience to orders is no defense against an accusation of war crimes. Of twenty-two defendants at Nuremberg, nineteen were convicted, although all declared they were following orders of the state —and no one doubted that a leader such as Hitler would have executed them on the spot had they disobeyed those orders.

The Tokyo war crimes trials produced a judicial precedent which went even further: Lieutenant General Tomoyuki Yamashita was convicted of responsibility for massacres committed by his soldiers in Manila, even though it was proven in court that at the time of the killings he was isolated in northern Luzon, completely out of touch with his troops, and in no position to maintain control.

When Lieutenant William Calley led his small platoon into Mylai on March 16, 1968, he, by his actions, was to explode the delayed-action bomb of the Nuremberg and Tokyo decisions in a U.S. military court, and for the first time in a major post-Nuremberg case, to force the American people to examine one of its own for a crime against humanity and decide where the guilt lay. With a young lieutenant of unprepossessing intellectual background? With his superior officers? Or, perhaps with the American people, who had supported a war which reduced its soldiers to savagery.

All these issues would unfold in a small courtroom in the zealously patriotic town of Columbus, Georgia.

March 16, 1968. The day began with nine black heli-
copters waiting in the chill dawn at Landing Zone
Dotti, home of the American Army's Task Force Barker in
South Vietnam. Their rotor blades gleamed in the sun as
Lieutenant William L. Calley, Jr., an extra belt of M-16
bullets slung over his shoulder, led the First Platoon of
Charlie Company aboard.

Charlie Company had been briefed on its mission the day
before by its commander, Captain Ernest Medina, after
funeral services for members of the company killed on a
routine patrol by booby traps. Already decimated by such
incidents, the men of the company were in a mood for
revenge.

But the men knew fear, too. For, as Medina had outlined
at the briefing, this would be their first pitched battle with
the Vietcong. One of the enemy's crack units, composed of
elements of the 48th Vietcong Battalion, was encamped in
the village complex known as Mylai. Intelligence reported
that by 7 A.M. women and children would be gone to the
nearby market in Quang Nai City. No civilians would be
left to get in the way. The orders given Medina by higher
headquarters reportedly were simple: kill the Vietcong;
destroy the village.

But because Medina's orders to his men at the briefing
were not that simple, an enduring controversy would develop over just what, in fact, he did say. One point everyone agreed on: Medina had told them to expect a real
battle, a tough fight in which men would be killed.

As Calley's men filled the helicopters, gunships already
circled over Mylai 4, one of several hamlets clustered on the
east coast of Vietnam in an area long known as a Vietcong
stronghold. Repeated attempts to "neutralize" or "pacify"
the area had failed. Minefields and booby traps still
cropped up, snipers still laid ambushes, American casualties
mounted. Now that rarest experience in Vietnam—an open
battle—seemed about to take place.

7:30 A.M. The first helicopter took off. To the west and
the north the men could hear artillery smashing into the

hamlet area. Gunships crackled automatic fire as Lieutenant Calley's helicopter landed in a rice paddy just west of the hamlet and his men rushed out, threw themselves down, and began firing into the village.

Other helicopters came in gently, the downdraft from their rotor blades flattening the brush, and more men piled out until the whole platoon was assembled. Their assignment was to enter the village from the south while the Second Platoon entered from the north. The Third Platoon was in reserve.

Overhead was a command galaxy of helicopters. The task force commander, Colonel Frank Barker, was at 1,000 feet. Major General Samuel Koster, commander of the parent Americal Division, was at 2,000 feet. Colonel Oran Henderson, commander of the Eleventh Brigade, was on top at 2,500 feet. So certain was the Army that this was to be a major battle that a photographer, Ronald Haeberle, and a reporter, Jay Roberts, were assigned to document the battle for public information. Haeberle, the Army would eventually admit, did just that in spades.

Walking in line toward Mylai 4, firing from time to time, Calley's platoon disappeared into the heavy brush and foliage surrounding the village. Some ninety minutes later Chief Warrant Officer Hugh Thompson arrived over the area in an observation helicopter to help locate the Vietcong. Instead of enemy soldiers, he saw dead women and children lying all over the village, other civilians running, and American troops cutting them down. Infuriated, Thompson radioed a report of the "wild" firing to brigade headquarters. But before the firing could be stopped, he saw the most horrifying sight of all—a ditch with bleeding corpses, and Americans firing into it.

In one of the most ironic battlefield incidents ever, Thompson landed his helicopter and rescued civilians from his own troops, taking two old men, five children, and two women to safety. When he turned, the carnage was still going on. This time he could find only one baby alive in the ditch, buried under its mother. Thompson took it away.

Thompson was later awarded the Distinguished Flying Cross for heroism. The citation credited him with rescuing fifteen children hiding in a bunker between Vietcong positions and "advancing friendly forces."

Captain Medina eventually told Lieutenant Calley to stop the shooting, and the men took a break for lunch, sprawling about in the sun among the corpses. During the whole morning, not a single enemy shot had been fired. The Vietcong had once again melted away, leaving a frustrated American force with no enemy to confront. But, this time the frustration culminated in tragedy.

Was the Mylai massacre "an aberration of the system" as General William Westmoreland was later to call it? Was it "standard operating procedure," as many Army men would later claim? Some support of the "aberration" theory may be determined by the visit two days later of Colonel Henderson to Captain Medina to tell him an investigation was under way. (Medina later told his troops, "It look like I'm going to get twenty years.") Why an investigation if these things happened every day? And why did Medina caution his troops to say nothing about the incident?

But the investigation mysteriously petered out; none of the scores of reporters in Vietnam even heard a rumor of the incident. It was not until a year and a half later that Robert Ridenhour, a former soldier who had not even been attached to Charlie Company, started the process of exposure. Rumors of the massacre had reached him in Vietnam. They had so shocked him that he had interviewed some of the participants on his return home. Now he wrote twenty-five letters to the White House and Congress. One of the two men who responded—Congressman L. Mendel Rivers, of South Carolina, Chairman of the House Armed Services Committee—swiftly called it to the attention of the Pentagon.

The Army began a secret investigation, and found that twenty-four officers and enlisted men should be tried by court-martial, either for "covering up" the incident, or participating in it. Subsequently, charges were dropped against everyone except Colonel Oran Henderson for the cover-up, and Captain Medina, Lieutenant Calley, and two enlisted men, Sergeant David Mitchell and Sergeant Charles Hutto, for the killing.

By now the press, at last, was onto the story. Pulitzer Prize-winning journalist Seymour Hersh journeyed to Fort Benning and interviewed Lieutenant Calley. The Columbia Broadcasting System managed to find Sergeant Paul Meadlo. His anguished story, told on television, brought angry Congressional demands for the punishment of the men of Charlie Company. President Nixon gave his own opinion, and as commander in chief it was not to be taken lightly by the Army. "What appears was certainly a massacre, and under no circumstances was it justified. We cannot ever condone or use atrocities against civilians."

On November 12, 1970, the eyes of the nation turned to Fort Benning where Lieutenant Calley stood to hear the charges against him: Murder with premeditation of no less than thirty Oriental human beings at a trail intersection in the south of the village; murder with premeditation of not less than seventy at a ditch on the east side of the village; and murder with premeditation of a monk and a two-year-old boy.

Captain Aubrey M. Daniel 3rd, the brilliant young prosecutor assigned by the Army, stood up to make his opening statement to support these charges.

"I want you to know Mylai 4. I want you to be there. We will try to put you there."

When Calley's platoon entered the village they found it to be undefended. "They found old men, women and children. None of them was armed. Some of them were still eating their breakfast."

In staccato style, Daniel told how one group of people were rounded up at an intersection of the two main trails that crossed through the village. Calley told Private First Class Dennis I. Conti and Sergeant Paul Meadlo: " 'Take care of these people.' So Conti and Meadlo had these people sit down on the north-south trail and started to guard them. That's what they thought they were to do."

But a few minutes later, according to the prosecutor, Calley was back, demanding " 'Why haven't you taken care of these people?' . . . 'Take care of them? We have taken

care of them.' . . . 'I mean kill 'em—waste 'em.' The people were sitting there unarmed, unresisting, sitting on the
trail. Conti stepped back. With full bursts of automatic fire,
Meadlo and Calley shot these people. Haeberle (the Army
photographer) saw people trying to run—they didn't
make it. They were shot down dead in cold blood on that
trail. Meadlo was crying he was so repulsed at what he had
to do at the direction of Lieutenant Calley."

At this point in the prosecutor's statement, Calley suddenly looked at Daniel and grinned, broadly. Daniel never
faltered. The story emerged as if in machine-gun bursts
from his lips. He told of James Dursi, Sergeants Meadlo
and Mitchell, rounding up another group of civilians. "Calley orders his men, 'Put these people in that irrigation
ditch.' And they were pushed and shoved into the ditch and
Calley ordered them executed—men, women, and children
— and they were. But James Dursi refuses. He won't. And
Meadlo cries and he fires. Conti wanders off in shock."

Helicopter pilot Hugh Thompson arrived over the ditch
and couldn't believe it. He landed and spoke to Lieutenant
Calley, but after he left, Calley went to Sergeant Mitchell
and ordered him to finish them off in the ditch. "So Mitchell
with single shots proceeds to finish off any survivors of the
initial burst of fire. Over seventy people were killed in that
ditch."

Daniel then told of an old man by a tree. "The man
began to plead for his life. Calley butt-stroked him in the
face with a rifle . . . at that point, someone yelled 'There's
a child getting away. There's a child.' A child somehow had
miraculously survived that fire into the ditch. Calley went
back and picked up the child, threw him into the ditch and
shot him—killed him."

Daniel paused, looked at Calley, then turned to the jury.
"At the conclusion of the evidence, I'm going to ask you in
the name of the United States Government and in the name
of justice to convict the accused of all charges and specifications."

Daniel's story had been so vivid that Judge Reid
Kennedy leaned toward the jury and said, "I want to

remind you that what you have just heard constitutes the government's allegations and is not to be regarded as evidence."

George Latimer, the seventy-year-old defense counsel, was on his feet. "Your Honor," he said. "You took the words right out of my mouth."

One of Daniel's first witnesses was the Army photographer, Ronald Haeberle, who by now had left the Army far behind. On a large map of Mylai 4 Haeberle showed the trail intersection where his pictures had been made. But, surprisingly, he never saw Lieutenant Calley in the village that day. What he had seen was killing:

"We were close to the village on the south side. I looked over and saw what seemed like a large group of people, fifty to seventy-five people. They were squatting. I didn't think anything of it."

"What happened next?"

"Okay, then I heard firing . . . the automatic firing was coming from one of two soldiers facing toward the people . . . some people were falling. I could see some people get up and run and they fell down. This woman, I think with a baby, stood up trying to make it with the small child in her arms. She didn't.

"There was a small child wounded in the arm and in the leg. I wanted to get a picture of him. I was looking through my viewfinder. I didn't notice that a GI next to me knelt down and he fired three bullets into him." The finished picture showed a dead boy.

Haeberle's pictures might eventually be important, but his testimony had not directly implicated Calley. And, indeed, on the way out of the courtroom Haeberle touched Calley's sleeve and whispered a word of encouragement— a sympathetic gesture on the part of a prosecution witness that was to occur time and again at this trial.

One of the major figures in the incident was First Lieutenant (formerly Chief Warrant Officer) Hugh Thompson, the helicopter pilot who had been decorated for rescuing fifteen children that day. But Thompson had come under criticism since then for allegedly false statements made to

qualify him for his decorations. Indeed, when the House
Investigating Committee had asked Thompson whether his
citation statements were true, Thompson declined to answer, claiming his constitutional right against self-
incrimination.

Now on the stand he was vague. Indeed, he never
admitted talking to or even seeing Lieutenant Calley that
day, although he had told the Congressional Committee
that he had spoken to a lieutenant at the ditch. When he
told of seeing the bodies in the ditch, his voice broke, and
he seemed near tears. "It was just a lot of bodies in there,
sir. Women, kids, babies, old men . . . 50 to 100 bodies,
sir . . . some dead, some alive, sir."

He said he put his helicopter down and spoke to an
infantry sergeant "who told me the only way he could get
them out of that ditch was with a hand grenade. I said,
'Hold your men. Wait up. I'll get 'em out.' "

Thompson's story of the rescue was affirmed by First
Lieutenant Jerry Culverhouse, who told how Thompson
had landed his helicopter and rescued civilians. Then Culverhouse had landed his own craft and helped pick them
up. "When we had them far enough from the village that
we thought they would be safe, we landed and had them
get off."

After seven days of prosecution witnesses, no one had yet
testified that Lieutenant Calley had shot anyone. Then
Daniel brought the first members of Calley's platoon to the
stand. Three of them, all civilians now, all blacks wearing
Afro hairstyles, implicated Calley in the incident. The most
damaging witness was former Specialist Fourth Class Robert Maples, who had been a machine gunner in Lieutenant
Calley's platoon. Maples testified:

"Lieutenant Calley herded the rest of the people
down into the hole. Him and Meadlo was firing into the
hole and Meadlo was crying. . . . It was women, babies, a
couple of old men."

"How do you know Meadlo was crying?"

"I saw him."

"Did you have any conversation with Lieutenant Calley at the ditch?"

"All I can remember is him asking me to use my machine gun."

"What was your response?"

"I refused."

On cross-examination Latimer brought out that Maples was "three-fourths the length of a football field" from Calley and Mitchell, and ridiculed his testimony.

"At seventy-five yards you saw tears in his eyes?"

But the witness was steadfast. "Meadlo was crying as he fired into the hole."

The next day, however, the prosecution suffered a major setback. The most important witness against Calley was Sergeant Paul Meadlo, whose nationwide television broadcast had done more than anything else to bring the incident to the country's attention. Now Meadlo was frightened. Calley was on trial. Perhaps the government could find some way of bringing *him* to trial even though he was now a civilian. Meadlo appeared in court and stunned everyone by refusing to testify, claiming his constitutional protection against self-incrimination.

Judge Kennedy was bitter. Looking down at Meadlo, he asked, mockingly, "Is this the man who granted the interview on TV? I didn't notice he had any great reticence to tell everything he knew about Mylai in great and nauseous detail on television."

When Meadlo stubbornly refused to testify, Kennedy turned him over to the local United States marshal "for whatever action he deems necessary—with my recommendation that you be prosecuted." (The legal basis for this move was certainly not clear—but in the end, it worked. Meadlo returned to the stand later in the trial.)

But meanwhile the parade of First Platoon members was bringing home the prosecution's case. Dennis Conti had been a minesweeper attached to the platoon. He told of rounding up prisoners at a trailside intersection with Sergeant Meadlo. Calley ordered them to "take care of them."

" 'We are,' we told him."

" 'No,' he said, 'I mean, kill them.' "

Conti said that he then watched Calley and Meadlo fire into the people. "They were pretty well messed up. Lots of heads were shot off and pieces of heads. Pieces of flesh flew off the sides and arms. They was all messed up. Meadlo was crying. He stuck his weapon into my hands and said, 'Here you do it.'

"I said: 'If they're going to be killed, I'm not going to do it. Let Lieutenant Calley do it.' Meadlo took back his weapon. At that time there was only a few kids standing. Lieutenant Calley killed them one by one."

Later, Conti testified, he found his commander once more, this time standing on top of a dike just east of the village with Sergeant Mitchell. They were firing their rifles downward.

"I went over to see what they were firing at. It was a ditch and there were people down in it. Calley and Mitchell were firing down on them . . . automatic bursts and single shots. As I looked down, I saw a woman try to get up and, as she tried to get up, I saw Lieutenant Calley fire and hit the side of her head and blow it off. So I left."

Charles Sledge had been a radio operator with Lieutenant Calley throughout that morning at Mylai 4. His testimony of the massacre at the trail intersection differed from previous reports. Sledge said that Calley gave the order to Meadlo to "waste them" but that he then walked off, and Meadlo shot them himself.

But Sledge helped the government's case with his testimony about events at the ditch. He said that Calley and Mitchell with their rifles outstretched were pushing people into the ditch. Then they fired into the ditch with automatic bursts. "People started falling and screaming," he added.

Sledge identified the old man whom Calley had butt-stroked as a priest because he was wearing white robes. Calley had asked the priest if any Vietcong were in the village.

"No Viet," the priest had said, and then he started begging for mercy.

"Lieutenant Calley asked him a few questions, then hit him in the mouth with the butt of his rifle. The priest fell back a little, bleeding from the mouth. He stood there, sort of pleading. Lieutenant Calley pointed his rifle point-blank, pulled the trigger and fired right into the priest's face. The priest fell. Half his head was blown away."

The next witness, Thomas Turner, startled the defense when he testified that the shooting at the ditch went on for an *hour*. Turner said that several small groups had been brought to the ditch "some screaming and crying" and told of Calley "pausing between groups of victims to insert a fresh clip in his M-16 rifle."

And once again there was an incongruous touch as Turner left the stand. He touched Calley's shoulder and said "Good luck."

The key witness, Paul Meadlo, was still missing as the government concluded its case.

On the day the defense was to begin its case, George Latimer, Calley's chief defense counsel, stood waiting for the court to be called to session. Apparently nervous, he did not sit while the jury filed into its seats. Instead he stood fiddling with the microphone, blowing into it, clearing his throat.

Then he began his opening statement. At the outset of his opening remarks for the defense, he said, his statement would be brief because "I am purposely not relating Lieutenant Calley's testimony at this time, for the very reason that his life is at stake and I prefer him to tell you first from the witness stand, rather than have it diluted by me."

Then Latimer went on to call Mylai "a death trap for American servicemen" where the young riflemen of Charlie Company really believed they would be killed, or at least lose their arms and legs to mines. Lieutenent Calley and his men, said Latimer, "were inadequately trained and instructed for this type of combat. The unit was under strength, and it was the first time some of the men were tested in an assault operation—which they were led to believe would be bitterly contested."

He pointed out that Captain Medina's briefing had come

right after a funeral for three of their comrades. "The nature
of the services was such that a feeling of revenge and
reprisal was created in the minds of all the men. . . .
The company commander stated that . . . every living thing in
that hamlet should be killed. No instructions were given on
the handling of civilians."

And then Latimer tried to implicate the Army hierarchy
in the massacre. The whole episode, he said, was observed
by higher commanders on the ground or in the air. These
higher commanders knew or could see what was transpiring
on the ground. But it was not until after *four hours* that an
order to cease fire was given. And that was given during a
lunch break.

With that, Latimer sat down. His opening statement had
taken only nine minutes. But the direction of the defense
was clear: untrained men, angry at the loss of their comrades, had been told that they must destroy every living
thing. Calley had been acting under orders. If not, why
hadn't the superior commanders on the spot stopped him
right away?

One of the first defense witnesses helped bolster the
defense's case. Chief Warrant Officer Scott Baker, a former
helicopter pilot, testified that a large group of dead Vietnamese along a trail in the southern part of the village had
been killed by fire from gunships or artillery *before* American troops reached the spot. This testimony conflicted
sharply with witnesses who had related that Meadlo and
Calley had shot the civilians. Baker further said that American troops were only about one-third through the village
when he observed the corpses.

The next witness did much to change the picture of
Mylai as an undefended area. Captain George White had
been leader of a platoon in Alpha Company, part of Task
Force Barker as was Charlie Company. White testified that
the whole area, known as "Pinkville," was a murderous
enclave before the incident. In the weeks preceding,
White's company had swept through the area—and been
decimated. Only one-third of his company was left. And
White testified that on these operations his unit had allowed

Mylai civilians to pass through their lines, only to find themselves trapped by the enemy. "When time of contact came, our back door was closed with sniper fire. We don't say these people did it, but they had something to do with it. There were times you could see bullets sweeping across the field like a gray shadow, a cloud—it was that thick."

White stood up and pointed to the map as he spoke. "I can see it like it was right today," he said, referring to an earlier battle at Pinkville. "Our machine gunner ran up to a hole and started firing his M-60 into it. A burst of fire from the hole ran up this man's leg and at about the same time a grenade or mine went off right next to him. The man didn't die, but it tore his body apart.

"The assistant machine gunner dropped his weapon. He turned into a complete vegetable. It was the first time I'd seen battle fatigue or shock. He didn't say anything. He couldn't walk or talk or move a muscle. He had to be dragged out of there."

Having established that Mylai was a hostile area, and implied that gunships and artillery might have been responsible for the dead civilians, the defense introduced its main theme: if anyone was to blame, it was Captain Medina, who had ordered Lieutenant Calley to kill the civilians.

Five witnesses (one of them with the wonderful name Steven Glimpse) came to the stand to report on Medina's briefing. Said Sergeant L. G. Bacon, "He told us to go in and kill all V.C., all V.C. suspects, all N.V.A. (North Vietnamese Army) suspects and destroy all crops and kill all animals."

Elmer G. Heywood agreed that Medina's briefing had told them that no "innocent" civilians would be found in Mylai and that the captain wanted "all living things destroyed."

"Destroy—that was the word," said Gene Oliver. "We were supposed to level the place."

Staff Sergeant Martin Fagan added: "Anyone remaining in the village—regardless, men, women or children— would be killed."

But on cross-examination, Daniel brought out that,

despite the briefing, not one of the five witnesses had killed civilians themselves. Some of them even admitted they were repelled by what they saw. Steven Glimpse, for instance, saw a youngster, already wounded in the arm and leg, killed. "I couldn't understand why this child was shot."

Heywood testified, "The reason I didn't shoot the people I picked up was I didn't have a reason to shoot."

But the witnesses did get across one important defense point, over and over again. When Captain Medina said all "innocent" people would be gone from the hamlet, they believed from their Army training and experience that women and children were included among the enemy combatants.

During the day-long testimony, two other themes emerged. One was the defense's fascination with the idea of marijuana as being the root of all the trouble. At Latimer's request, Sergeant West rattled off the names of soldiers who used marijuana, including a key government witness, Dennis Conti. When Daniel objected to the line of questioning, Latimer said he would bring forth evidence "that the troops had grandiose dreams as the result of marijuana, and their judgment was distorted."

West was permitted to continue, and he told of a night when, after smoking marijuana, he began seeing enemy movements. He called for flares "only to find it was just trees moving in the wind."

The second theme emerging this day came in the testimony of Michael Bernhardt, who gave the first hint in court of an army cover-up. Bernhardt testified that Captain Medina, a few days after the incident, told the men of Charlie Company to keep their mouths shut about the episode.

"He said if there was an investigation . . . we were not to volunteer any information."

Bernhardt, who had a reputation as a letter writer, said he had received a special warning from Captain Medina: "He took me aside personally and told me he didn't think it would be very good for me to write my congressman, or make a report to the Inspector General or anything. He didn't think it would be very good."

January 11th brought an important development for the prosecution. Paul Meadlo now was willing to testify. Judge Kennedy allowed the prosecution to bring him to the stand, interrupting the defense case. But the defense was not to be entirely displeased with the witness. Meadlo said that Medina had ordered them to search and destroy the village, "and that includes women, children, and livestock. We took it for granted that the people were Vietcong and I still believe they were Vietcong," he added, angrily.

But Meadlo did confirm the shootings at the trail intersection and the ditch. At the trail, "Calley backed off and started shooting automatic into the people, the Vietcong. He told me to help him shoot. He burned off four or five magazines [a magazine for an M-16 rifle usually contains about seventeen bullets]. I burned off a few, about three."

Later, Meadlo had gathered a group of seven or eight persons and was marching them past a drainage ditch when someone shouted to bring his prisoners to the edge of the ditch. There were about 75 to 100 civilians standing at the edge of the ditch. Calley told him, " 'We got another job to do, Meadlo.' Then he started shoving them off and shooting them in the ravine. He ordered me to help kill the people, too. I started shoving them off and shooting them."

He estimated that Calley reloaded his rifle ten to fifteen times—a total of more than 170 bullets poured into the ditch.

Defense counsel Latimer then asked, "Did you form any impression of Lieutenant Calley?"

"I thought Calley was doing his duty and doing his job."

Captain Daniel was angry at this statement, particularly since Meadlo had once proclaimed on television his horror at Mylai. Bitterly, he forced Meadlo to admit that he shot some babies in their mothers' arms.

"Were you afraid the babies might attack you?"

"Yes. Any baby might have been loaded with grenades that the mother could have throwed."

"Were they making any move to attack?"

"Not at that time, no."

"What were the mothers doing?"

"They were just squatting there."

"What were the babies doing?"

"They were in their mothers' arms."

"Is it true that you cried when you were shooting?"

"I could have. I was upset."

"Why?"

"Nobody really wants to take a human being's life."

With this answer (which brought a loud burst of laughter from an anteroom where Army personnel were recording the testimony on electronic tape) Meadlo was excused. Reluctantly or not, he had proved to be the prosecution's most damaging witness. He was the only man from Charlie Company's First Platoon who admitted killing people under Lieutenant Calley's direction—the same people who were specified in the Army's murder charge against Lieutenant Calley.

The defense resumed with a tall, dapper, mustachioed helicopter pilot, Dean Lind, who had piloted Colonel Barker during the Mylai assault. Once again the finger of accusation was pointed away from Calley and toward his superior officers—this time toward Colonel Barker, Colonel Henderson, and Major General Koster.

"From what I'd seen and heard in the helicopter made me realize he (Colonel Barker) knew what was going on."

Colonel Barker had gone back from Mylai to a conference with another officer, either Henderson or Koster, Lind could not remember whom. His impression was that Colonel Barker had said something about "noticing something wasn't right" and that he "wanted to relieve his anxieties." Lind testified that he had then taken Barker back to Mylai and landed just south of the village, but he did not know whether Barker had seen any bodies.

The defense then introduced a document which was to be a basic instrument in its contention that Calley was acting under orders: Colonel Barker's official report of the Mylai operation, filed about two weeks after the incident.

It was an action, the report said, that was "well planned,

well executed and successful." It went on to say that non-combatants had been evacuated and that the civilian wounded had been given medical aid. Specifically—and somewhat incredibly—it stated that American troops "were able to assist the civilians in leaving the area and in caring for and evacuating the wounded."

Enemy fire? The report said that American troops had encountered "two local force companies of Vietcong supported by two or three local guerilla platoons. Friendly casualties were very light, and the enemy suffered heavily."

Barker listed two Americans killed in action and eleven wounded (earlier witnesses had testified that the only American casualty at Mylai was a soldier who had shot himself in the foot to avoid taking part in the massacre). The enemy had suffered 128 dead and 11 captured, the report went on. And, as to civilians, "about 200 persons who were Vietcong supporters had created a problem of population control and medical care." These civilians, the report stated, had been caught in a cross fire between American troops and the enemy.

Only in his recommendations at the conclusion of the report did Barker hint at the actuality. He recommended that in the future there should be greater provision for caring for refugees. Medical and police teams should accompany the troops in operations likely to generate large numbers of refugees, and there should be, in addition, civilian affairs teams and psychological personnel.

Another document introduced by the defense also revealed the Army's apparent awareness of the Mylai massacre. This was a directive issued by the Americal Division, of which Charlie Company was a part, a month after the operation. The directive said that the phrase "search-and-destroy" would no longer be used because of "the emphasis placed on the word 'destroy.'" From now on operations would be termed "search and clear."

Colonel Henderson had taken command of the 11th Infantry Brigade just two days before the Mylai incident. Staff Sergeant Dennis Vasquez told of Henderson's briefing of company leaders, including Medina. Henderson wanted his men to "rush in aggressively, close with the enemy, and wipe them out for good." Then, in a chilling reminder of World War II atrocities, Henderson had said that he regarded the assault as the "final solution" to the problem of the 48th Vietcong Battalion.

The next defense witness underlined another defense theme: The state of mind of the troops that day caused by earlier losses to Vietcong mines and by bitterness at reports of Vietcong atrocities. To the stand came a crippled veteran, Robert Van Leer. Van Leer had stepped on a mine three weeks before the Mylai incident. His left leg had been amputated. Mines caused ninety-five percent of American casualties, but the troops were also stirred by rumors of atrocities, Van Leer testified. He told of a truck driver captured by the Vietcong who was "rat-trapped."

"A birdcage was put over his head, then rats were placed in the birdcage."

The next witness was Captain Kenneth Boatman, an artillery forward observer with Baker Company, which participated in the assault. Called to bolster a defense theme that the raid was a "search-and-destroy" mission in which "destroy" meant to kill every living thing, Boatman instead described how his own unit "detained" prisoners on the same morning that Calley's was massacring them. He said that his own company commander, Captain Earl Michaels (later killed in combat) "didn't condone indiscriminate shooting."

This setback to a defense case which had otherwise been proceeding without incident was a prelude to a calamity the following day. Defense counsel Latimer proposed to place three psychiatrists on the stand to testify to Lieutenant Calley's mental condition at the time of Mylai. Judge Kennedy was annoyed. He pointed out that defense attorneys had promised a year earlier that there would be no question of mental responsibility at the trial. Prosecutor Daniel said he had similar assurances a few days before.

The Judge consented to hear one witness at a hearing with the jury excused—and if Lieutenant Calley's mental responsibility were brought into question, he would adjourn the trial for a month while Calley was examined by a specially convened sanity board.

To the stand came Dr. Albert LaVerne, a senior psychiatrist at the New York University-Bellevue Medical Center in New York City. Almost immediately it became apparent that, among other things, he was a chief propagator of Latimer's theory of a marijuana-befuddled Calley. Earlier in the trial Latimer had suggested that Lieutenant Calley might have inhaled marijuana unconsciously when visiting the bunkers of soldiers who used it on the eve of Mylai . . . and that a marijuana hangover might have affected his brain. LaVerne testified that he had examined Calley for three days, and that on one occasion he had placed Calley in a smoke-filled room and introduced marijuana fumes along with the normal cigarette smoke.

"Lieutenant Calley . . . was quite upset toward the end. He felt I'd gotten him into some sort of trap. He became hostile, gesticulating with his hands. I assured him it wasn't a trap."

Daniel, in his cross-examination, asked: "He had a paranoid reaction?"

"Yes, in layman's terms."

Otherwise, LaVerne testified that Lieutenant Calley revered Captain Medina as a "father-figure" and the young officer could not disobey him. Given a Medina order, said LaVerne, Lieutenant Calley was "like an automaton, a robot."

That was enough for Judge Kennedy. He ordered the trial recessed—and Lieutenant Calley committed for observation by the sanity board. Outside the courtroom, Calley was glum. "I don't think we are trying to say I was insane so I don't like it."

One month later the board released its findings that Lieutenant Calley is "normal in every respect." Hearings resumed at Fort Benning on whether the psychiatrists' testimony could now be heard in court. Judge Kennedy ruled yes, but he also, finally, forced Latimer to give up on

his marijuana theory. As to Calley's inhaling marijuana near
his soldiers' bunkers, Kennedy remarked "there are not
many closed rooms in Vietnam."

On came three psychiatrists to say that Calley lacked the
ability to premeditate the slayings. He knew what he was
doing "in a narrow sense" when he shot at a Vietnam
civilian, but he did not "consciously understand" what was
happening. The stress of combat, plus his limited intellectual background, made it impossible for him to understand
the enormity of the killings.

Dr. LaVerne testified again to his robot theory, but when
Captain Daniel barraged him with a fusillade of questions
the eminent psychiatrist became confused. The trial
reached a point of absurdity when Dr. LaVerne asked if he
could consult the notes he had made during his interviews
with Calley. The notes he produced from his briefcase
turned out to be a mimeographed document of the Sanity
Board's findings—and no "notes" at all. Finally, LaVerne
told the Judge, "I'm under stress and fatigue." His testimony
was stricken from the record after the defense counsel
asked that he be "excused" as a witness.

All in all, the psychiatric testimony, as so often happens in
court, had left everyone more confused than before. Perhaps the one statement that everyone could agree on was
Dr. Wilbur Hannam's: "If you're going to blame someone
for war, the only person I can think to blame is God."

Latimer then announced that, at long last, Lieutenant
Calley would take the stand to tell his own story of the
happenings at Mylai 4.

At 2:10 in the afternoon of February 23, 1971,
Lieutenant William L. Calley, Jr. took the stand. He looked
smart but tense in his green uniform, and although he held
the Bronze Medal and a Purple Heart, he wore only his
modest Combat Infantryman's Badge. His defense counsel
led him gently through a narrative of his early life. It too
was modest. He had been in some trouble in the Seventh
Grade — "for cheating, basically, sir" — and had received
poor marks through military school and junior college. His
father had lost his business, his mother died of cancer,

and Calley was forced to take a series of menial jobs ranging
from dishwasher, short-order cook ("not that I know how
to cook" he said with a chuckle) to car drier in a minute car-
wash. After brief stints as a strike-breaking freight con-
ductor on a Florida railway and an insurance claims inves-
tigator, he ended up jobless in San Francisco and began
driving east with no goal in mind. His car broke down in Al-
buquerque and there he wandered into a recruiting station.

As the friendly interrogation continued Calley became
more relaxed, without losing his military bearing. He told of
his officer training and asked of Army classes on the Geneva Convention asserted "I can't remember anything of it,
sir."

Referring again to his training, Latimer asked, "If you had
a doubt about an order what were you supposed to do?"

"If you were given a mission to attack, you were to carry
it out immediately and if you had some discrepancy with an
order you would carry out the task and the mission first."

"What if you refused an order?"

"You could be court-martialed for refusing an order, and
for refusing an order in the face of the enemy, you could be
sent to death."

The defense counsel prompted him to tell of the eve of
the Mylai operation. Much of the attention of the defense
had been devoted to Captain Medina; now Calley began to
bring home in person the responsibility the defense accorded to Medina for the killings.

In the first briefing, according to Calley, "he started off
and listed how many men we had lost. Everyone was quite
surprised. I was quite surprised. We were getting low, fifty
percent down. The only way we could survive in Vietnam
was to be aggressive, we couldn't take any more casualties, and it was the people in the area who were causing
the casualties, and we should look on them as the
enemy."

Medina had shown them a map of the area. The main
target that day was Mylai 1 on the coast. But to get to it,
four other hamlets which surrounded it had to be neutral-
ized or the unit would be exposed to fire from the rear.

"Was anything said about civilians?"

"Yes, sir. There were no civilians in the area. Anybody there was enemy."

"Did you have a second briefing?"

"Yes, sir, for the platoon leaders."

"What was the substance of his remarks at that briefing?"

"He re-emphasized that under no condition should we let anyone get behind us. We leave no one standing in these areas."

"Going back to the first briefing, did anyone *ask* about civilians?"

"I believe there was a question."

"Did he respond?"

"He said he meant *everyone*."

Calley went on to add another point. Mylai was in a free-fire zone. That meant "We had political clearance to burn and destroy everything in the area. We could engage any target of opportunity."

He told of the events at Mylai, beginning with the helicopter lift-off in the morning. "H-Hour was 0730 and we were late getting off the ground. . . . Artillery preparation was still going on when we came in on the village, I could see it. . . . The gunship on the right side of our chopper opened up. The pilot of our 'copter said 'we have a hot one.' We landed, laid down a suppressive base of fire, and rushed up to the outer road. We started straight into the village. It was hard keeping everyone in formation."

"Did your troops have instructions about hooches?"

"No. Just quick neutralization as we went through. . . . Sergeant Mitchell asked me if I wanted him to check out the small part of the village to the southeast. I told him to gather his men, move on over, and check it out. The second squad leader told me there were bunkers on the north and east. I had the second squad leader check those out. Captain Medina called me and asked me what I was doing. I told him I had bunkers . . . and enemy personnel."

"Had you seen any Vietnamese dead bodies?"

"Many."

"Any live Vietnamese?"

"I saw two, sir. . . . Yes, sir, I shot and killed both of them."

"Under what circumstances?"

"There was a large concrete house, and I kind of stepped up on the porch and looked in the window. There was about six to eight individuals laying on the floor, apparently dead. And one man was going for the window. I shot him. There was another man standing in the fireplace, looked like he had just come down out of the fireplace—or out of the chimney—and I shot him, sir. He was in a bright green uniform, yes, sir, he was definitely—I took him as a NVA (North Vietnamese Army) cadre, sir."

"Did you see any other live individuals as you made your sweep?"

"Yes, sir. When I got to the eastern edge I saw a group of Vietnamese standing around. My recollection is there were GIs with them. Meanwhile, Captain Medina radioed: Get my people moving and get rid of people. I went to Sergeant Mitchell and told him to get his group of people moving."

Calley found Meadlo with a group of Vietnamese civilians. "I asked him if he knew what he was doing with those people. Get them on the other side of the ditch."

Then Medina called again.

"What was the substance of the next conversation between you and Captain Medina?"

"He asked me why I was disobeying his orders."

"All right. Was anything else said by him?"

"Well, I explained to him why—what was slowing me down, and at that time he told me to waste the Vietnamese and get my people . . . in the position they were supposed to be."

"What did you do?"

"I started over to Mitchell's location. I came back out. Meadlo was still standing there with a group of Vietnamese, and I yelled at Meadlo and asked him—I told him: if he couldn't move all those people, to get rid of them."

"Did you fire into the group of people?"

"No, sir, I did not."

And so Calley, for the first time, denied a specific charge: the murders at the trail intersection, which Sergeant Meadlo, among others, had testified to.

"What happened next?"

"I heard a considerable volume of firing to my north, and I moved up along the edge of the ditch and around a hooch and I broke out into a clearing and my men had a number of Vietnamese in the ditch and were firing, sir."

"What is your impression of how many of your men were there at the ditch?"

"Four or five, sir . . ."

"What did you do after you saw them shooting in the ditch?"

"Well, I fired into the ditch also, sir."

The words hung heavy in the court. The answer was a crucial one, and one of the jurors would later say that if he hadn't *admitted* the killings, they might have found some way to let him off.

"What did you see in the ditch?"

"Dead people, sir."

"Let me ask you, did you help anybody push people into the ditch?"

"Yes and no, sir. I came up as the last man was going into the ditch. . . . But, like I said, I gave the order to take those people through the ditch and had also told Meadlo, if he couldn't move them to waste them. It was my order."

"Now why did you give Meadlo a message or the order that if you couldn't get rid of them to waste them?"

"Because that was my order, sir. That was the order of the day, sir."

"Who gave you that order?"

"Captain Medina, sir."

"All right, now aside from what you have said about the shooting into the ditch, was there any other shooting you did in that general vicinity?"

"Yes, sir, I just saw a head moving through the rice and I fired. It turned out to be a small boy. I didn't know it at the time."

"Did you have an incident with a monk?"

"A man was brought to me for interrogation. I hit him in the mouth . . . knocked him down . . . I did not shoot him. I don't know if the blow knocked him into the ditch."

"What propelled him into the ditch?"

"Maybe somebody's foot."

"Was it yours?"

"No, sir."

"There is testimony on the record that a child ran from the ditch, and you threw him back."

"No, sir. The only child was the one I mentioned before."

Latimer once again brought up the trail intersection.

"Did you see any dead bodies at the trail?"

"No, sir, I didn't."

This flat contradiction of previous testimony led Judge Kennedy to ask: "What's the answer? That you were never down there?"

"I was never down there."

Latimer asked him whether he ever formed any specific intent to kill any Vietnamese civilian, and Calley said no. Later, Latimer drew from Lieutenant Calley his most ringing statement:

"I felt then—and I still do—that I acted as directed, I carried out my orders, and I did not feel wrong in doing so."

Lieutenant Calley's testimony had so far been impressive. In addition to his good appearance, he had managed to implicate Captain Medina as the real villain. But now Captain Daniel stepped forward to start his cross-examination and, in his soft, hammering voice, began to drill the Lieutenant with questions. Within minutes, with Lieutenant Calley shifting nervously in the witness chair, they reviewed the events when the First Platoon entered the village.

"What were your troops doing?"

"They were on line moving through the village."

"Were they firing?"

"Yes, sir."

"What were they firing at?"

"At the enemy, sir."

"At *people?*"

"At the enemy, sir."

"They weren't *human beings?*"

Pause, then reluctantly, "Yes, sir."

"They *were* human beings."

"Yes, sir."

"Did you see women?"

"I don't know, sir."

"Did you see children?"

"I wasn't discriminating."

"What do you mean you weren't discriminating?"

"I didn't discriminate between individuals in the village, sir. They were all the enemy, they were all to be destroyed, sir."

But later in his testimony Calley spoke of children rescued by a U.S. helicopter pilot and called them "definitely noncombatants." Daniel asked how he could recognize children as noncombatants at that point when previously he hadn't been discriminating.

Calley squirmed and answered, confusedly, "I had a means to discriminate and we were no longer firing—I had been given a no-fire order."

Then Lieutenant Calley admitted for the first time that Captain Medina hadn't wanted *all* civilians killed. This came when Calley testified he had intended to kill all the civilians except for the few Medina "told me to hang onto in case we hit a minefield."

"Did he elaborate or was that just understood by you?"

"Yes, just have them go ahead of us, that was understood. He didn't have to go into detail."

"How many civilians would you normally take to a minefield?"

"Never any larger than the front I was covering, sir. If I had five men on the front, I wouldn't use more than five, sir. If I had a twenty-man front I would use no more than twenty, sir."

But, Calley continued, sensing the contradiction between

killing *all* the civilians and saving some as minefield human detonators, "Captain Medina rescinded that order and told me to waste them, sir."

"Did he specifically tell you to disregard the previous order?"

"No, sir, he said those people were slowing me down, waste them, sir."

"Did you ever direct that anybody be searched?"

"No, sir. Not that day. No, sir."

"Had your platoon received any resistance in the village?"

"I don't know, sir."

"Did you inquire if they received any resistance?"

"No, sir."

"Have you ever been shot at before?"

"Yes, sir, I had."

"Did you know when you were shot at?"

"Yes, sir."

"Were you shot at that day?"

"I don't know, sir."

The cross-examination went on, but it was not all in Daniel's favor. Calley made a good witness, even under the prosecutor's relentless attack. He answered directly and quickly, and stuck to his theme: orders from above . . . the civilians were the enemy, not people . . . although, yes, they were human beings.

Interestingly it was Lieutenant Calley who confirmed the visit of helicopter pilot Thompson to the spot, and Thompson's rescuing of the civilians. What Thompson for some mysterious reason had equivocated over, Calley forthrightly admitted, although—for the first time—he equivocated, himself.

According to Lieutenant Calley, Thompson landed and came over to speak to him about rescuing the civilians.

"Did you tell him the only way you could get them out was with a hand grenade?"

"No, sir, I did not," Calley answered quickly, then stopped. "Let me retract on that statement. I believe I might have, yes, sir. I said about the only means I have to evacuate them out of there would be a hand grenade. . . . I had no means to evacuate the people. I believe I told him the only means I was supplied with were hand grenades."

But on the main details, Lieutenant Calley was steadfast. He was never at the trail intersection where civilians were killed; and as to the people in the ditch, he fired only "six to eight shots."

Finally the order came from Captain Medina to cease fire.

"Did you tell Captain Medina that you had shot the people in the ditch?"

"Yes, sir."

"Did he ask any facts about that?"

"No, sir."

Then, in another statement that was to be widely headlined, Calley added, "It wasn't any big deal, sir."

There was one more possible danger facing the defense: Captain Medina. All week long the courtroom had been filled with claims that Medina had ordered Calley to kill civilians. But Captain Medina was still not being called to testify. At this time the Army had not formally charged Captain Medina with murder in the Mylai incident. But the Captain, through his civilian attorney F. Lee Bailey, took action of his own. He filed an appeal with the highest military court, stating that he was being denied the opportunity to testify at the Calley trial and that, in fact, prosecutor Daniel had been *ordered* not to call him as a witness.

The Army's justification was that if Captain Medina were to be tried for murder, himself, he would not be a "credible" witness at another trial. But the appeal changed all that, and Captain Medina was informed that he could testify at the trial.

The following day the long-awaited confrontation took place. Into the court strode Medina, wearing the Silver Star among many other decorations on his chest. Relaxing in the witness chair with his knees crossed, turning his lined face to the jurors for most of his testimony, he was the image of an officer engaged in combat chatter with fellow veterans. He told of the horror of minefields in Vietnam.

In the weeks before Mylai his company had stumbled into such a field. It had cost three killed and sixteen wounded.

One of the casualties "was split as if somebody had taken a cleaver right up from his crotch all the way up to his chest cavity. I have never seen anything that looked so unreal in my entire life: the intestines, the liver and the stomach and the blood looked just like plastic. . . . the medic started to pick him up by the legs. I reached underneath his arms to place him under the poncho and we set him on top of *another mine!*

"The concussion blew me back. I fell backwards. As I got up the medic was starting to go to pieces on me. He was—he had blood all over him. I grabbed him as he started to pass me and I shook him and I said, 'My God, don't go to pieces on me. You are the only medic that I have got. I have got people that are hurt!' I hit him. I slapped him. I knocked him to the ground and I helped get him back up and I seen on his religious medal a piece of liver and I tried to get it off the individual before he seen it. The individual was very shook up."

With this bloody prelude, Captain Medina went on to tell of the untrained troops in his command, part of "McNamara's 100,000" referring to what many military officers felt was a below-normal standard of draftees while Robert McNamara was defense secretary. Charlie Company's training in Hawaii had not been very thorough, and its training in Vietnam wasn't much better. "The men affectionately called themselves 'Barker's Bastards.' We were illegitimate. Nobody wanted us."

A slight smile crossed Calley's face as he sat there, his left fist clenched near his mouth.

Medina's testimony moved to his briefing on the eve of the Mylai operation.

"All right. Were any questions asked of you at that briefing?"

"Yes, sir."

"Do you recall what they were?"

"Yes, sir. One of the questions that was asked me at the briefing was, do we kill women and children?"

"What was your reply?"

"My reply to that question was 'No, you do not kill women and children.' " (Medina looked straight at Calley.) "You must use common sense. If they have a weapon and are trying to engage you, then you can shoot back. But you must use common sense."

"Were any provisions made for the capture and collection of Vietnamese in that village?"

. . . "It was standard operating procedure in other operations that we had conducted that the sweep elements, when they moved through the village . . . would push any of the inhabitants to the far side of the village, collecting them in an open area."

On cross-examination Latimer drew several admissions from the captain, who candidly admitted trying to cover up the incident. He gave four reasons for this. First, what took place at Mylai "was a disgrace upon the Army uniform I am very proud to wear. Number two, I also realized the repercussions it would have against the United States of America. Number three, my family. And Number four, lastly, myself, sir."

Medina also admitted that, even though he had not told Lieutenant Calley to kill civilians, he had authorized him to "utilize prisoners to help lead his unit through the minefield." He also conceded that he had shot a Vietnamese woman, explaining that he thought she was reaching for a rifle. He denied however that he had killed a wounded little boy who came running up the trail. But he said he was so confused that he might have commanded the shooting by others.

"When the child was shot I became very emotional. I felt very bad about this and I grabbed the radio and I says: Be sure you inform all your personnel that they don't shoot innocent civilians."

Then Medina, military to the end, stepped down from the witness box, turned, gave a smart salute to a rather startled military judge, and marched past Calley's table without glancing at him.

So ended the testimony. The Judge announced that he

would be prepared to hear summations on both sides, after a weekend recess.

Daniel's summation first established that there had been a massacre at Mylai. Not less than twenty witnesses told of seeing some thirty dead at a trail intersection south of the village; another dozen witnesses remembered some seventy dead in an irrigation ditch east of Mylai.

Daniel then attacked the main defense argument: that Calley had been acting on orders from his captain, and that he had been under too much emotional stress to know the orders were illegal. "We submit to you the accused in fact received no order. . . . Even if such an order had been given, it would not constitute a defense if a reasonable man in similar circumstances would know it was illegal. . . . He put over seventy people into a ditch like a bunch of cattle—men, women, children, and babies. Is that a reasonable order?"

When it came the defense's turn, counsel Latimer rose wearily to his feet. Exhaustion was in his voice as he began his closing remarks. It was an emotional speech, and it hammered over and over again at the role in the massacre played by Captain Medina, whose testimony had so damaged the defense case.

Latimer referred to the reasons Captain Medina had given for his failure to report the deaths of civilians at Mylai and told the jury, "I am sorry, gentlemen, but those reasons seemed very hollow to me. . . . I do not believe there was an area in that village where a shot could be fired that Medina couldn't hear. Gentlemen, if you believe that story, well, you can believe that the man was not fit to be company commander. But between him and Lieutenant Calley, they are both running the last yards to a life-or-death sentence, and when the stakes are that high, somebody has got to try to escape the responsibility."

With this implication that Captain Medina was lying, Latimer continued; "Gentlemen, I don't see how you could take a group of twenty-thirty men—all good soldiers, all good men—and put them over there and have an incident like this, unless it was suggested, ordered, or commanded by someone upstairs. And I need go no further than Captain Medina."

During the investigation of Mylai, immediately after the massacre, Latimer pointed out, the "finger was pointing at Captain Medina, who himself said he would 'probably get twenty years.' And all of a sudden things changed. Who becomes the pigeon? Lieutenant Calley, the lowest officer on the totem pole in this entire business."

His voice rising to an emotional peak, the seventy-year-old attorney announced that in the course of the long trial he had come to regard the twenty-seven-year-old lieutenant as an adopted son — "and I would not adopt a murderer." He then turned to the jury and cried: "I ask that you let this boy go free."

With this emotional appeal ringing in the court, Daniel jumped to his feet. "There has been talk of the accused as a poor kid sent over there, but there hasn't been anything said for the victims. Who will speak for them? . . .Would any tribunal in this world have found one of those children guilty of any offense and then ordered his execution? . . . When the accused took the oath of a United States officer, he was not given a license to slaughter unarmed, innocent men, women, and children." To condone Calley's action, Daniel charged, is "to make us no better than our enemy, to legalize murder."

Lieutenant Calley, he said, "assumed responsibility for their deaths so now he must assume responsibility for this unlawful act." Daniel faced the jury directly. "You gentlemen are the conscience of the United States Army. You are the conscience of this country. Your duty is clear . . . to find the accused guilty as charged."

Three years to the day after American troops walked into Mylai 4 the Calley case went to the jury.

The Judge instructed the jury that they must decide these issues:

1) Did Calley actually order or participate in the killing of any civilians at Mylai?

2) If he did kill, did he act with premeditation?

3) How many people were killed?

4) The Nuremberg dicta—was he acting under orders, and if so, did he know as a reasonable man in such circumstances that such orders were illegal?

The jurors began their deliberations and the young lieutenant retreated to his apartment on the base, decorated with a U.S. flag that had flown at the Battle of the Bulge, a reindeer pelt, and a "No More War" sign. Apparently, he had retained his sense of humor. *TIME* magazine reported that he was keeping a "body count" of roaches he killed in the kitchen. And when one of his friends asked him if he had shot the reindeer whose pelt hung on the wall, Calley replied: "God, no—I wouldn't kill a reindeer."

Military juries in court-martial have often been accused of hasty deliberation, sometimes reappearing in court with a verdict in less than an hour. Such was not to be the case at this trial. Instead the jury deliberated for days, returning time and again to have whole sections of the record reread to them . . . a process which infuriated Latimer, especially as most of the testimony it wanted to hear was unfavorable to his client. "They're retrying the case," he fumed.

As the days went on, Calley became noticeably more nervous and Latimer louder in his impatience. At one point he heard that the jurors had had two cocktails one evening, and complained to Judge Kennedy that they were "wining and dining." By the time the jurors filed back into the courtroom to announce their verdict, nerves were at the cracking point. Lieutenant Calley was escorted before the jury box as the courtroom fell silent. The jury had deliberated thirteen days, a conclusion that befitted what was already the longest court-martial in the history of America. Lieutenant Calley saluted the President of the Court, stout, graying Colonel Clifford Ford, a fifty-three-year-old veteran of World War II and the Korean War, with three rows of ribbons on his chest.

In a surprisingly gentle voice, the Colonel began reading the verdict:

"Lieutenant Calley, it is my duty as President of this

Court to inform you that the court, in closed session, and upon secret written ballot, two-thirds of the members present at the time the vote was taken concurring in each finding of guilty, finds you:

"Of specification one of the charge: guilty."

Specification one referred to the trailside killings, which Calley had denied. But because the exact number of victims was not known, the jury had convicted Calley of premeditated murder of "an unknown number, no less than one."

Calley visibly sagged.

On specification two, referring to the alleged killings at the ditch, Calley was judged guilty of premeditated murder "of no less than twenty." On the additional charges of murdering the monk, he was found guilty, and of the small child, guilty of assault with intent to murder.

Calley listened to the verdict, standing stiffly, his face flushed, staring at Colonel Ford. When the Colonel finished, Calley saluted crookedly, turned and walked stiffly back to the defense table.

The sentence for premeditated murder could only be death or life imprisonment under the Military Code.

Judge Kennedy told the jury "Gentlemen, we will go into the sentencing phase tomorrow."

Half an hour later Lieutenant Calley was escorted out of the building between military guards into a waiting crowd of 100. A woman shouted "We're with you, Calley." He was taken to the stockade, while Latimer told reporters "Take my word for it, the boy is crushed."

The next day brought one of the most emotional moments in the trial. In front of the jurors who would decide his life or death, Calley made a final statement.

Standing behind a microphone, his hands jammed into his pockets, he spoke in a choked voice, very near to tears, pausing between sentences:

"Let me know if you can hear me, sirs. Your Honor, members of the court, I asked my attorney, George Latimer, and my other attorneys not to go into mitigation in this case. There's a lot of things that aren't appropriate, and I don't think it really matters what type of individual I am. And I'm not going to stand here and plead for my life or my freedom. But I would like you to consider a thousand more lives that are going to be lost in Southeast Asia, the thousands more to be imprisoned, not only here in the United States, but in North Vietnam and in hospitals all over the world as amputees.

"I've never known a soldier, nor did I ever myself, wantonly kill a human being in my entire life. If I have committed a crime, the only crime I've committed is in judgment of my values. Apparently I valued my troops' lives more than I did that of the enemy. When my troops were getting massacred and mauled by an enemy I couldn't see, I couldn't feel and I couldn't touch—that nobody in the military system ever described them as anything other than Communism.

"They didn't give it a race, they didn't give it a sex, they didn't give it an age. They never let me believe it was just a philosophy in a man's mind. That was my enemy out there. And when it became between my men and that enemy I had to value the lives of my troops—and I feel that was the only crime I have committed.

"Yesterday, you stripped me of all my honor. Please, by your actions that you take here today, don't strip future soldiers of their honor, I beg of you."

Captain Daniel rose to his feet and addressed the jurors.

"You did not strip him of his honor. What he did stripped him of his honor. It is not an honor—it has never been an honor—to kill unarmed men, women, and children."

But the prosecutor pointedly did not ask for the death sentence. Undoubtedly he was already aware of the fantastic outbreak of public revulsion at the conviction, symbolized by Latimer waving a mass of telegrams at the jury that day and shouting that the case had "torn America apart."

In fact, the Judge instructed the jury that under military law they could reduce the charge to involuntary manslaughter as had been done in a previous murder case involving civilians in Vietnam and thus give Lieutenant Calley a lighter sentence. But the next day the jury announced its sentence. There was to be no compromise:

"First Lieutenant William Calley ... the Court ... sentences you to be confined at hard labor for the length of your natural life. To be dismissed from the service. To forfeit all pay and allowances."

The verdict and the sentence opened up the final — and greatest — drama of the long-drawn-out trial of Lieutenant Calley.

Epilogue

Perhaps never before in this nation's history has a judicial trial provoked such an enormous outcry of rage against the verdict. Within minutes of the announcement of Calley's conviction, telegrams began inundating the White House, running 100 to one against the verdict.

The Gallup poll revealed that 79 percent of the American people disapproved of the verdict. In Michigan and other States, members of draft boards resigned. State legislatures passed resolutions urging the President to grant executive clemency to Calley. Protest marches took place in Dallas, Kansas City, Jacksonville, Corpus Christi, and Los Angeles. Two hundred and fifty high school students in Saint Louis held a five-mile "Support Calley" march. In New York hundreds of persons stopped by a table in the Port Authority building and signed "Free Calley" petitions. Veterans' organizations throughout America passed resolutions, sent messages to President Nixon, and began raising funds for Calley. In Vietnam, televised interviews with servicemen showed that an overwhelming majority of them were angry at the conviction.

Politicians leaped into the act, none more swiftly than Governor George Wallace of Alabama. Within two days of the sentence he was visiting Calley and then appearing at a giant protest rally in Columbus, Georgia.

The outcry seemed to catch everyone by surprise, perhaps most of all the President, who was vacationing at San

Clemente, California. He reported later that he, himself, was so troubled by the verdict that he could not sleep. The next morning he rose and issued the first of two Presidential edicts: He ordered Calley to be removed from the stockade and kept under house arrest pending his appeal. Few seemed to be against that action: Gallup reported that 83 percent of the people polled supported it.

But the telegrams and protests kept pouring in. The New York *Post* headlined an incredible fact: "CALLEY BRINGS US TOGETHER." Right-wingers and new-left liberals joined in calling the verdict a farce, for widely different reasons. The conservatives maintained that Calley was only shooting the "enemy"; the liberals claimed he was a "scapegoat" for his military superiors.

In the midst of the uproar, President Nixon issued his second edict, which seemed to capitalize on the nation's emotion for political reasons. He announced that he, as commander in chief, would personally intervene and decide what action should be taken on the case. He stated that in his judgment the case "having captured the attention of the American people to the degree that it has," required "more than the technical review" provided by the Code of Military Justice.

Whatever the political need—or expediency—of that statement, it destroyed in one stroke the entire court-martial which had operated in such a judicially correct manner to arrive at its verdict. Six jurors had listened to the testimony; six jurors had pondered over the testimony for thirteen days; and the six had decided that Calley, on the evidence, was guilty and should serve a life term. Now the President was saying, in effect, he would completely disregard the trial.

Military justice, so long subject to the claim that command influence was its major flaw, now saw that claim substantiated in spectacular fashion. And none saw it more clearly than the prosecutor at the trial, Captain Aubrey Daniel. Daniel fired off a letter to President Nixon which exploded on the front pages of the nation's newspapers.

"On November 26, 1969, you issued the following statement . . . : 'An incident such as that alleged in this case is in direct violation not only of United States military policy, but is also abhorrent to the conscience of all the American people. . . . Appropriate action is and will be taken to assure that illegal and immoral conduct as alleged be dealt with in accordance with the strict rules of military justice.'

"On December 8, 1970, you . . . made the following statement: 'What appears was certainly a massacre, and under no circumstances is justified. . . . We cannot ever condone or use atrocities against civilians.' "

The letter continued:

"In view of your previous statements . . . I have been particularly shocked and dismayed at your decision to intervene in these proceedings in the midst of the public clamor. Your decision can only have been prompted by the response of a vocal segment of our population. . . .

"Your intervention has, in my opinion, damaged the military judicial system and lessened any respect it may have gained as a result of the proceedings.

"You have subjected a judicial system of this country to the criticism that it is subject to political influence. . . . The image of Lieutenant Calley, a man convicted of the premeditated murder of at least twenty-one unarmed and unresisting people, as a national hero has been enhanced. . . . The greatest tragedy of all will be if political expediency dictates the compromise of such a fundamental moral principle as the inherent unlawfulness of the murder of innocent persons. . . ."

No one could doubt the young attorney's sincerity, and his reasoning was solid. The military boards which would review the case could hardly review it impartially with the President's words in their ears. Interestingly, it was one of the foremost critics of military justice—Senator Birch Bayh— who quickly came to Daniel's assistance. Senator Bayh had a bill pending in Congress to eliminate command influence. This bill had been aimed mostly at military commanders, not the *Commander in Chief*. Bayh told reporters that although he "shares the deepest compassion for Lieutenant Calley," President Nixon "by his premature actions has made a truly impartial review impossible. Reluctantly I have concluded that the President is determined to play politics with the Calley decision and the entire Mylai tragedy."

Aides to the President quickly reacted to the criticism by confiding to reporters that Mr. Nixon had acted only because of the unprecedented wave of protest across the country; that he felt it his duty as President to "cool" that emotion before it got out of hand.

The controversy about the verdict may never be resolved. Everyone has an opinion, but the case is complex, on too many levels, almost impossible to grasp whole. General Telford Taylor, the Chief U.S. Counsel at Nuremberg, has said an acquittal would have been "disastrous"—at the same time he found the sentence "opaque and harsh."

But—the final irony—it now seems that Lieutenant Calley may have served the cause of peace when he leveled his rifle at defenseless women and children in that small hamlet in Vietnam. Two weeks after the verdict pollster Louis Harris found that, for the first time, a majority of Americans—58 percent—thought that the Vietnam war was immoral and that Americans should end it and come home.

For students of military justice the case involves one more intriguing aspect. Two centuries of courts-martial had shown military justice evolving slowly into a legal system of which military men could be proud. But there were constant flaws—and constant absurdities such as the Presidio cases—which brought military justice into disrepute. The Mylai trial was the most important, most spectacular, most challenging trial in our nation's history. As prosecutor Daniel said in his letter to President Nixon:

"The trial of Lieutenant Calley was conducted in the finest tradition of our legal system. It was in every respect a fair trial in which every legal right of Lieutenant Calley was fully protected. It clearly demonstrated that the military justice system, which has previously been the subject of much criticism, was a fair system."

True. But in the end, what happened? The American people protested against the verdict, and the President announced he would completely disregard the trial and make his own decision. It is hard not to sympathize, for once, with the hard-working military legal personnel who are laboring to make military justice a workable system. And a system which produces judges such as Reid Kennedy, and prosecutors such as Aubrey Daniel, is certainly a system on its way to achieving respectability.

But the system still faces the giant mistrust of the American people, inspired by so many notorious cases in the past which highlighted its flaws. Few would disagree that we have come a long way from the flogging and peremptory executions and other brutal practices associated with military justice in an earlier era. The trial of Lieutenant Calley was, in a way, the apogee of a long road upward to genuine protection of individual rights in a judicially correct trial in the military. But the aftermath of the trial showed that the system is still not perfect, still does not work, and perhaps can never function consistently until the factor of command influence is eliminated.

Index

287